Telephone : MOUntview 3343.

HIGHGATE LITERARY & SCIENTIFIC
INSTITUTION
11, SOUTH GROVE, N.6.

920
smy

10303

Time allowed FOURTEEN Days

Date Issued	Date Issued	Date Issued
M NOV 1959		
DEC 1959		
MAY 1960		
2 JUN 1960		
JUL 1960		
1960		
-7 SEP 1960		
OCT 1960		
15 OCT 1960		
25 OCT 1960		
NOV 1960		
19 AUG 1967		

2000-5-58

THE
PRETTIEST GIRL
IN ENGLAND

✻

'Mrs. Wat [Smythe] says the Duke of
Orleans is very much in love with Cou.
She dances constantly with him and [he]
says she is the prettiest girl in England.'

Mrs. Fitzherbert, in a letter to
Mrs. Dawson-Damer, May 17, 1833

THE
PRETTIEST GIRL
IN ENGLAND

❈ ❈ ❈

The Love Story of Mrs. Fitzherbert's Niece
from Journals edited by

RICHARD BUCKLE

❈

JOHN MURRAY
ALBEMARLE STREET LONDON

Made and printed in Great Britain by
William Clowes and Sons, Limited, London and Beccles
and published by John Murray (Publishers) Ltd.

TO MY MOTHER
and to all the other descendants of
the first Walter Smythe,
living and unborn

CONTENTS

ILLUSTRATIONS

*Reproduced from ' Mrs. Fitzherbert and George IV ', by W. H. Wilkins. By courtesy Longmans, Green & Co.

ix

ACKNOWLEDGEMENTS

My first thanks are due to Mr. Edwin Kersley, who rescued the journal of Georgina Smythe from some forgotten sale-room and eventually delivered it to me. In snapping up this 'unconsidered trifle' he made amends for the negligence of whatever member of the Craven family sent it once so ignominiously to be sold; and if the journal proves interesting to posterity he must be remembered with gratitude.

Next I must express my thanks to the late Sir Frederick Hervey-Bathurst, to Lady Hervey-Bathurst and to the present Sir Frederick Hervey-Bathurst for lending me and allowing me to quote from the journal of Georgina's elder sister, Louisa Smythe. The miniatures by Holmes of the two Smythe sisters and of the former Sir Frederick are also reproduced through their kindness.

For permission to reproduce other pictures I should like to thank Cornelia, Countess of Craven; the Marquess of Downshire; the Marquess of Bristol; the Earl of Tankerville; Sir Shane Leslie; Captain Denison; Major Trotter; the Corporation of Brighton and the Parker Galleries.

To Helen, Duchess of Northumberland, Lady Diana Cooper, Lady Saltoun, Miss Nancy Mitford, Mr. and Mrs. Christie-Miller, the Duke of Northumberland, the Marchese d'Aix, the Marquess of Hertford, the Earl of Harewood, the Earl of Verulam; the Earl of Mount Charles, Mr. David Erskine, Mr. George Kinnaird, Sir Iain Moncreiffe, Sir Shane Leslie, M. Charles de Beistegui, Mr. Clifford Musgrave and Mr. Hector Bolitho I am also indebted for help and advice, and I thank them sincerely.

xi

For much constructive criticism and advice on the book in its final stages, as well as for help with the proofs and Biographical Notes, I should like to record my thanks to Mr. Mario Amaya.

RICHARD BUCKLE

PREFACE

It cannot be a common thing for a man to fall in love with his great-great-grandmother: but that is what happened to me when I first read the journal of Georgina Smythe during the summer of 1954. I did not inherit her journal: I came upon it by a series of chances so extraordinary that if I believed in Fate I should think I had been specially elected to save this interesting document from oblivion. If, eight years before, I had not published in a magazine I was then editing an article by my friend Iain Moncreiffe on the first Quadrille at Almack's, and if I had not, on an impulse, inserted a frivolous footnote to that article, mentioning that a Lord Craven referred to in it was my ancestor; if Mr. Edwin Kersley, the print-seller, had not read this footnote and been kind enough to offer me some Craven horse pictures, which he had acquired at a sale long since; and if, years after I had bought these, I had not called unexpectedly on Mr. Kersley in Paddington to see if he had anything to lend me for an exhibition I was organising—then, I think, the journal of Georgina Smythe might have been lost for ever.

On this last occasion Mr. Kersley said he had turned out a few more Craven relics. He handed me some old prints and a leather-bound note-book, the lock of which had been broken open. "I'll give you the prints," he said, "and you can have the note-book for a pound." Of course I jumped at his generous offer.

The note-book contained the intimate journal of my ancestress, Georgina Smythe, for part of the years 1832 and 1833. I had known nothing of this lady until then, except that she was a niece of the celebrated Mrs. Fitzherbert, that she had married first my great-great-grandfather, Augustus Craven, and secondly the duc de la Force. One of my aunts had a silver-gilt dressing-case that had belonged to her. However, Georgina Smythe—or 'Cou', as her family and friends called her—wrote so vividly and with such lack of artifice or pretention that I soon came to know her well. Her diary was not concerned with great men or great events. Born in the year before Waterloo, she made her début in the very month the Reform Bill was passed: but her comment that a ball at Apsley House was overcrowded or that she found one at Lady Sefton's or the Duchess of Bedford's dull or entertaining is the nearest we get to meeting the victor of Waterloo or witnessing the triumph of the Whigs. The diaries may be disappointing to the student of art and letters. Cou shared a box with Samuel Rogers on the second occasion that Taglioni danced *La Sylphide* in London, but she was too busy flirting to pay any attention to the banker-poet or to the divine dancer, so that we learn nothing about either.

To the student of manners, however, the journal is certainly of interest, and indeed for anyone who likes to read about love it holds an irresistible appeal. Although it begins by being—and continues to be, on and off—a lively chronicle of social occasions, Cou's journal turns into a love story. It was a love story never meant to be read. Georgina Smythe was a sort of Jane Austen heroine, but what she wrote was true.

Cou was high-spirited, with a great sense of fun, as her grand-daughter, my grandmother Sandford, had been; she was acutely critical of her friends' and family's behaviour in a way that reminded me of my mother: but what most attracted me to her was her single-minded and whole-hearted pursuit of love, once she had found it for the first time on first sight of Augustus Craven.

The journal was broken off—in mid-sentence—after Cou's mother finally gave her consent to the marriage with Augustus. Was the leather-bound note-book ever unlocked again until it came into Mr. Kersley's possession? Did the diarist ever show it to her husband? Did either of her sons read it? Neither my grandmother nor my great-uncle, Caryl Craven, ever mentioned it. If it was sold as junk, which seems likely, on the death of my elder great-uncle, Augustus, whom I never knew, it was probably still locked up, and the key lost; for surely no one who had read it could let so precious a document pass out of his family. I like to think that I was the first to read the love story of Georgina Smythe since she locked up her note-book for the last time in the summer of 1833, one hundred and twenty-one years before.

I naturally began to try to find out as much as possible about everyone mentioned in it. I also hoped to find portraits of Cou and her friends. Her elder sister, Louisa Smythe, married Sir Frederick Hervey-Bathurst: I discovered that their grandson, another Sir Frederick, was living in Hampshire. He and Lady Hervey-Bathurst produced more rabbits out of hats for me. Not only had they, among other relevant pictures, the miniature of Georgina Smythe which is reproduced facing page 76 of this book—and in which I immediately recognised the attractive and headstrong author of the journal—but they had diaries kept by Louisa Smythe from 1827 to 1831, and a few letters of Louisa, Cou and their mother to the former Sir Frederick.

I thought at first that Louisa's journal should appear in full with Cou's. Continuing as it did for several years, and ending immediately before her younger sister's began, it formed an admirable introduction to the latter; but Louisa was not telling one complete love story as her sister was, and even when she came to record her relations with Frederick Hervey-Bathurst she left out many of the most important scenes. Above all, she wrote much less vividly than Cou. So I decided to use only the most interesting passages from Louisa's journal as an introduction to Cou's.

Miss Mary Craven, the last surviving grandchild of Georgina Smythe, sent me from her villa in Italy photographs of portraits of Georgina in later life and of her father, Wat Smythe. Unfortunately, both she and her second cousin Sir Frederick died while I was working on the book. The portraits of Augustus Craven and of the other Cravens came from Hamstead Marshall in Berkshire, which Cou describes visiting. It was exciting to examine there, as well as at Clarendon and Combe, the rooms in which she sang, danced, laughed, hoped and despaired during the crucial year of her life. Likenesses of two of her admirers were found in London houses as close to each other as Lyall Street and Wilton Crescent: that of her first beau was traced to Mells in Somerset. It was a chance examination of the celebrated print after Sir Francis Grant's *Melton Breakfast* at my barber's one afternoon, which revealed to me that I had been familiar with the face of Cou's devoted cousin, Rowland Errington, since I was a child. My own club, it turned out, had been Lord Craven's London house at 16, Charles Street.

Working in the Bodleian, in the British Museum and the British Museum Newspaper Library in the mysterious suburb of Colindale, poring over old *Peerages* and copies of *The Landed Gentry*, writing letters to people who might be alive or dead, I enjoyed my quest for Georgina Smythe and my attempt to throw light on the background of her life in 1832 and 1833.

A journey into the past is perhaps the most enticing of adventures; and the heroine of my pursuit seemed none the less irresistible for being of the same flesh and blood as myself. A century and a quarter after meeting Augustus Craven on his yacht at Greenwich Georgina Smythe had found in me another beau.

R. B.

Overstrand, December 1957

NOTE

Whereas the spelling of the two diarists, whether peculiar to their period or to themselves, has been retained, their punctuation has been edited.

PRINCIPAL CHARACTERS

MAMA
: Mrs. Wat Smythe, widow of Walter Smythe and mother of the two diarists.

LOU
: Louisa Smythe, elder daughter of Mrs. Wat Smythe.

COU
: Georgina Smythe, younger daughter of Mrs. Wat Smythe.

AUNT FITZ
: Mrs. Fitzherbert, aunt of the two diarists on their father's side. A Roman Catholic, widow of two Catholic gentlemen and secretly married to—but long since separated from—the Prince of Wales, now King of England.

MINNEY
: Mrs. Dawson-Damer, *née* Seymour. Adopted daughter of Mrs. Fitzherbert.

MARY
: Maryanne Smythe, also an adopted daughter of Mrs. Fitzherbert. Probably the illegitimate daughter of Jack Smythe, second brother of Mrs. Fitzherbert, but believed by some to be the child of the latter by the Prince of Wales.

AUNT CHA	Miss (Charlotte) Boycott, only unmarried sister of Mrs. Wat Smythe.
WILLIAM	William Stanley, cousin of the Smythe girls. His maternal grandmother was sister to Mrs. Fitzherbert and Walter Smythe.
ROWLEY	Rowland Errington, brother of William Stanley. He had changed his name from Stanley to Errington on inheriting from an uncle. Considered a match for Georgina.
FRANCO	Francis Seymour, Minney's nephew. A Guards officer and close friend of Georgina's.
MR. VILLIERS	'Hyde', 'Mr. Ville'. A young man about town and a beau of Louisa's.
LORD OSSULSTON	'Lord O'. Heir of Lord Tankerville. Loved for a time by Louisa.
SIR FREDERICK HERVEY-BATHURST	'The Elu', 'The Innominato'. A cricketing Guards officer put forward as a match for Louisa.
MR. TROTTER	An officer in the Life Guards and an early beau of Georgina's.
LORD GEORGE HERVEY	Son of Lord Bristol. In love with Georgina.

xviii

LORD HILLSBOROUGH	'Mountain', 'La Montagne'. An officer in the Life Guards, heir to Lord Downshire. Georgina's chief preoccupation during her first season, until she meets Augustus Craven.
LORD ALBERT CONYNGHAM	'Longues jambes.' Third son of Lady Conyngham, George IV's last favourite. For some months in love with Georgina.
COUNT TOLSTOY	A Russian diplomat. Nephew of Princess Lieven.
LADY CRAVEN	'Dapper.' Widow of the first Earl of Craven, formerly the actress Louisa Brunton. Mother of Lord Craven, Augustus, Frederick and Louisa Craven.
LORD CRAVEN	'Uffy.' Second Earl of Craven, Viscount Uffington, an eligible landowner.
AUGUSTUS CRAVEN	'August', 'The Emperor'. Second son of Lady Craven. In love with Georgina.
FREDERICK CRAVEN	'Freddy', 'Fatty'. Lady Craven's youngest son.
LOUISA CRAVEN	'Lupo.' Only daughter of Lady Craven and Georgina's close friend.

PART ONE

THE ELDER SISTER

*Extracts from the Journal
of Louisa Smythe
1827–1831*

1827

In May 1827, Mrs. Wat Smythe, a widow of forty-nine, brought her two daughters up to London from Brighton with the intention of launching the elder of them on the world. To promote this aim she had taken what we should now consider quite a large house, number 6, Great Cumberland Place, where she kept two carriages, eight or nine indoor servants and a governess for the younger daughter, thinking herself very poor. Part of Great Cumberland Place is standing as it was, although the houses have been renumbered; and the Smythes' house is still there to be seen, in the very middle of the crescent, the gulf of a bombed site yawning beside it. The tall house had a fine staircase with iron bannisters spiralling up to a skylight; and the big back drawing-room on the first floor had a bow end with three windows, which distinguished it from the others in the crescent. Mrs. Wat's twelve-year-old younger daughter, Georgina—or Cou—was delicate and nervous, so it was naturally considered an advantage to have 'le bon air of the Park' at their front door. The elder daughter, Louisa, was sixteen, however, and about to 'come out', so that for the time being she must have been the focal point of the household.

If the immediate prospect for Louisa Smythe was one of unmixed pleasure, her mother was probably not free from anxiety. It was essential that her girls should marry well, and she was staking more than she could afford on a house and clothes in order to give them every opportunity. For centuries the London season had served its purpose—as it still does—of bringing together the children of the nobility and gentry with a view to marriage: and for centuries parents had weighed up the comparative merits of their children's dancing partners in terms of breeding, fortune, fecundity, character and looks.

It may be instructive to consider what reasons other parents might have enumerated for or against an alliance of their sons with one of the Smythe girls.

Their birth was respectable, if not brilliant. The Smythes were a Roman Catholic family from County Durham, who came into property in Shropshire through the marriage of Sir Edward Smythe, the first baronet, to Mary, daughter and co-heiress of Sir Richard Lee, in the time of Charles II. From then (until 1949, when it became a convent) Acton Burnell was the seat of the Smythe family. On their father's side the girls were also descended from worthy north-country Catholic families such as Errington, Levesey, Widrington, Carnaby, Molyneux and Selby, and from the even more eminent west-country families of Cary and Blount.

Because of the difficulty for Roman Catholic gentlemen to find appropriate wives—for until Emancipation in 1830 they were prevented by law from earning a living in any of the professions then considered suitable to their birth—the Church of Rome came to allow mixed marriages, on the understanding that male children should be brought up Catholic, female Protestant.

Walter, or Wat Smythe, the girls' father, had consequently married a Protestant wife, Louisa, one of the five daughters of a Shropshire neighbour, Thomas Boycott, squire of Rudge. Mrs. Wat, who was widowed in 1822 and obliged to resign the Hampshire house of Brambridge to her husband's next brother, descended from several Shropshire families who were much intermarried, including those of Jenkins and Puleston. Through her Wingfield, Leighton, Devereux and Bourchier ancestors she derived, though she may not have known it, from Edward III.

That their father had been a Catholic was a fact that would probably weigh little against the Smythe girls, for they had been

4

brought up in the safe and cosy bosom of the English Church. There was, however, a more sensational skeleton in the family cupboard. Their father's sister had married the King of England. Mrs. Fitzherbert's story is too well known to be more than briefly summarised here. The eldest of five children, Mary Anne—or Maria—Smythe was married, when she was eighteen, to Edward Weld of Lulworth Castle, a Catholic twenty-six years her senior. Weld died within a year, and Maria married another Catholic gentleman of property, this time only ten years older than herself, Thomas Fitzherbert of Swynnerton. Within three years he too was dead.

It was during the season of 1784 that the Prince of Wales first saw Mrs. Fitzherbert and fell in love with her. The young widow was then going out for the first time in London society: she had inherited from her second husband the lease of a house in Park Street and had taken the villa, Marble Hill, at Twickenham. The Prince was attractive, but the 'lass of Richmond Hill', as she was inaccurately called in the ballad, was both virtuous and devout. In November of the same year he staged a mock suicide, and the alarmed Maria consented to go to his bedside in the company of Georgiana, Duchess of Devonshire. The promise of marriage he extracted from her in these circumstances she held not to be binding, and the next day she fled abroad. It was illegal under the Royal Marriage Act, for the Prince to marry without his father's consent, and in marrying a Catholic he could forfeit succession to the Throne. It was not in his character, however, to look far ahead. He sought to persuade Maria Fitzherbert into a marriage which, though illegal, would be recognised by her Church: whether this ceremony would have to be kept secret for ever was a problem the future would decide. Mrs. Fitzherbert undoubtedly returned his affection. After a year abroad, in response to the longest love-letter in the English language, she came back to London. The Prince of Wales and Maria Fitzherbert were married by a Church of England clergyman, John Burt, on December 15, 1785, the bride's uncle, Henry Errington, and her brother, Jack Smythe, being witnesses. The marriage took place in Mrs. Fitzherbert's house in Park Street, near the Oxford Street end, the garden of which stretched towards Park Lane. The block of flats called Hereford House stands on the site today. For over eight years the Prince and Mrs. Fitzherbert lived happily, though under separate roofs, together.

In June 1794, under the influence of Lady Jersey, the Prince left Mrs. Fitzherbert. In April 1795 he married his cousin Caroline of Brunswick. His new wife, however, disgusted him, and Lady Jersey failed to retain his affections. Three days after the birth of his heir, Princess Charlotte, the Prince of Wales made a will leaving everything he had in the world to Maria Fitzherbert. The same month he separated for ever from the Princess of Wales. It was over four years, nevertheless, before Mrs. Fitzherbert could be prevailed upon to take him back, and this she only consented to do after receiving the Vatican's decision that she was the canonical wife of the Prince.

Mrs. Fitzherbert told Lord Stourton that the next eight years, much of which time was spent at Brighton, 'were the happiest of her connection with the Prince'. Her curious position was accepted as an honourable one; she was treated with the deference due to Royalty; even the Queen respected her and recognised her disinterestedness. The Dukes of York, Clarence and Kent—particularly the first and last—were her dear friends, and remained so after her final separation with the Prince. For, in 1808 the volatile Prince fell in love with Lady Hertford, and in 1811 he parted with Mrs. Fitzherbert for good.

Few women have ever been placed in such awkward situations as Maria Fitzherbert, though many have been badly treated by those they loved: none ever lived down an imprudent action—for her consent to marry the Prince must count against her—with greater discretion. The Duke of Wellington said she was 'the most honest woman who ever lived'. Certainly, the fate of political parties, of the Throne and the country rested on her silence about the illegal marriage, and she never spoke. That she was content to appear disreputable and even ridiculous in the eyes of the world earned her the respect of all those who ultimately learned her secret.

Now, at the time of Louisa Smythe's coming out, Mrs. Fitzherbert's illegal legitimate husband was on the Throne. Aunt Fitz had long lived in dignified semi-retirement, moving between her house in Tilney Street, Park Lane and her house on the Steyne at Brighton. She had always been kind to Mrs. Wat and the Smythe girls, having them to stay and introducing them to her friends. If most people in society looked upon Mrs. Fitzherbert as a long-discarded mistress of their unpopular monarch, her life had always been so placidly respectable that I doubt if the mothers of gilded bachelors could have considered her relationship to Louisa and Cou as rendering them unsuitable daughters-in-law. On the contrary, she was comfortably off—on his accession the King raised her allowance from £6,000 to £10,000 a year—and she presumably had intentions for her two nieces.

Aunt Fitz was now in her seventies, so she liked to be a good deal at home, and was only persuaded to parties on special occasions. Her adopted daughter, Minney Seymour, now Mrs. Dawson, was, however, a member of the smartest and gayest set in London. She was of great help, when she could spare the time, in finding the Smythe girls the most eligible dancing partners and securing them invitations to the most sought-after balls.

Minney, now thirty, and a mother, had always been unusually fascinating: everyone loved her, and she had long been the centre of Mrs. Fitzherbert's life. As a girl, she had had many suitors. She refused her cousin Beauchamp (later Lord Hertford), Prince Jules de Polignac, Lord Glengall, Lord Frances Leveson-Gower (later first Earl of Ellesmere), and Lord Arthur Hill, a younger son of the Downshires, who was an intimate friend of Mrs. Fitzherbert and her family, and who will be met frequently in the following pages. Neither Beauchamp nor Arthur Hill ever married: perhaps they continued to love her. The most touching of Minney's rejected suitors was George Fitzclarence, later Lord Munster, the eldest illegitimate son of the Duke of Clarence and Mrs. Jordan. Although he married and had children, Munster never loved anyone but

Minney and his end was tragic. When it had come to thinking of marriage, Mrs. Fitzherbert could not bear the thought of losing Minney, but since this was inevitable she was anxious for her to make a great match. She probably had her eye on the bachelor Duke of Devonshire, as most mothers and guardians would have over a number of years; but the good-natured, artistic Duke was to remain a bachelor.

When Minney met and fell in love with George Dawson, a younger son of Lord Portarlington, Mrs. Fitzherbert was outraged. George had fought at Waterloo, but he had no prospects and was considered to be rather a rake. The King too, though he had long since parted from Mrs. Fitzherbert, continued to take an active interest in Minney's welfare, and he was equally opposed to the match. When Minney was a girl he had invested £10,000 for her: this had become nearly £20,000, and he was not anxious for the money to fall into the hands of a spendthrift. Every possible means of parting the lovers was attempted. Dawson was posted by the Duke of York to St. Vincent, Minney was sent to France and Germany. One of the go-betweens they employed in their long, clandestine correspondence, was the Countess of San Antonio,* later Duchess of Cannizaro, a great amateur of music and a hostess of the time, who appears frequently in the Smythe journals.

In the end, George's aunt, Lady Caroline Damer, who had frequently paid his debts, announced her intention of leaving him her Dorset property of Came; Mrs. Fitzherbert softened; and the King gave his consent providing the money was tied up in such a way that Dawson could not get hold of it all. Minney

* Countess of San Antonio (1785–1841), daughter of Governor George Johnstone of Pensacola. Inherited a fortune from her brother, Sir John Lowther Johnstone, 6th Baronet, in 1811. Married a Sicilian, Francesco di Patanone, Count Sant' Antonio, later Duke of Cannizaro, sometime Minister in London of the Kingdom of the Two Sicilies. A great musical hostess of the period and patroness of singers, mainly Italian. Fat, lively and good-natured, she was evidently fond of the Smythe girls, particularly Georgina. She is referred to in the journals as 'the Countess', or 'the Tessa'. Greville tells the story of her husband's desertion, and of her taking up with a young tenor. She was so jolly that Society connived at her gigolo.

Seymour was married to George Dawson at St. George's, Hanover Square, in August 1825, after a courtship of over five years. By the time Louisa Smythe's diary begins, their eldest child had already been born in Tilney Street. It is probable that George Dawson was unfaithful to her, for Louisa Smythe speaks of her in one passage as 'ravaged with jealousy'. One imagines her, when she was older, as thin and exceptionally smart, her vitality used up in social intrigue.

Aunt Fitz had another adopted daughter, who had come to live with her a few years before the journals begin. Maryanne Smythe, a slightly dim figure, was given out to be the daughter of Mrs. Fitzherbert's second brother Jack, lately dead, but was believed by many to be her child by the Prince of Wales. Mrs. Fitzherbert never showed the same passionate devotion to Maryanne that she did to Minney: both called her 'Mama'.

If their Catholic forebears and the Royal associations of their aunt would be no severe handicap to the Smythe girls, Mrs. Fitzherbert's wide circle of acquaintance and Minney Dawson's charm and popularity would be positive advantages to them. To what extent their own mother would be a help or a hindrance in society was more of a problem.

Mrs. Wat Smythe, born Louisa Victoria Sobieska Boycott, had been left with little money to bring up her daughters, so that life cannot have been easy for her. She seems to have been a difficult and occasionally hysterical lady. It is clear that she liked to live in an extravagant way, and Mrs. Fitzherbert refers in a letter to her fondness for finery. She was inclined to self-pity, and tended to be socially pushing but these were perhaps the inevitable concomitants of small means and two daughters. She was jealous and temperamental; and there is even a suggestion that she drank too much.

An idea of Mrs. Wat's difficult nature may be had from the following letter. On January 18, 1828, after staying with her niece, Lady Stanley,* at Hooton in Cheshire, Mrs. Fitzherbert

* Mary Haggerston, only daughter of Sir Carnaby Haggerston, 5th Baronet, and Frances Smythe. Married 1805 Sir Thomas Stanley-Massey-Stanley, 9th Baronet, by whom she had three sons and one daughter. She was first cousin to the diarists, but much older than them. Died 1857.

wrote to Minney: 'Pray do write to Louisa [Mrs. Wat Smythe]. Her extreme jealousy of me is owing to my visit to Hooton where I was treated with great affection and kindness, and her hatred of Maryanne she makes no secret of, as she has taken into her head people take more notice of her than of her girls. She says Lady Stanley and I hate her and her children, and that she only has one friend left in the world, which is Lord Arthur [Hill], and she supposes very soon he will be set against her. She vows she will never set her foot in Lady Stanley's house again, though after I left Hooton she remained there three months with every kindness and attention shewn her and her girls. You would not know her, her character is so changed. . . .' Later in the same letter, Mrs. Fitzherbert quotes a significant remark of Charlotte Boycott's, the diarists' only unmarried aunt—'Aunt Cha'—who spent much of her time between her brother's seat at Rudge and Mrs. Wat's house in Great Cumberland Place, and with whom Aunt Fitz evidently shared confidences over the excesses of their mutual sister-in-law. 'Pray do write to Louisa, who is in such a state with everybody, and I am sure if you don't write she will think I have prevented you. Charlotte [Boycott] says she is very much reformed with respect to—(I cannot bear to say the word, but you will understand it). She worries her family and all about her by her extreme degree of jealousy and suspicion and really makes us all quite uncomfortable, I have determined to take no notice and shew her and the girls every kindness and attention in my power, for really I have a very sincere affection for her and would do everything on earth I could do, both for her and her children, but I really think if she has left off her old customs she is not right in her mind.'

In another letter, undated, Mrs. Fitzherbert writes: 'I am very sorry to hear of Mrs. Wat's accident. If you recollect, a similar circumstance happened about this time last year when she returned home from having dined with me at Norwood. I shall say no more about it.' Cou records, during the visit to Clarendon, her mother being taken suddenly ill and put on a diet which excluded wine; and it is perhaps not malicious to imagine that sometimes, when Louisa or Cou describe their mother as being too tired to take them out to a party, they are dutifully attributing to fatigue a condition more likely resultant from other causes. Nevertheless, when Mrs. Wat was in good form, she was sufficiently unselfish to sit up with her dancing daughters till six in the morning.

It is a pity that I have been unable to find a portrait of the diarists' 'Mama'. I feel sure, however, from various intimations, that she was a handsome and imposing woman, with something of a grand manner. She was used, from the time of her marriage, to associating on intimate terms with the Royal Family. She certainly brought up her daughters admirably. Both girls break easily into French and Italian in their journals: both seem to have dressed well, danced well, and known how to make themselves agreeable in society. Both were God-fearing; and the expressions of piety which occur from time to time in their journals ring true. If Louisa, being more reserved, seems to stand more for Sense, and the impetuous Cou for Sensibility, the two girls were equally expert at hiding their feelings. Indeed, they kept their own counsel to the extent of withholding certain confidences from their mother; and I cannot help feeling that if she had been an easier mother to confide in the diaries might never have been written.

A slightly dragonish mother and a lack of great fortunes were the gravest handicaps Louisa and Cou could complain of. If the right prince came along, with the right bank balance, the dragon might easily be braved. The chief reason to hope all would be well was that both girls were extremely pretty. Louisa was fair, Cou shorter and dark; both were musical, but Cou was the one with a voice; both had a sense of humour, but Louisa kept hers more to herself; both had learned the utmost circumspection in handling their mother.

✢   ✢   ✢

From the first, Louisa was discerning between the merits of the parties she went to.

11

Friday, May 11, 1827

... We took the trouble of dressing for a disagreeable, hot and crowded ball, where I knew three people, and where to say I was ennuyéd is to say nothing. It will be with difficulty I shall be persuaded to return there.

Sunday, May 13, 1827

... At 11 o'clock we went to Ly. Salisbury's where we found the rooms nearly empty and looking very formidable. However, people in general were very goodnatured to me and I liked it much better than I expected. Mr. Byng and Mr. Fitzclarence were there. The former, though goodnatured, is far too complimentary to please. Lord Arthur was very amusing. He introduced me to Mr. Shelley. *

But a débutante was evidently not considered to have come out until she had appeared at Almack's. Every Wednesday during the season a ball was held at Almack's Assembly Rooms in King Street, St. James; and tickets to these very exclusive dances were only to be had—at ten guineas each—by favour of one of the Lady Patronesses. These included the Whig hostesses Lady Cowper and Lady Sefton, the tyrannical Lady Jersey, and the Austrian and Russian Ambassadresses, Princess Esterhazy and Princess Lieven.

Wednesday, May 16, 1827

The day of my entrée into this gay world: everything but the weather was propitious to me. I set off to Almack's a little before 11 with Mama, Minney & Capt. Dawson. When we arrived the rooms were already full; they are beautiful & far surpass what I had imagined them to be. I began to valtz with Capt. Dawson. I felt not a little frightened at first. I then

* John Villiers (1808–1867), eldest son of Sir John Shelley, 6th Baronet. Married 1832 Louisa Elizabeth Anne, daughter of the Rev. Samuel Johnes-Knight. He succeeded his father as 7th Baronet in 1852, and leaving an only daughter, was succeeded by his brother.

Louisa Smythe
From the miniature by James Holmes

(*Above L.*)   Mrs. Fitzherbert in old age. From a water-colour drawing

(*Above R.*)   Minney Dawson-Damer, Mrs. Fitzherbert's adopted daughter
                From the miniature by Jean-Baptiste Isabey

(*Below*)   Mrs. Fitzherbert's house at Brighton. From an engraving *c.* 1810

danced with Ld. Clanricarde,* Baron Oxenstierna, Mr. Fane, Prince Stanislaus Potocki, Mr. Hutchison, Mr. Knutzen, Comte Chrétien Danniskiold,† Ld. Worcester, & Ld. Arthur Hill. I came away a little tired but perfectly charmed with my first Almack's. The only thing I disliked was Mama having to chaperone Miss Beauclerk.

In spite of a preponderance of Scandinavian diplomats this might be accounted a fairly good beginning.

Morning visits were the fashion. Among Louisa's most regular callers at this time were Brooke Greville, cousin Charles of the diarist, Miles Stapleton, nick-named 'the Baron' though it was thirteen years before he successfully claimed the Barony of Beaumont, which had been long in abeyance, and who Louisa once described as being 'infinitely more unintelligible than ever', and the Danish Count Danniskiold-Samsøe 'qui fait des compliments à ne pas finir'. Brooke Greville was destined to remain for some time a favourite, and so was another beau of her first season, the ten-years-younger John Shelley, who was nick-named 'Ivy'.

Louisa's enjoyment was not unmingled with ambition, for, one night, after going on from Harrington House to a musical party at the Countess of San Antonio's, where 'Princess Esterhazy was particularly gracious', she complained that she had 'not as yet succeeded in getting introduced to Lord Castlereagh, who was at both parties'. Castlereagh, nephew of the statesman, and Lord Chesterfield were among the most eligible bachelors available, though the latter was living openly with the attractive Mrs.

* Clanricarde, Ulick John, 14th Earl and 1st Marquess of Clanricarde (1802–1874). Succeeded to the earldom in 1808; created Marquess in 1825. Married 1825 Harriet, only daughter of George Canning, the statesman, and Viscountess Canning. He was supposed to have been made a Marquess for marrying Canning's daughter; and in 1826 had earned the disapprobation of society for making a young man under age drunk and winning £8,000 off him.

† Lensgrave (Count) Christian Conrad Sophus Danniskiold-Samsøe (1800–1886). Married (1) in 1833 Lady Elizabeth Brudenell-Bruce, daughter of the 1st Marquess of Ailesbury; and (2) in 1850 Hofdame Anna Amalie Louise Øllegard von Zytphen.

Lane-Fox. They were shortly to be hosts, together with some other bachelors, at a breakfast—that is, an afternoon garden-party with dancing—at Boyle Farm, Richmond, and when Louisa heard about this from Maryanne she was 'dying to be asked'. Next day 'all my fears respecting the Breakfast were quieted, for Minney told me I was already asked'.

Not every evening was enjoyable, however. One night the Smythes dined with a Mr. Giffard, and although they were served a 'magnificent dinner, I certainly was not amused, placed between a Naval officer with light hair & pointed face with sharp eyes, who I had never seen & a fat red faced Hunting esquire, in consequence I was reduced to eat Turtle pour passer le temps . . .'

June, 1827, ended in a whirl of dissipation. On the 25th: 'We went to a very large party at the Duke of Clarence's, which ought to have been perfect to reward us for spending an hour [in a traffic jam] between Carlton House and the Admiralty. The first person we saw on entering was Sir John Shelley* and his son. We were presented to the Duchess, qui n'est pas trop belle, . . . and proceeded to Ly. Stanley's—a nice quiet party with the Tyrolese.' The Tyrolese were four brothers and a sister brought over by Prince Esterhazy and much in demand as entertainers this season. Why their singing, dancing and pre-sumably yodelling should have made Lady Stanley's 'a nice quiet party' is not clear.

On the 28th Louisa went to Almack's 'with a Flamingo coiffure, which was universally admired', and danced with

* Sir John Shelley, 6th Baronet (1772–1852); married 1807 Frances, heiress of Thomas Winckley of Brockholes, Lancashire, by whom he had four sons (one of them being Louisa Smythe's friend 'Ivy') and two daughters. He was a famous sporting character and a friend of the Prince Regent's. He sold his estate of Michelgrove to pay debts, then bought with his wife's money the smaller property of Maresfield in Sussex. He was, before his marriage, the lover of Lady Haggerston, Mrs. Fitz-herbert's sister. His wife was an intimate friend and hero-worshipper of the Duke of Wellington and her memoirs are interesting. Sir John's was a senior branch of the poet Shelley's family. He was probably the only person ever to kick the Prince of Wales in the backside. (See the memoirs of Frances, Lady Shelley.)

Henry Cox, Mr. Trotter, Mr. Montgomerie, and Mr. Shelley, who is 'excessively entertaining and good-natured'. On June 28: 'Could not persuade Mary[anne] to go to Lady Ravensworth's which was the most lively ball I have as yet been at, & with reels and country dances was kept up till 5 o'clock. I danced twice with Thos. Liddell, who is a most goodnatured, amiable little person. I have often heard him called affected, but think it is very unjust. I also danced with Lord W. Thynne, Ld. Clanricarde, Mr. Shelley & [her cousin] William Stanley. . . . I was much delighted at Ly. Londonderry asking to be introduced to us that she might ask us to her Ball: this put me in high good humour and was one of the reasons I liked the Ball so much.'

At last the day of the Breakfast at Boyle Farm arrived, but Louisa was nearly done out of her party when news reached the household that her great-uncle Errington had been so inconsiderate as to die in Northumberland two days before.

Saturday, June 30, 1827

In the morning everything went wrong. We had to wait for both the coiffeur and dressmaker till near three o'clock; and at last Aunt Cha received a note from the Stanleys to say that Mr. Donkin was going to the North instantly upon hearing very bad accounts of poor Uncle Errington; and half an hour after we received the intelligence of his death. It certainly was not an unexpected event, and it is only to be wondered at that he arrived to such an advanced age; but however expected the event I could not help wishing it had not happened today, as it agitated dear Mama very much. We did not get to Richmond Hill till after four, where we found Aunt Fitz very cross & the rest of the party rather in a fuss; however we all arrived quite safely at Boyle Farm, where we proceeded down a little winding path till we reached the house where Lord Castlereagh & Ld. Chesterfield met us & presented us in the most graceful manner with bouquets. We then proceeded through the house, where the prospect that was unfolded to our eyes is worthy to be described by the pen of a Poet. . . .

In a passage of prose which seems half-intended to take off the inflated journalism of the period, Louisa goes on to describe what must have been a very successful party given on a lawn sloping down to the Thames in beautiful weather. The company was summoned by a *carillon* to dine in tents to the sound of military music and 'village bells'. After the Rosière Quadrille had been performed, dancing became general; then at nightfall the trees were lit up, there were fireworks, supper, and more dancing till three in the morning. 'It was a most brilliant winding up of the month of June.'

During July it becomes evident that the stock of both Danniskiold and Stapleton was falling. The Dane annoyed Louisa by being too ingratiating and possessive; the future Lord Beaumont she often referred to as 'the sentimental Baron'. Louisa was bored with them both. Brooke Greville and Shelley remained in the running, and Prince Gortchakoff, a Russian diplomat some years older than herself, began to flatter Louisa's vanity by paying her regular visits and talking to her in a grown-up way. Meanwhile Hyde and Charles Villiers, two attractive and cynical young men, brothers of the future Foreign Minister, Lord Clarendon, had appeared on the scene.

Uncle Errington had left the Smythes some money, but it was a bore having to go to balls in black. The season was not yet over.

Wednesday, July 4, 1827

We went to Tilney Street, and drove all over the Town to get black beads. Mama did not go to Almack's, therefore Mary & I went with Minney. We went en noir, but did not look so triste as our costumes bespoke us. . . . My partners were Mr. D. Kinnaird, Lord Clanricarde, Mr. Danniskiold (who is very indignant that it is possible to think or look at anything but himself), Lord Russell, the Bar[-on] of course, Mr. C. Villiers, Chevalier Fouella, Mr. Macdonald, Mr. Trotter. . . . Je me suis fort amusée. I did not get to bed until a very late hour on account of telling all my adventures to Mama. . . .

On the 17th there was a 'rowing party', and Louisa in a group composed of Mama, Maryanne, Lady and Miss Mildmay, Shelley, Fairfield and Fred Molyneux found themselves in 'three rowing boats, owing to the failure of the steam . . .' It was a long, exciting day, but apparently no one was too tired to enjoy a 'lively dinner' at Richmond, to walk about 'au clair de la lune', listen to the Tyrolese and dance. On their return to London they went on to another dance at the Mitchells' which lasted until five in the morning: and Louisa commented, 'We had 14 hours of uninterrupted pleasure, which I think might satisfy the most exigeant'.

The next day, Louisa wrote, '. . . We spent the day in endeavouring to recover the fatigue of the preceding day & to prepare ourselves for those of the night'. They attended the last Almack's of the season, and 'four o'clock nous a trouvé prenant la dernière tasse de thé à Almacks'. Louisa ends the entry on the hopeful note that 'we may all be as well & happy at the beginning of Almacks next year as we are at the conclusion of it in the year 1827'.

Shelley, now referred to as 'Ivy', and Prince Gortchakoff, who was in later years to become an eminent statesman, and Foreign Minister to the Tzar, were at this time in constant attendance.

On Friday, after an excursion in the open carriage to Putney with two of her favourites, Ivy Shelley and Hyde Villiers, to attend a picnic which was slightly spoilt by the importunities of Mr. Ogle, who 'was so dreadfully civil I could not get rid of him', there was a ball at Chesterfield House. At this, Louisa recorded tartly, 'I danced with . . . Mr. Ogle for the first and last time'. She was, however, full of admiration for the famous old mansion, which stood (till 1934) at the corner of Curzon Street and South Audley Street, but any daydreams she may have had of becoming its mistress were probably dashed at the sight of Lord Chesterfield's unconcealed devotion to Mrs. Lane-Fox. 'We had a country dance, which Ld. Chesterfield led with Mrs. Lane-Fox, and which nearly succeeded in knocking me up. However, at last I was prevailed upon to dance the Cotillon, which lasted till broad daylight. I was not a little flattered at Ivy valtzing with me after having put half the room behind his chair. We returned home I think I may say a little fatigued after all my dissipation, & I really wonder that dear Mama is not quite done up with it all.'

On August 2 the Smythe girls heard that the only son of their only surviving Boycott uncle had died at an early age. This meant that in the male line the Boycott family was extinct.

So the season petered out sadly for Louisa. The thirteen-year-old Cou, on the other hand, could raise sufficiently high spirits, one night after dinner with Aunt Fitz in Tilney Street, to join the gentlemen in 'smoaking' on the balcony.

Canning, the Prime Minister, and father-in-law of Louisa's dancing partner Clanricarde, also died at this time. Driving in the Park on August 14, Louisa met Lord Castlereagh, who told her about the formation of the new Government: but when she got home she wrote in her journal, 'I am ashamed to say, all I can remember is that Lord Goodrich [sic] is Premier'.

London was emptying; only a few relations and Prince Gortchakoff remained. Going to the play was Louisa's only diversion; and she was always a critical playgoer.

Louisa's first season had, perhaps very naturally, been inconclusive; she had formed no distinct preferences and received no direct proposals. The evening before their departure Mrs. Wat, driving in the open carriage with Louisa, injudiciously took her to task and quoted Count Danniskiold-Samsøe's remark that she had no heart. Louisa wrote, 'I think he made a little mistake, for though I do not think myself sentimentally inclined, to say that I am void of heart or affection is I hope a false accusation.' Did Mama think that, given a little more encouragement, Danniskiold, Shelley, Brooke Greville, 'the sentimental Baron', or even Prince Gortchakoff, might have proposed?

Mrs. Wat had taken a villa at Hammersmith, and the Smythes remained quietly there until November 9.

Only a few days before, Prince Gortchakoff had set about probing Louisa's character. ' He is an extraordinary person, & certainly frightens me a little by his penetration,' wrote Louisa. ' His wanting me to confess my partialities, weakness, character,

18

& in short everything is rather odd for a person so little acquainted with me as he is. What amuses me very much is the stress he lays upon my not throwing myself away upon a person older than myself. ... He did all he could to make me confess my faults, & when he found I would not, he told them me & also advised me to guard against what he thought was my côté faible, as he thought the love of admiration was the rock which I was most likely to split upon. He could not, he said, exactly describe my character, as he said no enigma was more difficult than a young lady of 18. I was delighted that with all his penetration he had not discovered my favourite, & that he placed Mr. Liddell, Hyde Villiers & H. Mildmay in the first rank. . . .'

Who was the favourite Gortchakoff failed to name? Shelley? The penetrating Prince was not far off the mark for Hyde Villiers soon came up into first place. The fascinating Russian diplomat was posted to Rome and disappeared thenceforth from Louisa's life.

Back at Cumberland Place life was slightly gayer. Louisa struck up a friendship with Georgina Elphinstone, daughter of Lady Keith and granddaughter of Johnson's friend, Mrs. Thrale. She also acquired a new beau in Mr. Fairfield, whom she was to see much of in Brighton during the winter. One morning the Smythe girls and Fanny Hayman were escorted by Hyde Villiers and Henry Cox to visit Deville, a fashionable phrenologist, the absurdity of whose proceedings seems to have struck Louisa. 'The room . . . was dark, high, hung with lamps decorated with skulls. . . . Cou was pronounced to have great capacities, strong feelings, strong sense of justice. . . . Fanny wanted exciting and inwiting. . . . Extensive powers were my lot, strong passions when let loose, organ for poetry, good temper, strong attachments, etc. Mr. Villiers had, I think, a finer set of organs than the rest of the party. . . . We were all musical, talents for languages and drawing. We returned in the snow, not a little elated with our fine organs, and I have formed a resolution to begin miniatures as soon as possible!'

1827 ended with the Smythe family paying their winter visit to Mrs. Fitzherbert at Brighton.

1828

*Life at Brighton – Louisa's flirtation with Hyde Villiers –
Maryanne's engagement and marriage – Louisa embarks on
her second London season – She meets Sir Frederick
Hervey-Bathurst – Lady Londonderry's fancy-dress dance –
Sir Frederick proposes – Louisa's doubts – A trip abroad.*

To stay with Mrs. Fitzherbert at Brighton was to feel slightly
Royal, for if in London she was just another old lady living off
Park Lane, she was still treated as the uncrowned Queen of the
little seaside town. People 'ma'am-ed' her and stood up longer
for her than for others, Creevey wrote to his wife.

Whether it was Mrs. Fitz or the Prince who first 'discovered'
Brighton, it can safely be asserted that Brighton became what
it did—that is to say, the most fashionable of English watering-
places, the seat of a court, the largest city in Sussex and a name
famous throughout the world—as a result of their curious union.
They first stayed there together in July 1786, poor under the
burden of the Prince's debts, but happy in playing the favourite
eighteenth-century game of love in a cottage. In those days the
'Marine Pavilion', gracefully designed by Holland, though not
yet accounted a Royal Palace, was a simpler building. The Royal
Pavilion may be said to have owed its being to the Prince's
passion for building and his love for Maria Fitzherbert. Yet he
abandoned the lady long before the house had undergone its final
Indian metamorphosis, and by the time Nash's rebuilding was
finished it was no longer his home.

Although Ackermann had glorified the final state of the
Pavilion in his splendid volume of views by Nash and the elder
Pugin in 1825, and although the King had paid what was to
be his last visit to the town in 1827, Brighton had fallen
from Royal favour some years before. Too conscious of his

girth and his unpopularity to risk appearing in public more often than was absolutely necessary, the one-time Prince Charming, who could be charming still, screened by the woods of Windsor, basked in the cosy presence of the Marchioness of Conyngham. But his 'dearest and only beloved Maria' had remained faithful to the town where she had been happy with him in younger days. She was popular in Brighton, not only for the fashionable crowds that followed her there, bringing prosperity to the tradespeople, but because of her steady benevolence to the poor. Brighton in 1828 was, from a social point of view, the winter capital of the country.

Mrs. Fitzherbert's house at the corner of the Steyne and Steyne Lane had been built for her by Porden, the architect of the Royal Stables, in 1804. It still stands, though much chopped about, refaced with red brick, and in use by the Y.M.C.A. This house, though unpretentious, was bigger than it appears in old prints or than it looks from the Steyne today. The entrance was in the side street. There was a fine double staircase with a cast-iron balustrade in the Chinese taste, like those in the Pavilion; a large first-floor drawing-room, eighteen feet high and running the whole width of the house; and a covered verandah facing the broad and cheerful Steyne, from which Mrs. Fitz could look south towards the sea, and north towards the gardens of the Royal Pavilion where the King walked no more, and where in its gayer if less gorgeous days she used to receive the guests.

It is hard to imagine a more agreeable way for a girl such as Louisa to spend the winter: for at Brighton she could enjoy the simplicity of country life without the boredom of provincial society. People were up and down from London all the time. After walking on the Chain Pier (which stood some way to the east of where the Palace Pier stands today) Louisa and her cousin Maryanne Smythe would dine at home and receive visits from their various beaux. If there were no evening parties, or if there was none they wished to go to, they could always make music or play games as a pretext for decorous flirtation: but there was a dance nearly every night. The 7th Lancers were stationed in Brighton; and a number of London hostesses such as Lady Fremantle, Lady Marian Sotheby, the jolly, musical Countess of San Antonio and the not quite respectable Duchess of St. Albans* had taken houses and were giving parties. Every Wednesday during the winter season balls known as the local Almacks were held at the Old Ship Hotel: of these Mrs. Fitzherbert was Patroness, and tickets could only be secured through her.

Mrs. Fitz was evidently happy in the thought that her nieces enjoyed staying with her, for she wrote to Minney's husband in Paris 'there never was anything so delighted as the girls in this house'.

On January 1, Mrs. Fitzherbert had a dinner of twelve people, and Louisa decided that Captain Fremantle of the Coldstream Guards was 'the nicest of our Brighton beaux'.

Hyde Villiers did not make his appearance till Sunday, January 20. From then on, he and Louisa met daily, and it was with him that she had her first serious flirtation.

Sunday, January 20, 1828

This day was crowded with events. We took a little walk after Church, and the first person we met, to our surprise was Mr. Fairfield [who had left Brighton a few days before]. I was not less astonished to see Mr. Hyde Villiers, who arrived with the former at a late hour last night. They walked with us and then came to pay their respects to Aunt F. & Mama. . . .

Monday, January 21, 1828

Mary & I walked with Mrs. Dawson. It was a lovely day, but we did not meet a soul we knew. At last Mr. Fairfield

---

* Harriot (1777–1837), daughter, possibly legitimate, of Lieut. Matthew Mellon (who died in India eight months after she was born) and Sarah, a wardrobe mistress. She became a famous actress and from 1804 the mistress of Thomas Coutts, the banker, who was nearly seventy. In 1815 she married Coutts, who died in 1822. In 1827, being fifty, she married the twenty-five-year-old Duke of St. Albans, who was said to be simple-minded. Sir Walter Scott liked and respected her. After her death, the immense fortune of Thomas Coutts passed to his granddaughter by his first marriage, Angela, Baroness Burdett-Coutts, the philanthropist.

joined us. Mr. Villiers was nowhere to be seen, till we came in. I suppose he thinks it is the best policy to make himself wished. . . .

At this time Mr. Fairfield began to be referred to as 'Perfide', either for reasons of assonance or because he was paying more attention to Maryanne than to Louisa.

Wednesday, January 23, 1828
. . . Mr. Villiers and Perfide dined here . . . Aunt Fitz thought the dinner went off very pleasantly. We played at écarté & remained éveillé rather too long to please Aunt Fitz.

On January 25, Mrs. Fitzherbert gave a ball at Steyne House.

Friday, January 25, 1828
The celebrated day of our charming Ball. We went to the Pier before dinner to restore our faded roses. We all dined at three, & by half past ten we were dressed & in the drawing room. Our costumes were exceedingly admired. Mary opened the Ball with Mr. Fairfield & I with Mr. St. John. In the course of the evening I danced with Mr. Fairfield, Mr. Browne, Mr. Streatfield, alias Rosebud, Mr. Beauclerk, who most amiably arrived in time for the Ball, Mr. Hyde Villiers, Mr. Bathurst & Mr. Mildmay. There was a wonderful blaze of beauty, of which [the] Miss[es] Sheridan, Fremantle and Bagot were the most brilliant ornaments—not to forget the lovely little Endimion [unidentifiable]. We kept up the Cotillon, which Mary led with Perfide, till near 5. The Ball was universally considered charming. Aunt F. looked à merveille, & everybody seemed in high force.

Saturday, January 26, 1828
We did not make our appearance at breakfast till after two, when Mr. Villiers and Perfide came to talk over last night's ball. It was a heavenly day, quite like Spring. We walked on the Chain Pier, where we met all the world, who all seemed pleased with our Ball. Charles le Bienaimé, as Mr. Villiers

styled Mr. Beauclerk, walked with us. Perfide dined here—
he was quite knocked up—& Aunt Fitz retired at tea. Mr.
Villiers came to tea, but we were all sacrificed to the *Treasures*
[the servants, who would want to go to bed early] & sent to
bed by eleven. Today was rather agreeable considering it was
the day after so agreeable an evening.

Monday, January 28, 1828

A very disagreeable day. Mr. Villiers left Brighton for the
meeting of Parliament. . . .

Louisa was out of spirits until Hyde Villiers returned, a few
days later, with his brother, for a ball given by twenty-five
bachelors at the Old Ship to return hospitality they had received
during the winter at Brighton. 'The Miss Smythes', according
to a local paper, 'wore Swiss costumes of red and blue, chip hats
and flowers.'

The Assembly Rooms at the Old Ship Hotel consisted of a
handsome barrel-vaulted supper-room and a long ballroom with
a musicians' gallery: they were at the back of the hotel and
approached by their own separate double staircase. They still
exist and are still used for dances.

Friday, February 1, 1828

Friday, the day of the Grand Fancy Ball given by 25
Bachelors . . . Aunt Fitz, I am sorry to say, was unable to go
to the ball owing to a severe attack of rheumatism, which was
a great disappointment to the whole party. . . . By 11 we
arrived at the Almacks rooms, & were received on the staircase by the Gentlemen, who presented us with Bouquets. It
was a most brilliant & beautiful sight: the dresses were most
of them very pretty, & there was a very small share of
quizzes [provincial freaks]. . . . I danced the Cotillon,
Country dances, Valtz & Sauteuse, all of which I led, with
Mr. Fairfield, who did the honors quite beautifully, & exerted
himself to the utmost to keep up the Ball with spirit. His
fatigues were crowned with success, for the dancing was kept

up till half past 5, & the *Second* Supper was not over till 6. . . . The two Mr. Villiers came down on purpose for the fancy Ball. Mr. Villiers took me in to Supper, & Perfide took the young Circassian [probably Maryanne]. It was a very agreeable gay Ball, & was certainly the best, with the exception of Aunt Fitzherbert's, that we have had at Brighton.

People now began to take Louisa's flirtation with Hyde Villiers seriously.

Saturday, February 2, 1828
   We did not make our appearance till two, but I can not say I felt the worse for the fatigue of the preceding night. Aunt F. talked to me very seriously of Hyde Villiers, & said that the general report at Brighton was that he was come down to see how I should receive him, & that it was talked of as a settled thing. She also put me on my guard as to not showing him any particular preference if I did not wish to give him encouragement. . . . Mr. Fairfield & Mr. Villiers staid here till near dinner time, and were indignant at our refusing to be at home in the après-diner, but we were inexorable. I wonder Aunt F. does not remark Perfide & Nina [Maryanne], as I think they *occasionally* make themselves rather particular.

Sunday, February 3, 1828
   . . . in the evening we had a Thé. I observed Aunt Fitz's orders with regard to Hyde, who looked *rather* triste. This little reunion was not half so agreeable as that of last Sunday.

The next day Hyde Villiers appears to have made some pronouncement to Mrs. Wat which was either a declaration of his affection for Louisa or a renunciation of her on the grounds of her cold shoulder on the previous two evenings.

Monday, February 4, 1828
   An eventful day, but a most wretched one. I could not help suspecting from Perfide's manner the cause of Mr. Villiers'

interview with Mama: his letter quite overpowered me, & it was not without a *strong* effort that I contrived to get through the long hour of dinner. Of course I did not go to the Ball, & poor Mary was in consequence made a little victim. His letter was indeed *much* too touching, I cannot help feeling hurt, at having obeyed Aunt Fitz's injunctions too closely last night; however I hope it was and is all for the best, I am quite at a loss to imagine from what quarters he could have heard that I disliked him & that his presence was disagreeable to me,— that indeed is very far from being the case, as I always thought him a most agreeable charming person. The report I heard certainly was the cause of my being more cautious & less prévenante in my manner to him than I should have been towards a totally indifferent person.

Any sort of declaration of affection or proposal of marriage would always upset the Smythe girls far more than the death of a close relation.

Tuesday, February 5, 1828

The thoughts of answering Mr. Villiers' letter made me quite nervous, but with dear Mama's assistance I contrived to get through it. I am truly sorry it ever went so far, as notwithstanding all Hyde says about forgetting what has passed & behaving to him, when we meet, in the same unconstrained manner that I usually do to my other acquaintances, I feel it will be quite impossible, & though I would not for worlds lose his agreeable society, yet I must confess I dread the first meeting. Perfide came to see us at luncheon, after which he left Brighton. We then drove about in the open carriage, & the day really was much too triste.

Thursday, February 7, 1828

Mama had a most affecting letter from Mr. Hyde Villiers, in which was enclosed a short note to me. I cannot express how unhappy the whole business has made me, & how much I dread the meeting in London. We walked on the Pier, &

26

much malgré nous were obliged to go to a Carpet Dance at the Duke of Roxburgh's. We d'abord went to the Play, which was patronised by the 7th. Hussars & their Band, which made it rather agreeable.

It is not clear exactly why Louisa's romance with Hyde Villiers came to an end. Either he had never had any serious intentions for Louisa, and her sudden coldness to him, assumed on Aunt Fitz's instructions, forced him to show his hand—that is, to apologise for having made her conspicuous, and to beat a dignified retreat: or else he was quite sincere in his devotion, and the Smythe family considered him an inadequate match, being a younger son. (The then third Earl of Clarendon was an old man with an only daughter: the title would therefore descend to his nephew George, Hyde's elder brother: and to marry a Villiers was not nothing.) At any rate, Hyde died unmarried four years later.

All the attention of the Brighton household was suddenly concentrated on the courtship of Maryanne Smythe by Edward Jerningham. This proceeded at a lightning pace, despite what Louisa considered the dullness of the two lovers. In her journal, and perhaps in conversation with Cou, she nick-named Jerningham 'the Stick'. He was only a younger son of Lord Stafford, but he was a Catholic, and Aunt Fitz seemed to be delighted.

Maryanne was pretty in a rather silly way, good-natured, lethargic and uninteresting. She had none of Louisa's or Cou's appetite for amusement and flirtation. Mystery envelops her early years; she had only made her first appearance in Mrs. Fitz's household in 1820, at which time she was probably about fifteen. Whether she was really a daughter of Jack Smythe, as was given out, or whether she was the child of Mrs. Fitzherbert and the Prince of Wales, is uncertain to this day. Sir Shane Leslie points out that it is extremely doubtful that Maryanne was a daughter of Jack Smythe by his wife, the widow Strickland, for family tradition holds that this lady died childless, and we know that in later years Maryanne did not defer a journey to

Norfolk at the time of Mrs. Jack's death. Mrs. Fitzherbert was to write to Minney in November 1831 'Mary [Maryanne] starts for Cossey tomorrow. She is quite well and I shall be glad when she is settled there. I have just had a letter from Charles to announce the death of Strickland *alias* Mrs. Jack Smythe . . .' Mrs. Jack cannot have been Maryanne's mother. On the other hand, Mrs. Fitzherbert was not so passionately fond of Maryanne as she was of Minney, which is odd if she were her only child. It seems to me probable, if not certain, that Maryanne was an illegitimate daughter of Jack Smythe.

Sunday, March 9, 1828

Mama went to Church for the first time since her illness. We had an excellent and affecting sermon. On our return we found that Mary had received a proposal from the Stick, which I must confess rather astonished me, as I never saw any Châteaux en Espagne realised so soon. The accomplishment of them now certainly depends on Mary, as he is devoted: the connection in every way desirable. In short, nothing now remains but Mary's private sanction, which is certainly rather necessary. I was much amused by Mama & Aunt Fitz not only settling the wedding, but deciding what the pretty little couple were to do afterwards, as if Mary were the person least concerned. One is never a proper judge of the sentiments of others, till one's own have been called forth in a similar manner, but at present it seems to me that nothing could induce me to pay the slightest attention, much more to—but enough of this; I have no time for moral reflections.

The Smythes left Brighton at midday on March 13, arriving in London at half-past five, to find Aunt Charlotte Boycott with a bad cough. Louisa's dreaded first meeting with Hyde Villiers was soon over. 'I was writing in the drawing room quite by myself when Mr. Villiers was announced. I was taken quite by surprise; however we shook hands, and I immediately left him to call Mama. I think that hazard managed our meeting beautifully. I thought him looking very ill, but I felt much too nervous

Sir Frederick Hervey-Bathurst
From the miniature by James Holmes

Lord Ossulston with his sister Emma (Lady Fitzharris)
From a painting by an unknown artist

to return to the drawing room till his visit was nearly over.' The same day 'Mama affronted Uncle Hunter'.

Aunt Fitz brought Maryanne up to London at the end of March. There was a question of whether Maryanne and Jerningham could afford to get married. 'The young man is Edward Jerningham, second son of Lord Stafford,' Mrs. Fitz wrote to Minney in Paris, 'very amiable, good-looking and gentleman-like. . . . There are unfortunately ten younger children, their fortune five thousand each, which is so very trifling that though I shall give Mary at present twenty thousand added to this, they could not exist without a further addition. I have written to beg they will do something more. If this is not acceded to, the marriage cannot take place. However I do not as yet quite despair. Fortunately Mary has not seen enough of him to be much attached and feels the smallness of his fortune would be a great drawback to their mutual comfort, for it really would not enable them to have the common necessaries and comforts of life, and if they should have children they would absolutely be beggars.' It was certainly not a very furious love-match on Maryanne's side. Everything, however, was settled satisfactorily, and preparations for the wedding went ahead.

Mrs. Fitzherbert gave her servants a ball on the night of Maryanne's wedding, going out herself with Minney to spend the evening at Lady Stanley's. A letter she wrote to Maryanne at Tunbridge the next day gives an amusing glimpse of the sort of mishaps to which Mrs. Wat was prone. Mrs. Fitz clearly thought her sister-in-law rather a joke, and imagined her household to be run in a haphazard manner. 'Mrs. Wat brought me home from Lady Stanley's and her new footman was so extremely in liquor that we were obliged to get one of Sir Thomas' servants to hold him behind the carriage to keep him from breaking his neck. Her carriage wheel broke down as she left this house in the morning. There never was anything so unlucky as she is with her Establishment. . . .'

Monday, June 16, 1828
The day of Mary's wedding, which we all attended as

Bridesmaids. The Bride looked very pretty and behaved remarkably well. I never saw anything half so nervous as the
whole ceremony; the meeting in the vestry room beforehand
is only too awful—it made me and Maria very nervous. The
Miss Jerninghams laughed all the time. After the ceremony
we returned to a fine breakfast in Tilney St., where Mary
remained till four o'clock. We drank tea with the Stanleys.

Of the four Misses Jerningham who attended Maryanne as
bridesmaids, only one was ever married and she died a nun.
Their giggling did not get them very far.

Shortly before the Jerningham wedding, on the day after her
nineteenth birthday, Louisa had met Sir Frederick Hervey-
Bathurst. He was a cadet of the house of Hervey, his great-
grandfather having been eighth son of the first Earl of Bristol.
His parents were dead, but his grandmother had married in
1797 Sir William Fremantle, who held a position at Court. Lady
Fremantle had been one of Louisa's hostesses at Brighton during
the winter, and her nephew by marriage, Captain Fremantle,
Louisa had described on New Year's Day as 'quite the nicest of
our Brighton beaux'. Frederick, though, was of far more consequence, besides being eighteen years younger; he was a
baronet with a fine property in Wiltshire; he was twenty and an
officer in the Grenadier Guards.

It is evident that the Fremantles had spoken of Sir Frederick
to Louisa, for on Wednesday, June 11, she wrote: 'I was at last
introduced to Sir Frederick, who is very handsome, but appears
dreadfully shy.'

A week after her meeting with Frederick Hervey-Bathurst
Louisa was walking with him in Kensington Gardens, chaperoned by her Aunt Emma Ravenscroft. That night at Almack's
he pressed her to make up a water-party for Greenwich on the
next day, and 'it was in vain that we raised objections, Sir
Frederick a applani toutes les difficultés'. Rain, however, prevented this excursion.

Although from now on Frederick took up more and more of
her attention, Louisa was also attracted by 'le très aimable'

William Ashley, brother of the famous philanthropist Lord Shaftesbury. He had a good voice and pleasant manners. Her confidante during these agitated and indecisive seasons—or at least her chief female friend, for it is doubtful if Louisa was the type of girl to confide all her secrets even to her diary—was Georgiana Elphinstone.

Sunday, June 29, 1828

Drove with Mama after Church to Percy's Cross, to settle finally about our costumes [for Lady Londonderry's fancy dress ball at Holdernesse House on the next day], & after a little conversation we succeeded in understanding each other. We found all the Ashleys there. Mr. Ashley était aimable comme à l'ordinaire, he certainly is a most charming fascinating person, & I never yet saw anyone who upon so short an acquaintance I liked so much. What bad taste of Ly. Mary Brudenell! [who had presumably rejected him]. If report does not err in saying she behaved ill to him, I cannot forgive her for it. He seems to be so mild & perfectly amiable—then such a voice!

Monday, June 30, 1828

The day of Ly. Londonderry's celebrated Fancy Ball, which by far exceeded in magnificence anything I have ever seen. We went very early to Ly. Fremantle's to fetch Sir Frederick who belonged to the Turkish Quadrille, & a little after ten we proceeded to Ly. Londonderry's, where the coup d'oeil really was most splendid. Ly. Londonderry's dress as Queen Elisabeth was magnificent & very becoming; not so was the dress of Mary Queen of Scots, Ly. Ellenborough, who did not look at all well. The whole court was dazzling in magnificence & splendor. . . . I thought I never saw people look so well or so handsome as they did that night. Besides the Court, there were three Quadrilles; two remarkably pretty, namely the Turkish & Grecian, & the other, in the Court dress of George the third, very eccentric. The dancing did not begin till a late hour, & was kept up till 8. I danced a great deal.

The Quadrille I danced with Sir Frederick; my other partners were, Mr. Villiers, l'aimable Mr. Ashley, Mr. Brooke Greville, Ivy, who was as gay tonight as autrefois, & took me to supper, Ld. Arthur Hervey, Mr. Edwardes &c. I think it would be quite impossible to say who looked the best, or whose costume was the most becoming or splendid. One Quadrille consisted of 2 Miss Liddells, 2 Johnstones, Miss Elphinstone, Ly. E. Kerr, & Miss Kinnaird & myself, so I flatter myself it was not a little admired. I enjoyed the Ball of all things. Mama went all in black with a veil, & looked remarkably well.

No wonder Louisa enjoyed the Ball; for it was a kind of apotheosis of her first two seasons. She was surrounded by her three old admirers, Brooke Greville, 'Ivy' Shelley, and Hyde Villiers, she danced a Quadrille with Frederick Hervey-Bathurst, who was, as it were, her fiancé-elect; and she was able to indulge the melancholy but delicious thought that perhaps she liked William Ashley best of all. Yet she could not foresee what Fate held in store for her. Two days later she was to meet the beautiful young Lord Ossulston, with whom in the course of time she was to fall in love, and who was to be one of the reasons which prevented her from being united to Sir Frederick for nearly four years.

Wednesday, July 2, 1828
. . . We went to Almack's. . . . The only drawback to my amusement was our having Miss Beauclerk to chaperone, who scarcely danced the whole night. My partners were F. Seymour, Ivy, Mr. Villiers, . . . Ld. Ossulston, Mr. Ashley, Mr. Edwardes, & twice [with] Sir Frederick.

Poor Charlotte Beauclerk, whom Mrs. Wat had been obliged to chaperone at Louisa's first Almack's the year before, and who must have been very plain as nobody asked her to dance, lurks as a sad shadow in the background of the Smythe girls' brilliant London seasons. She died unmarried.

Louisa began to refer to Sir Frederick in her journal as 'the Elu'. This seems to suggest that he was chosen or 'elected' for her by Lady Fremantle and Mrs. Wat.

Next Monday Louisa went on her 'first Steam Party' up the river to the Castle Inn at Richmond. 'The *Elu* was much annoyed at our telling him that we were advised to avoid him as one of the most dissipated men in Town. We were on the brink of a quarrel, but he thought better of it. . . .' The following day, though, he was 'très charmant'.

Saturday, July 12, 1828
. . . Aunt Stanley spent the evening here. She talked of nothing but my marriage with Sir Frederick, who she praises highly. He is certainly the only one of my acquaintances or intimate friends who I would accept instantly, without a scruple; that is if I thought he was really attached to me.

Later in the month Frederick wrote to ask Mrs. Wat if he might propose to Louisa. She wrote back to him at Hungerford, where he was stationed.

> 6, Gt. Cumberland Place.
> August 1st.

My dear Sir Frederick
    Though your letter did not very much surprise me, yet I confess it has agitated me more than I can possibly express, feeling that the future happiness or misery of a Being so dear to my heart entirely depends on the result.—At the same time I can with truth assure you that as far as I have been able to judge of your character upon so short an acquaintance, you seem to possess those good qualities & principles which I should most desire in a son in law—therefore you have my answer which I have reason to think will not be a very unfavourable one; but on an Event of such importance I wish her to be guided entirely by her own judgement & feelings.
    You are both very young & I perfectly agree with Lady Fremantle in thinking that things had much better remain as

they are till you return from Ireland; & I promise you a cordial reception when or wherever we may meet.—My Autumn plans are undecided but I think the Rhine will be our attraction. The disputed Berline is arrived & Miss Boycott has bought it.—She & Louisa desire me to add their kind regards to those of yours very truly,

Louisa Smythe.

Pray take care of your health & do not kill yourself with cricket.

This presumably was read as a provisional acceptance. Louisa was taken down on a visit to the Fremantles' at Englefield Green, a village on the edge of Windsor Great Park. This ordeal of inspection by Frederick's grandmother, unmarried aunt, youngest sister, step-grandfather, step-great-uncle and step-first-cousin passed off well, although 'the first ½ hour before dinner was particularly gênant'. Next day the party drove through Windsor Park to see the first giraffe—or camel-leopard, as it was then called—ever to reach these shores. (George IV was so fascinated by this strange beast that when it died shortly afterwards he had it stuffed.)

Sunday, August 31, 1828
. . . The events of this month still appear to me as a dream & I cannot as yet believe in the reality of them.

Thursday, September 4, 1828
. . . I am *very* sorry to hear my little affairs are becoming the general topic of public conversation.

Saturday, September 6, 1828
. . . Heard from Sir Frederick.

Monday, September 8, 1828
Received a very kind letter from Ly. Fremantle who I am sorry to say has received a very bad account of Sir Frederick's health.

Friday, September 12, 1828

. . . Mama had a much better account of Sir Frederick from Ly. Fremantle. . . . I made myself almost unhappy at the thought of my fate being so soon settled. Nobody, more than myself can be aware of the *very* happy life that I have hitherto led, & excepting occasional little désagrémens, which it would be impossible to go through the world without experiencing, I have indeed had a most unusual share of happiness. The current of my life has hitherto run most smoothly, & I have not a wish to change my present happy state—but I must think more seriously than of amusing myself for the passing hour, & give a time to these sombre reflections.

Mrs. Smythe wrote again to Sir Frederick.

6, Gt. Cumberland Place.
Sept. 13.

My dear Sir Frederick

I assure you we have been very unhappy about you for some time past hearing you were *very* ill—but a lr. from Ly. F. yesterday assures us you are much better—& I hope soon to hear from yourself that you are quite well, that you obey Dr. C-s orders & do not over-fatigue & over-heat yourself at *Cricket*, Tennis, &c. If you will write a few lines by return of post we may receive it before we go, which I intend doing on Thursday the 18th & after that you may direct to Post Restante à Bruxelles—I intend going there first & if the weather is fine perhaps we shall go a little way up the Rhine & then to Paris, & return here early in Novr. & about the end of the month or the beginning of Decr. I hope we shall have the pleasure of seeing you here in high *health* & *beauty*. It is rather an arduous undertaking going abroad without a Gentleman but I hope my Courier will prove a treasure & we shall find numbers of people we know at Bruxelles & Paris—I assure you we were charmed with our visit to E. Green. Nothing cd. equal the kindness & attention of dear Ly. Fremantle, Sir Willm. & all the family—& I was particularly gratified by their approbation of my dear *Child*. She was rather nervous about the Visit at first, but their goodnature soon put her at ease. . . . London is a perfect Desert & we are all longing for Country Air—a few *odd Men* call sometimes, & that is all.—I wish you were here to go abroad with us. I have engaged Ld. A. Hill to cross the Channel with us.—Louisa is very busy with her Drawing Master, & begs you will read the second series of the Canon Gate by Walr. Scott as she is making sketches from the 'fair Maid of Perth'. She desires me to say everything kind for her & we both desire you to recall us to the memory of yr. Bror. Lionel.

Believe me, dear Sir Frederick, very truly yrs.

L. Smythe.

I hope change of air will do us all good. Louisa has still a bad cough & cold, & Cou has been very unwell with a sore throat & is *still* languid.

Whatever Mrs. Wat might write to Sir Frederick before the Smythes left London for the Continent Louisa had made up her mind not to consider herself engaged.

Wednesday, September 17, 1828

. . . I am now going to leave London, where I have this season been *very* happy & much amused. Had I it within my power to recall the last four months I think I should have acted very differently to what I have done in many instances, but that alas! I can not do. I wish I had shewn more firmness & resolution, but no one except myself is to blame. It strikes me more forcibly every day that my answer ought to have been in very different words, but I since have had time to reflect, & it constantly comes across me that I was too precipitate in my answer, & I am quite unhappy that I did not take my dear Mama's advice. I still hope to be able, without many disagreements to be able to rectify the effects of my hasty & inconsiderate conduct. I did not reflect what it was to leave one of the happiest of homes, & the kindest & best of Mamas. No, I must endeavour with composure to hear my conduct

36

blamed by the world, for I cannot make up my mind to leave my dear Mama, & so young to quit my happy home.

Either Louisa had decided that Frederick was rather a bumpkin, that she was not in love with him, and that she would not marry somebody she could not whole-heartedly admire and respect: or she wanted to enjoy the gaiety and admiration of one or two more London seasons.

Louisa's journal of the foreign tour is not remarkable for any original observations on places, people or pictures. The Smythes stayed at Brussels, where Louisa was much attracted to Emila Bagot, the daughter of the British Minister, and visited the battlefield of Waterloo, which provoked philosophical reflections. They went up the Rhine. At Frankfurt, Mama heard from Lady Fremantle. Louisa recorded: 'I can only say how sorry I am to find that she considers everything in so settled a state, as *I* am far from doing so.' They continued through Lausanne and Geneva, returning home by Lyons and Paris.

Back in London Mrs. Wat was obliged to write an awkward letter to Frederick Hervey-Bathurst.

> Cumberland Place.
> Wedy. 3rd. Dec.

My dear Sir Frederick,

We have returned here about a fortnight after a most delightful tour through France, Belgium, Germany & Switzerland—Your letter arrived on Monday & we were very glad to hear such a good acct. of your health & that you are so soon likely to return to your friends in England.—

I must now tell you candidly why Louisa did not answer your second letter as she promised to do—After the flattering preference you expressed for her, to which you know her answer, we thought the subject was to rest between those most interested, & consequently I never named it but to two of our nearest Relations—you may guess therefore how much she was annoyed and frightened at being wished joy by everyone she has seen both before & since her return upon an

Event they hear of as finally decided, when we only look upon it, & I am sure you must do the same, as depending upon mutual liking on longer acquaintance—this has made her quite unhappy as she feels herself much too young & too sensible of the responsibility of so serious an engagement to enter upon it hastily—& though her sentiments for you have not changed, you have known each other so short a time, it is impossible you can either of you judge whether your characters are suited to each other, & certainly a decision of such importance can only be made in a hurry by those who think lightly on the subject.

Though I feel confident that you must look upon what has passed in the same way that we do, my dear Sir Frederick, I think it best to explain myself that we may meet without restraint, & I am sure you will agree with me that nothing can be more distressing to the delicate feelings of a young girl than all these premature congratulations.

Believe me, we shall be very happy to see you again, & I am sure you have too much goodness & delicacy of feeling not to understand the motives that have induced me to write this explanation instead of waiting till we meet.—

Believe me dear Sir Frederick
                    Very truly yrs.
                              L. Smythe.
We shall be glad to see your Brother again if he has not forgotten his Brighton acquaintance.

Christmas found Mrs. Wat and her girls once more with Aunt Fitz at her house on the Steyne; and the round of Brighton gaieties was resumed.

1829

Cou's first admirer – Mrs. Fitzherbert's Grand Fancy Ball –
Sir Frederick and Mrs. Fitzherbert – Louisa's third season –
A gap in the journal.

Cou could not make her début for three years, but she was allowed to go to dances at Brighton, and at fourteen she already had a beau. This was a young Frenchman, the vicomte de Flavigny, who, although he rather bored the superior Louisa, seems, in a touching way, to have experienced all the delicious pains of first love for her fascinating little sister. Maurice de Flavigny was the brother of Mme d'Agoult, who lived with Liszt and bore him three children, including Cosima Wagner. It is curious to think of Cou's first admirer becoming uncle by marriage to the composer of 'The Ring'. I like to imagine Cou at this time jumping up and down with excitement and running to meet the years as they advanced inexorably towards her.

'Ivy' Shelley, William Ashley ('the Guglielmo') and Charles Villiers, who seemed to be replacing his brother Hyde, were Louisa's favourites of the moment, with Sir James Ogilvy, Sir Vincent Cotton, and Lord Porchester as runners up. Charles Villiers's sharp tongue earned him the title of 'Le Vipère'. The celebrated diner-out, 'Poodle' Byng, and the faithful Lord Arthur Hill were as ever regular visitors at Mrs. Fitzherbert's house; these, however, were older men. Byng played a game with Louisa, pretending to be a rejected admirer.

Mrs. Fitzherbert was to give a fancy-dress ball, and preparations for the Rose Quadrille, which was to be the set piece of the evening, began several days ahead.

Thursday, January 8, 1829
. . . We drew lots for the Rose Quadrille. Some of the roses

came up as if they had been previously arranged & not left to Il destino, but I believe all save Flavigny was abandoned to fate. Mr. Byng m'amuse fort. I do not mind his playing the part of the ci-devant.

To Louisa's consternation, Sir Frederick, undaunted by her evasive behaviour in the last six months, returned to the charge and arrived on the very evening of the ball at Steyne House.

Monday, January 12, 1829

The day of our grand fancy ball. The morning was of course spent in preparation, & we all dined together at an early hour. Flavigny on his arrival came to us immediately in a great state of fuss to know who fate had assigned to him for the first Quadrille; however we soon quieted his fears. Mama received a note just before the Ball from Sir Frederick to say he was arrived and wished for an invitation. This, as can easily be imagined, put me in a very nervous uncomfortable state, & though I am reported to possess but a small share of feeling, I confess I dreaded the meeting. I danced . . . twice with Sir Frederick, four times with Mr. Ashley, three times with Ivy, who was tout aimable ce soir-là. . . . I heard afterwards that the Poodle & others had watched my meeting with Sir F. & pronounced me void of feeling, as they declared I met him like an indifferent person & was not in the least embarrassed.

The *Brighton Gazette* reported the dance with superlatives typical of journalism of the period. 'Mrs. Fitzherbert's grand Fancy Dress Ball was not only the most splendid party given during the present season, but the most splendid probably ever seen in Brighton. There were more than two hundred present, including all the Fashionables now residing in the town. No magnificence can be conceived greater than that displayed in the various dresses, which were exceedingly rich. . . . The fine rooms of the noble mansion, thus lighted up, presented a most brilliant and dazzling appearance; and on the supper table every

40

delicacy was seen in profusion. . . . We do hope that Mrs. Fitzherbert may long enjoy health to promote the prosperity of the town. . . . Mrs. Fitzherbert, who we are happy to say, looked in excellent health and spirits, wore a rich dress of white satin trimmed with blonde, and a white dress hat; the Hon. Mrs. Dawson-Damer, a handsome black fancy dress, head-dress of diamonds; Hon. Mrs. Jerningham, a black velvet dress, with a richly ornamented stomacher. . . . Miss Smythe, a beautiful Turkish dress, with handsome turban of scarlet and gold and a profusion of diamonds; Miss C. Smythe looked most lovely in a simple white fancy dress, with a veil confined with a chaplet of white roses. . . .'

That Frederick Hervey-Bathurst, once—if briefly—the official fiancé of Louisa, and now put on trial, should have been content to share her company with Ashley and the others, resigning himself to being one of a band without making scenes or doing anything to arouse adverse comment from Louisa in her diary, raises him in our estimation. He seems to have had staying power, and to have submitted with good grace to his apprenticeship. Perhaps Lady Fremantle had ordered him to persevere; perhaps he loved Louisa.

Mrs. Fitzherbert, however, did not love Frederick Hervey-Bathurst. She thought him a bore, and she made this clear. She probably did her best to influence Louisa against him, and it appears that, some time during March or April, she found an opportunity of indicating to the poor young man in a personal interview that he would not be welcome as a nephew. She cannot have minded his lack of intellectual pretensions for she had none herself: it can only have been his awkward manners that annoyed her. Even the kindest old ladies can sometimes be formidable. She had warned off Hyde Villiers. She warned off Frederick.

Soon after the Smythes' return to London, at a ball given by the Duchess of St. Albans, William Ashley criticised Louisa. He 'had rather a singular conversation with Mama respecting me, & I sadly fear from what he said to her that he thinks me a Coquette & a flirt, & that the generality of the world give me credit for following Mrs. Dawson's example & walking in her footsteps. All this I should have avoided if I had been able sooner to make up my mind, but I shrink with horror at the thought of being seized with repentance when my affections are once placed.'

Louisa had made her own decision. She would keep on dancing, in the hopes of finding someone (suitable) whom she liked better than Sir Frederick. Her third season began. Louisa became so overwhelmed by the social whirl that she abandoned her diary at the beginning of May, not to resume it until the following year.

Sir Frederick continued to visit her and to dance with her while he was in London, but he and Louisa drifted apart. Watching her pursuit of gaiety, he probably decided she was hopeless and gave up the chase. On November 27, Mrs. Fitzherbert wrote from Brighton to Maryanne, '. . . Sir Frederick was of the party, grown so very ugly, thin and ill that you would not know him again. He never speaks, and is as stupid as possible. Everything is at an end between him and Lou, and I hope this year, we shall have neither lovers or *idiots*.'

Frederick may have been looking thin and ill because he was unhappy, and it is not unlikely that he was frequenting Mrs. Fitz, who he must have known disliked him, simply to have news of Louisa.

Mrs. Fitzherbert was over-optimistic in hoping for no more 'lovers or idiots'. Louisa had a flirtation at Brighton with an amusing Frenchman called Charles de Mornay.* He was certainly most unsuitable: he had neither money nor prospects, and had come over to England on the look-out for an heiress. Aunt Fitz sent him packing.

* Charles-Henri de Mornay (1803–1878). In the French diplomatic service. Minister in Stockholm under King Louis Philippe. Created Count 1845. No relation to the duc de Morny, half-brother of Napoleon III, with whom Sir Shane Leslie confuses him.

1830

Trouble over Charles de Mornay – Louisa's fourth season not recorded – Death of the King – Lord Ossulston – William Stanley – The new King at Apsley House – Visits to Ravensworth, Chillingham and Hooton – Mrs. Fitzherbert and William IV – The missing miniature.

February 1830

We spent the beginning of this year at Brighton on a visit to Aunt Fitzherbert, where, with a *few* exceptions we spent our time very agreeably, and had we not remained so long I think we might have avoided the disagreeable occurrences which terminated our visit. The few last days were so *extremely* unpleasant, that they nearly effaced the recollection of the previous part of our séjour, which I had enjoyed very much. Our amiable Aunt is decidedly very capricious, in nothing is it more evident, than in the way she varies her treatment and manner towards those she lives intimately with. At the beginning of our séjour at Brighton Aunt Charlotte was everything in opposition to Mama, who unfortunately never succeeded in doing anything to please her; then she became tired of Aunt Cha's brusque manner, & though she pressed her to stay, was evidently not sorry when she went away; Mama had by this time become a great favourite & all went on smooth till a short time before we came away when the amiable Charles de Mornay put us all de travers. I had every reason to be delighted, & in good humor, as luckily I always contrived, & happily succeeded in constantly remaining a favorite. Everything I did was right; she delighted in chaperoning me—enfin for some time I was all perfection. But at last her behaviour & whole absurd conduct to & about Mr. de Mornay made me so indignant that I

43

could not help shewing how *very* much I was annoyed by it. Therefore instead of regretting my departure from Brighton, I quite sighed to find myself once more at home. I know nothing more truly disagreeable than a family reunion when everyone seems to be in a constant state of fear & restraint, dreading lest a word should escape them.

Such was the agreeable way in which we ended our visit, & most delighted I was when the day of our departure was fixed. I could scarcely persuade myself to tell Aunt Fitzherbert that I regretted leaving Brighton. It was such an egregious falsehood. We had a lively *dispute*, which was nearly terminating in a quarrel, after dinner the last Sunday, & in which I took a very active part.

Back in London, Louisa found her Aunt Charlotte Boycott very melancholy, having just attended the death-bed of her sister Sophia Bowen.* However, 'we found our house very clean and nice, & a new Pianoforte added much to the ornament & agrément of the drawing-room'.

Louisa's diary again fell victim to the onslaughts of London society.

King George IV was dying at Windsor under the eye of his last favourite, Lady Conyngham. Few people were sorry. Mrs. Fitzherbert, however, who had not seen her fantastic, caddish but attractive husband for nearly twenty years, felt the stirrings of old love and duty. Under cover to Sir Henry Halford, the King's doctor and her own, she sent him a letter. This he is said to have snatched and read eagerly, then thrust under his pillow: but by then he was too weak and wandering to reply. Mrs. Fitzherbert had come up to London, ready for a summons. She waited in vain. Her husband died on June 28.

The new King, William IV, sent the Duke of Sussex to Mrs. Fitzherbert, telling her to put her household in mourning.

* In recent editions of Burke's *Landed Gentry*, under the entry for the Wight-Boycott family, who descend in the female line from Thomas Boycott of Rudge, the date of Mrs. Bowen's death is wrongly given as 1848.

By the time Louisa's diary is resumed in mid-July the season is nearly over, but she is in love with Lord Ossulston. Charles Augustus Bennet, Lord Ossulston, was the son and heir of the fifth Earl of Tankerville. Lady Tankerville came of an even older and more distinguished family, the house of Gramont: her parents, the duc and duchesse de Gramont, had been émigrés, and Corisande was one of the mixed bag of children brought up at Devonshire House. She was now a formidable dowager, and probably thought a mere Miss Smythe not nearly good enough for her handsome son.

Monday, July 12, 1830

Received a note from Minney this morning to scold me for not going to the Countess last night. I only regretted it for an instant, & that was when I heard *who* I had missed seeing by not going. I went to Tilney St. this morning but did not see Aunt Fitz. Minney was there, I never was more struck by anything than the change in her appearance, anxiety and jealousy have aged her to a degree which I should not have thought possible. However, we went together this evening to a little musical reunion at Mrs. Bradshaw's * and from thence proceeded to Ly. Tankerville's which I liked better than any party I have been at this year. Lord Ossulston was most amiable & looking *so* handsome—at the end of the evening he sung quite beautifully with the Guitar, I never heard so touching or so lovely a voice—he seems to be adored by his family & I am *sure* not without reason. Ly. Fitzharris [his sister] said we had behaved very ill in not going to Chillingham as we proposed last year. I told her we had some thought of going to the North this year, upon which she begged we would take them en passant. We remained there till late.

* Ann Maria Tree (1801–1862), the actress. A favourite star at Covent Garden from 1819 to 1825. Married Capt. James Bradshaw, R.N., in 1825. She gave up the stage and he went into Parliament. She continued to act privately, however, for Greville mentions her acting at Bridgewater House, in 1836, as 'perfection itself'. Her sister Ellen Tree married Charles Kean the younger.

Louisa now took to riding in the Park, and found it a convenient means of seeing more of Lord Ossulston. Her *confidant* and companion on these predatory excursions was her cousin William Stanley. A match between William and herself was considered possible, just as one between Rowland, William's next brother, and Cou came to be discussed two years later. Stanley inherited a great fortune, which he was to dissipate on the racecourse, and a property which had been in his family since the reign of Richard II, which he was to sell. He never married.

Tuesday, July 13, 1830
   . . . Saw Lord O. on horseback & returned early to prepare for riding. William wished me to try his horse again, which I did & liked it, as it went very quietly. . . .

Wednesday, July 14, 1830
   Had a very pleasant ride in the Park this morning with William & Mrs. Ellice. Mr. de Mornay paid us a tolerable long visit. We went in the evening to Ly. Cowper's—a nice party but nothing *particularly* amusing. The Master of the Rolls gave us tickets to go to the King's funeral, which we gave away, as of course we did not go—drove about in the morning. Cecil Forester was at Ly. Cowper's, just returned from canvassing. . . . Minney I thought looking a figure. It was remarked in Tilney St. as *odd* of Ly. Cowper giving a party the night before the King's funeral. Minney's soirée was thought nothing of.

Friday, July 23, 1830
   Quite a relief to wake without having to go to the Prorogation. Mama & I went to see the Procession, escorted by Mr. Edwardes. We had a very good view from Ld. Kensington's house on Carlton Terrace. The cream-colored horses are beautiful. Went to Tilney St., but did not see Aunt Fitz; found Maryanne sitting in her bedroom, & not attempting to get down. [Maryanne's second child, her first son, had been

born on June 28.] Oh! how I should get bored, with such a life & such an amiable, goodnatured, stupid husband. Mais qui se ressemble s'assemble. I rode late in the Park with Mrs. Ellice. Mr. Forester rode most of the time with us—*nothing* so attentive as new acquaintances. . . .

Cecil Forester, who came of a very handsome family, at this time looked like becoming a favourite.

Monday, July 26, 1830

The anniversary of dear Cou's birthday. We began our day by going early to the Grand Review in the Park. Cou & Mama went to see it from Ld. Hertford's,* & I foolishly en-countered the fatigue & heat of walking in the midst of the crowd. Ly. Georgina Wortley was my chaperone, besides which we were very well escorted, & escaped, most fortun-ately, without being run over or crushed to atoms. We were amply repaid for our trouble, for the sight was splendid. I was rather anxious for an invitation to the Duke of Wellington's Ball, but it came *so* late that I do not think the Ball at all compensated me for the trouble and worry I went through about it. We went in Black with crepe veils; I think I never was so ill coiffed or looked so atrociously ugly in my life—I was quite out of conceit with myself. Apsley House is very splendid, but the Gallery did not answer my expectations; it is too narrow for the length. His Majesty was very gracious

* Francis Charles Seymour, 3rd Marquess of Hertford (1777–1842), K.G. His mother was the Lady Hertford who supplanted Mrs. Fitzherbert in the affections of George, Prince of Wales. Married 1798 Maria Fagniani, illegitimate daughter of the Duke of Queensberry ('Old Q') and an Italian noblewoman. Celebrated for his unconcealed lubricity; caricatured by Thackeray as Lord Steyne in *Vanity Fair* and by Disraeli as Marquess of Monmouth in *Coningsby.* One of the richest men in the country.

Lord Hertford had three London houses: Hertford House in Manchester Square, now a museum of his family treasures and known as the Wallace collection; Dorchester House in Park Lane, on the site of which now stands an hotel; and a villa in Regent's Park. The house from which Mrs. Wat Smythe and Georgina watched the Review was of course Dorchester House.

to Mama, & broke through a large circle to come & speak to her. Those who were in uniform looked remarkably well, while those in Court dresses & weepers looked exactly like the Apothecary in 'Romeo & Juliet', or Undertakers just returned from a funeral—the Duke of Devon & Mr. de Mornay in splendid costumes looked perfectly frightful. The conversation of the night was Ly. Strachan and her daughter having been to the Palace without an invitation, & that, like all other illnatured stories, was spread about with great rapidity.

The journal seems continually petering out, and starting again in spurts, only to cease once more. At the end of the summer the Smythes were still in London. One night 'Rosa dined with Cou'. This was Mlle Laharpe, a former governess who had been sent away for developing an excessive devotion to Cou. Louisa was having drawing lessons from one artist and sitting to another. Charles de Mornay teased her one day about her friendship with William Stanley: 'he is determined upon *le Cousin* being très épris de *la Cousine* & thinks it du dernier mauvais goût that he should prefer la chasse aux perdrix to escorting me, to which of *course* I agreed . . .'

Suddenly, on September 26, Mrs. Wat and the girls are staying with the Ravensworths in Northumberland. They were in the course of a north-country tour which was to include Lord Ossulston, the Stanleys and the lakes.

Monday, September 27, 1830
We left Ravensworth this morning between nine & ten. I was sorry to go, as our visit had turned out very agreeable, & I felt nervous about Chillingham; however I tried to show it as little as possible. We reached Whitlingham early in the afternoon, where Mama stopped to lunch; & there we left dear Cou & Miss Delisle. It was a rainy dull evening & the Inn certainly looked most wretched. The road to Chillingham is very dreary, & the Castle certainly did not present a very lively appearance as we drove up to it. We got out of the

carriage, mounted a flight of steps, had to cross over a large old-fashioned court, then began to ascend a winding stone staircase, which I thought never would end, & at last we found ourselves in the drawing-room. Lady Tankerville soon made her appearance, received us très gracieusement, said she feared we might find it dull as they had only a family party in the house, consisting of Ld. & Ly. Fitzharris, Mr. Harris, & Ld. Ossulston. I was not sorry to hear this, thinking it much more likely to be agreeable. We took a turn in the flower-garden which is excessively pretty, & though so late in the season it is filled with roses and violets. We found Ld. & Ly. Fitzharris & Mr. Harris trying their skill in shooting Pistols. I was introduced to the two Harris, of whose conceit I had heard so much, & I was now left to judge whether reports had done them justice or not. Lord Ossulston soon returned from shooting, in high good looks. They dined punctually at 7, & I luckily was in very good time. Dinner went off very agreeably. Ly. Tankerville enquired for Cou & on hearing she was at Whitlingham immediately desired she might be sent for, to arrive in time for luncheon on the following day. We spent the evening in working, talking, écarté; & Mama & the Tankervilles played at Whist. We went to bed before 12, & I confess I retired the first night under the impression that Chillingham was not near so gay or pleasant a house as Ravensworth.

The next day Cou made her appearance with Mlle Delisle; Sir Mathew Ridley with his son, who Louisa thought 'anything but agreeable additions', came to dinner; and John Trotter, who was destined to strike a spark in the heart of Cou.

Wednesday, September 29, 1830
A very fine morning. All the gentlemen went out shooting immediately after breakfast, except Mr. Harris, who most amiably remained to escort the ladies in their rambles. I was much afraid that Mama would *really* go tomorrow, for I was beginning to like my Séjour most extremely. We had a very

long walk after luncheon; our party was composed of Cou, Ly. Fitzharris, Mr. Harris & myself. Cou, by her repeated tumbles & excessive gaucherie, occasioned much laughter. It was a regular country walk, & we had the satisfaction of returning home wet through & above our ankles in mud. I was greatly delighted to find, on my return, that Mama did not intend leaving Chillingham till Sat. Lord Ossulston brought me home some beautiful heather from the Moors, for my coiffure; I appeared in it at dinner & was complimented on the pretty way it was put in. Dinner went off very agreeably; luckily Mr. Ridley was too late for dinner therefore Mr. Harris took his place. I am quite revenu from the disagreeable impression I had of the Harris'—I like them both. . . .

Thursday, September 30, 1830

 . . . It was given to me to decide what we should do to amuse ourselves—riding, walking, driving, all were proposed, discussed & all alike rejected. It was put to the vote, & a *scrambling* party was given the preference to. Accordingly, after luncheon we set off, that is, Ly. Fitzharris & I, for we could not prevail upon Cou to be of the party, Ld. Ossulston, Mr. Trotter, & Harris. We started in the pony carriage & the gentlemen on ponys. We continued in our vehicle till we reached the foot of the craggs, & then we commenced our scramble. Ld. Ossulston looked *so* handsome in his plaid jacket & cap; the mountain air had given him a color, & he reminded me of the description Walter Scott gives of the Hero of 'the Pirates', only en plus beau. We reached the top of the cragg in safety, & then wandered for some time on the Moor, which is covered with heather. It was perfectly charming & our expedition would have been too agree[able]: had it not been for an accident that happened to dear Lord Ossulston, who, eager in pursuit of a fine black-cock that he had *winged* but not killed, rushed from rock to rock &, in seizing the bird, unfortunately sprained his ankle violently. This, of course, prevented our pursuing our excursion, as he could only reach home supported by Mr. Trotter & Mr. Harris, the latter of whom rose considerably in my estimation by the affectionate interest he showed to his friend. Poor dear Ld. O. must have suffered very much, but he bore it with the most cheerful goodhumor. The evening s'est passée comme à l'ordinaire. Ld. Ossulston, seeming to forget the pain he was in, sung most touchingly for us. While the music was going on Mr. Harris said "I wish I could sing; there is no knowing what is to be done with a fine voice." I said I had no doubt were he to try he would find he was gifted with a bel voce. "Oh! but that is only *one* among the numerous accomplishments that I fear are requisite." . . . I was not a little pleased when this conversation ended as I dreaded being accused of entering into a flirtation with Mr. Harris, which I certainly did not intend; & I went to my room with the intention of avoiding him during the remainder of my visit. Our evening ended très gaiment, & we danced till one o'clock. . . .

From the following day's entry it appears as if the Chillingham party would have been gladly rid of Mrs. Wat, even if Louisa's continued presence might have been welcome.

Friday, October 1, 1830
The day looked cloudy & anything but propitious for the Battue, & I went down to breakfast prepared to give it up de très bonne grace, thinking that dear Lord O. would be obliged to stay at home in consequence of his sprained ankle; but he came down rather less lame & determined upon accompanying us, and as the day cleared up we set off at 12 o'clock. That is, Mama & Miss Delisle remained at home, & our party consisted of Lord & Ly. Tankerville, Lord & Ly. Fitzharris, Mr. Harris, Mr. Trotter, Cou, Lord O. & I. We at first beat the covers in vain—nothing but hen pheasants made their appearance; but happily by dint of beating the bushes & wading through plantations & bean fields we roused the Pheasants, & though not very plentiful, the gentlemen seemed satisfied with their day's sport, & we were very much amused. We walked for five successive hours, with

51

the exception of occasionally getting into the pony carriage to move from one field to another. There was no drawback to the pleasures of the day but the lameness of Lord O., & though he used every exertion to conceal the pain he suffered, every hour of fatigue made him look more souffrant. Ly. Tankerville & I drove down in the pony carriage to the covert side, & the whole way she entertained me with the praises of *her dear* Charley, saying he was *so* amiable, such a delightful temper, with a most affectionate heart—all this looked as if she wished me to think him perfect, qui ne le faisait déjà que trop. Under any other circumstances all these eulogiums would only have struck me as the effects of maternal affection, but after all I had heard I confess it seemed odd to me. They did all in their power to make our visit agreeable to us, & Lord Ossulston said he hoped we really did not intend leaving them so soon. However, certainly we were not *much pressed* to remain, which seemed extraordinary, but the whole family appeared to act as if they would not for *worlds* appear too anxious about our remaining. I said as little as possible about the beauty of the place, & was rather sur les épines when Mama said she would like to live there. Ly. Tankerville proposed Mama's going on to Edinburgh & leaving me at Chillingham till her return—that I was thoroughly pressed to do; but Mama declined for me. Ly. T. said if I was allowed to remain she would give me a room close to her own that I might be under her special protection. When Mr. Harris heard of this plan he said "Oh, for God's sake, stay." Even Ld. Fitzharris persuaded me to remain, & said he would be as good a chaperone & keep as much out of my way as he had done that morning at the Battue. Lord O. did not at all appear to object to the proposed plan & I honestly own that at the moment Edinburgh, the Lakes & Scotland I would willingly have dispensed with seeing, could I have remained at Chillingham. It would not however have been right, & of course I did not accept. I retired to my room that night with a heavy heart, for so completely happy & at home did I feel that it certainly was painful to me to part.

After a sight-seeing tour, of which Louisa left no record, the Smythes went to stay with their Stanley cousins at Hooton near Chester. Lady Haggerston, the younger sister of Mrs. Fitzherbert, of Wat, Jack and Charles Smythe, was the mother of an only daughter who had married Sir Thomas Massey-Stanley, a Catholic like herself. Lady Stanley had three sons, William, Rowland and John (each of whom was to succeed to the baronetcy in turn) and a daughter Maria. Rowland had changed his name to Errington on inheriting the property of an uncle.

'A fine, calm November day' brought to Louisa's mind thoughts of the 'affectionate and adored Father' she had lost. She reflected on death, the passing of time, and the uncertainty of her future, concluding her melancholy meditations with a prayer.

The Smythes spent the end of the year in London.

Mrs. Fitzherbert had passed some worrying weeks after the King's death. His executors were the Duke of Wellington and Sir William Knighton.* The former, though eminently fair, was not over-sympathetic towards her, the latter she mistrusted and would have no dealings with. The only security for her allowance was a mortgage on the Royal Pavilion at Brighton. However, the new King was anxious to do whatever was possible for her, and after some negotiation it was arranged that the annuity of £10,000 should be continued on condition that she gave up all further claims on the estate of George IV.

On August 29, she had retired to Brighton; the King and Queen went down to the Pavilion on the following day. There were festivities, in which Mrs. Fitzherbert, of course, took no part. The King sent his eldest son, George Fitzclarence, whom he was soon to create Earl of Munster, to ask Mrs. Fitzherbert why she had not been to visit him at the Pavilion. This was her

* Sir William Knighton (1776–1836), Keeper of the Privy Purse to George IV. Beginning life as a doctor and accoucheur, he was appointed physician to the Prince of Wales 'because he was the best-mannered doctor he had ever met'. In 1822 he succeeded Sir Benjamin Bloomfield as confidential adviser to the Prince, all of whose secrets he must have learnt, and whose financial affairs he put in order. If he was a sinister figure, he at least abjured financial rewards in favour of the secret exercise of power.

opportunity to regularise her position with regard to the Royal Family. She wrote to say that she had something to show him before she could obey his command.

On September 4, according to the *Brighton Herald*, 'His Majesty honoured Mrs. Fitzherbert with a visit of about three-quarters of an hour'. We know from the account she gave Lord Stourton, and which he wrote down, what passed between them.

'Upon her placing in his hands the documents which have been preserved in justification of her character, and especially the certificate of her marriage, and another interesting and most affecting paper, this amiable Sovereign was moved to tears by their perusal, and expressed his surprise at so much forbearance with such documents in her possession, and under the pressure of such long and severe trials. He asked her what amends he could make her, and offered to make her a Duchess. She replied that she did not wish for any rank; that she had borne through life the name of Mrs. Fitzherbert; that she had never disgraced it, and did not wish to change it; that, therefore, she hoped His Majesty would accept her unfeigned gratitude for his gracious proposal, but that he would permit her to retain her present name.

' "Well then," said he, "I shall insist upon your wearing my livery," and ended by authorising her to put on widow's weeds for his royal brother.'

From that time Mrs. Fitzherbert's footmen wore scarlet and blue.

Four days later Mrs. Fitzherbert went to the Pavilion, never having entered it, as she wrote to Minney, 'since I was drove away by Lady Hertford'. The King came to the door to greet her, and she was 'overwhelmed with kisses from male and female'.

It is strange that Mrs. Fitz had lived for twenty years next door to the Pavilion without ever going inside it. She had seen rising the Mogul domes and minarets of Nash, but the splendours of the crimson music-room with its scaly golden ceiling and the painted banqueting hall with its dizzy dragon chandelier, were new to her. 'I cannot tell you,' wrote Mrs. Fitz, 'my astonishment at the magnificence, and the total change since my first acquaintance in that house. They live a very quiet life. . . .' Into the flamboyant décor created by 'The First Gentleman of Europe', 'The Sailor King' had settled happily down, with good, plain Queen Adelaide and his brood of bastards. 'I think I counted today eight Fitzclarences.'

Mrs. Fitzherbert's honour had at last been vindicated in the eyes of the Royal Family, as it was to be, later, in the eyes of the world: but she felt herself grown old and a survivor from another age. 'I never saw this place so full in my life,' she wrote to Minney a few days later. 'You can scarcely get along the streets for the number of carriages, very smart, and the owners dressed out as if going to some entertainment, but not a face you ever saw before.' It was increasingly hard for her to get about. At the end of the year she decided to give up being patroness of the weekly balls at the Old Ship Hotel, and had, as she wrote, 'some trouble to get ladies to take my place'.

One further source of comfort remained to Mrs. Fitzherbert after all her trials. When William IV returned to her all the jewelry and miniatures which she had, over a period of years, given the late King, she found there was one miniature missing. This was the picture of herself, only three-quarters of an inch high, framed in brilliants and covered in half a diamond, which in his will of thirty years before, the Prince had desired to be buried with him, suspended round his neck with a ribbon, as he used to wear it when he lived. Mrs. Fitzherbert had the pair to the miniature, the Prince's portrait, covered by the other half-diamond. Had the King been buried with her picture on his heart?

George Seymour, Minney's brother, was ordered by the new King to make enquiries; and he was able to write to Mrs. Fitzherbert that he had every reason to believe that it was *not* removed from the late King's neck. It had also been seen on the King 'a twelvemonth back'.

Confirmation of her hopes came in a curious way. The Duke

of Wellington, meeting Minney Dawson-Damer at dinner some time after the King's death, took her aside and made a halting confession. He had promised King George IV that nothing should be removed from his body after his death, and that he should be buried in the nightshirt he died in. It happened that he was left alone with the body, and saw something hanging round the King's neck on a worn black ribbon. Overcome by curiosity he drew a locket out of the clothes. It was Maria Fitzherbert's miniature.

The Iron Duke blushed in admitting to his curiosity, but seemed relieved to have made his confession: he left it to Minney whether to tell the eighty-year-old Mrs. Fitzherbert or not. Minney bided her time. One day when she and her 'Mama' were alone together the conversation turned to the late King, and she took the opportunity of repeating the Duke of Wellington's words. Mrs. Fitzherbert received the story without comment; but presently Minney looked up and saw that she was silently weeping.

1831

*Louisa's change of heart – Ossulston back in London – The
Smythes give a Ball – Louisa meets Frederick again – Cou's
amusements – Mrs. Fitzherbert reverses her policy –
Engagement of Frederick and Louisa.*

'What an extraordinary thing is the human heart!', Louisa
observed. Some time during the last two months of 1830 she
had decided that she only loved Sir Frederick. She began to
refer to him in her journal as 'the Innominato', the One who
shall be Nameless.

On January 1, the Smythes were given the Duke of Gloucester's box for *Henry IV* at Drury Lane. Mrs. Smythe took her
sister Charlotte Boycott and her two daughters; they were
escorted by Rowland Errington. A pantomime followed the
play, and during the unfolding of the panorama, Louisa indulged
in sad reflections.

. 'The warlike air that is played while these beautiful scenes
are passing, made me think of this time last year when Charles
de Mornay was singing it at Brighton, or of this day 12 month
when I met the said individual at an evening party at Ly.
Downshire's, where he attacked me with compliments during
a whole evening. At the Pantomime I had no one to talk to, &
I *thought* of my *former* friend & of *him* amongst my admirers
whose affection *so far* exceeded them all, who now I think *I
might* be worthy of, though at the time most certainly I was
not; & most indignant did I feel when I reflected that Aunt F.
by her untimely interference had prevented the possibility of
it *ever* taking place. I fear I have by my own indecision—no,
I will not blame myself; it is to the *supposed* kindness of Mrs.

F. I owe it all. Most deeply do I regret it, as also that by her foolish conduct she has prevented me ever having an opportunity of justifying my conduct to *one* who behaved so *beautifully* to me. Quelle singulière chose que le coeur humain! . . .

Tuesday, January 4, 1831

Errington dined with us, & left town in his Britshka & four at ten o'clock. I am sorry he is gone, though I confess I wd. rather have someone else for a beau frère. He told me he had been walking for some time with the *Innominato*, who, selon lui, was most agreeable, but looking *so ill*. I wish I could know if I am ever destined to renew my acquaintance. In this one point I think it would be more agreeable to know one's fate. I am sufficiently vain to think that were *he* to know the present state of my feelings, it might give him satisfaction at least—the Old Proverb is right—

Wednesday, January 5, 1831

Le Beau Cecile called very late. . . . I think Miss Elphinstone must end in marrying Augustus Villiers, though, as Mr. Forester remarked, it does not follow that matrimony is to be the final result of presenting a riding whip to a young lady. Nevertheless the Turquoise handle looked *ominous*. . . . Mr. F. likewise informed me that he had heard it reported that *I* was going to be married. Naturally I enquired who to? Fearing I might be affronted, he reluctantly complied with my request, & said 'to Ossulston'. A short time ago this would not have been unsatisfactory. *Now* I only thought of Frederick. . . .

In spite of her renewed preoccupation with Frederick, Louisa could not help being moved by the knowledge that Ossulston was in London. A visit to Lady Tankerville during which that great lady avoided all mention of her son set Louisa wondering how she really stood with the Bennet family. It was tantalising not to know whether he had ever cared for her, even if he did so no longer.

An unexpected call from Lady Fremantle and her daughter heralded a renewal of relations with Frederick Hervey-Bathurst. It was nearly two years since Louisa had spoken to him, and nearly three since she had stayed at Englefield Green as his bride-elect. Could it be that he was still fond of her, that his thoughts coincided with hers?

Monday, February 28, 1831
. . . I was sitting in the drawing room on my return [from the riding school]; I heard a knock. Great indeed was my surprise when I heard Ly. Fremantle & Miss Hervey announced. They have never called since the fracas at Brighton, & little did I expect they ever would renew their intercourse with us. They were both very gracious in their manner, & I tried to put on a manner totally unconcerned & free from agitation, which certainly I did not feel. I was so surprised at seeing them here that I scarcely knew what to say or think, so various were the reasons, motives etc that crowded at once upon my imagination. *The* acquaintance may be renewed!

Tuesday, March 1, 1831
A very seasonable but unpleasant day, with a cold easterly wind. I got up late & walked in the Park with Aunt Charlotte, & likewise paid some visits with her after luncheon, by which means my day was entirely wasted in the Dolce far niente of a London morning, from which is derived no present enjoyment or after satisfaction. I confess it to my shame that of late my time has been spent in total idleness. It is true that I have not been quite so happy as I used to be, but the fault is my own & I have no one to accuse. However, for the future, by constant occupation I will endeavor to improve the time allocated to me. . . . I wish I could know the motive of yesterday's visit. It can, I think, proceed only from two causes. I am at present in a state of indecision difficult to describe but too keenly felt.

During the next three weeks, Louisa was too busy to keep up her Journal. The *Morning Post* helps us to fill the gap. On March

10, Mrs. Wat and Louisa were presented by Minney Dawson-Damer at the Queen's second of four Drawing Rooms. Mrs. Wat wore white and gold with a violet velvet train. Louisa, described as 'Miss Wat Smythe' had on 'a white crepe dress, embroidered in silver, with blond epaulettes; train of white satin trimmed with silver lama. A plume of feathers, brilliants, and blond lappets'.

On March 17 the Smythes gave a ball. The *Morning Post* rose to the occasion.

Mrs. Smythe's Ball

A brilliant ball was given by the above distinguished lady, at her elegant Mansion in Great Cumberland Place, on Thursday evening. At half-past eleven one Ball-room was thrown open, and dancing commenced to WEIPPERT's delightful music with a very effective set of new Quadrilles, entitled *The Royal Quadrilles*, performed before their MAJESTIES at the Marchioness of LONDONDERRY's Grand *Fete*. . . .'

At last Louisa set eyes on Sir Frederick again.

Thursday, March 24, 1831

A wretched cold dry day. We went in the evening to a party at Ly. Sefton's, which was tolerably agreeable; there I met Miss Hervey & Sir William. They were both very gracious in their manner. The Fitzharrises came in for a short time; she I think is much gone off in looks. We went on to a Ball at Ly. Hampden's, which was hot & crowded. When I was dancing the first Quadrille the first person I saw on turning my head round was Sir Frederick; he *did* not or *would* not see me. I was most anxious for an opportunity to speak. I then valtzed with Tolstoy, & after the first round we stopped close to the musicians, I looked up & saw the person I most wished to see standing close behind me; there was an opportunity to renew our acquaintance. What I had *so long* wished for. It was of no use, I could not avail myself of it; I trembled so, my heart beat so violently, that I think had my life depended upon it I could not have spoken to him, yet I am furious with myself for having lost so favourable an opportunity in the crowd. We should not have been observed, & I was dancing with a foreigner who, knowing none of the circumstances, would not have remarked it. What contributed to lessen, or rather make me still more nervous, was fearing that *he* might scarcely answer me; yet had he been *very* anxious to avoid me he would not have remained in the same place the whole time. He did not speak to a creature, but remained in his pensive way looking at the dancing. Tolstoy must have thought me stupid to excess, but I certainly did not bestow a thought on him. I turned round several times intending to speak, but each time my voice faltered. I *could not* speak. At last the Valtz ended & roused me from my abstraction. I was determined, en passant, to say how d'you do to Sir F. He answered me in the same manner. If we ever meet again I will endeavour to be more composed, & whatever exertion it may cost me I must renew my acquaintance. Coming out of the supper room, Mama spoke to him & accused him of having cut us of late. I was then with Lord Boringdon. Lord O. was not there. I find the youngest of the Miss Cadogans is suspected of having written *the* Beloved O. Ly. Londonderry was at the Ball in high goodhumor. The Mazurka was very ill danced.

Monday, March 28, 1831

One of those lovely Spring days that feel so mild & delightful, that one is happy malgré soi & in good humor with the world in general. I drove in the open carriage with Aunt Cha, paid several visits & then went in to the Park. There I saw Sir Frederick, who for the first time depuis des siècles bowed most graciously to me. I only wish he would renew his visits, & I confess it would give me a feeling of great satisfaction to know that his feelings *now* correspond with mine.

> Ingiustissimo amor, perche si raro
> Correspondente fai nostri desire?*

* Most unjust love, wherefore so seldom
  Dost thou make our desires correspond?

It is now exactly a month since Ly. Fremantle & Miss Hervey surprised me so much by calling. For various reasons I would give the world to ride again.

Wednesday, March 30, 1831

I find I have been talked over & I am generally thought to be too reserved in my manner, which at first is very taking, but people complain that I am not open enough & that they cannot get on with me. Henry Cox I find is one of these. All these are indifferent people, about whose opinion I do not care. I wish I could know how I stand in the opinion of *him*, the only person whose approval would give me pleasure.

Good Friday, April 1, 1831

Went to Church & staid the Sacrament; a very long service, which lasted more than three hours. Remained at home all day and did not see a soul, with the exception of Errington, who called in the evening. Mama told me this evening what had been said of me. I conclude by it that I am not popular; my conversation is not interesting enough; people are disappointed in me; they say my eyes look intelligent, yet I have not sufficient interest to make people cultivate my society. I know not what is to be done. People in general are much annoyed at my not being a *love-sick* girl, yet if those who find fault with me on that account are not anxious that I should fall in love with them, what can it be to them?

Wednesday, July 27, 1831

A very fine day & we all went to a small breakfast at Ly. Farquhar's. . . . Lord Ossulston did not at all *seek* our society. He must have heard of my refusing his—I will not say friend. He is a singular individual, & after all that passed has conducted himself strangely. *Once* I wished it, but now I do so no more: indeed I do not think he ever cared for me. For a time, I own, I wished that he might like me; I thought him amiable in the extreme: but he is too young, & I think too fickle in his tastes & preferences to ensure my happiness. I now regret extremely that ever there was a question of it, as it has been to me an ignis fatuus, shining only to mislead.

With these words Louisa abandoned Lord Ossulston for good and all. She was ill for a few days at the end of July and the beginning of August, and when she went out again felt dispirited and detached from the surrounding scene. But she was soon to be happy.

Cou's life, meanwhile, had been becoming more and more amusing as she grew nearer to the time of her coming out. She still had lessons from her governess, Mlle Delisle, with whom she got on very well; but there were also delightful mornings when friends came to sing and practise the piano with her, and evenings when she was taken to an opera or play. Mr. Mitford or the high-spirited Countess of San Antonio—now Duchess of Cannizaro—would often join her in making music; and Vincenzo Gabussi, an Italian pianist and composer who had settled in London, would come in the evenings to coach her and improve her style. She had been going to the riding-school, too, and was gradually overcoming her fear of horses. In March she had been confirmed at the Chapel Royal; and on July 26, had 'attained the long wished for age of 17'.

In September the Smythes were burgled. 'A little before eleven,' wrote Louisa, 'I went to fetch Cou and Aunt Cha from Tilney Street, & on our return we found the Crescent filled with Policemen . . . on entering the house the first thing we heard was that we had been robbed of all we possessed . . .!' Mrs. Fitzherbert wrote to Minney 'Of all the things that could have happened to Mrs. Wat nothing could be more distressing to her than losing all her finery. Luckily for me and for her she sent my diamonds to me when we went to Tunbridge, for I feel losing other people's property is worse than losing what belongs to oneself. . . .' On September 8, however, King William IV was crowned, and Mrs. Fitzherbert was able to write 'The Smythes all went to The Coronation in the Chamberlain's box and were quite delighted. It was a little amusement and diverted their minds.'

The nervous Cou was the one to suffer most from the robbery, for as late as the middle of October Mrs. Fitzherbert was writing, 'Poor little Cou is looking ill, not from any love-affair, but from the fright of their house being broke into. It has had such an effect on her that she never dares go to sleep and is often obliged to have things given her in the night to quiet her nerves.'

On September 20 Louisa went with her mother to the wedding of her great friend 'Elphi', Georgiana Elphinstone, to Augustus Villiers. The present of a riding-whip with a turquoise handle *had* led to matrimony. There was a party at Lady Keith's house in Piccadilly afterwards. This we only know from the *Morning Post*, for Louisa abandoned her diary for ever in the middle of a sentence at the time of the burglary.

It is a pity that we cannot follow the final stages of Louisa's chequered courtship by Frederick in her journal: but we learn from her letters, which he kept and which his family have preserved, what happened.

It seems that Mrs. Fitzherbert changed her role from that of Witch to that of Fairy Godmother. She it was who, at Louisa's request, asked Lady Fremantle to find out what Frederick's sentiments were. Strange, after her previous dislike of Frederick, that an appeal to her good nature should have been immediately successful. She was a kind-hearted woman, but she had held out for five years against her beloved Minney's marriage to George Dawson—and then become devoted to him. Now she was suddenly all in favour of Louisa's union with Hervey-Bathurst. Perhaps she was afraid of Louisa, now twenty-one, being left on the shelf.

Sir Frederick's sentiments for Miss Smythe were unchanged. During the autumn he proposed and was accepted. Frederick and Louisa were engaged at last. Everyone appears to have been relieved and delighted. The Smythes spent December and part of January at Brighton, and Frederick travelled up and down from London. Aunt Fitz wrote to Minney, 'Fred Bathurst was obliged to go to town, being upon guard, and told me he should call upon you, but I don't think he will have the courage to do so. Lou is completely happy and delighted and I am half in love

64

with Fred Bathurst myself. I think him so good-looking and so amiable. I wish he was not quite so shy but I hope he will upon better acquaintance get the better of that. I think dear Lou has a great prospect of happiness of which she, you know, is so deserving. There are many reasons why I am pleased with this match. He is not what is called rich at present but all Lady Fremantle's property will come to him at her death. . . .'

Louisa sensibly began by having an explanation with her diffident lover.

[Undated: probably November or December, 1831.]

My dear Sir Frederick,

I received your letter this morning with much pleasure, as in answering it, I shall have an opportunity of writing to you on a subject which I have always felt too nervous to enter upon in conversation.

I own to having felt hurt at hearing you did not believe I was *really* attached to you, but that I had been persuaded into it. That, believe me, is not the case, but after my past conduct I am not surprised at any conjecture you may make. Your conduct to me at a time you had every reason to hate and abuse me was so kind & generous that I *never* can forget it. Believe me, it was entirely by my own desire that Mrs. Fitzherbert spoke to Ly. Fremantle, as I have long been most anxious to renew our acquaintance; therefore pray, dear Sir Frederick, do not for a moment imagine that I *could* have been persuaded, or that I should so earnestly have requested Mrs. Fitzherbert to ascertain what your sentiments were if I had not preferred you to all. I have no doubt you often think my manner towards you cold & reserved. Forgive me for it. I do not deny that after what has passed, I feel an awkwardness in your society which I am far from with those indifferent to me. It would be difficult for me to express how much I feel your constancy and continued attachment. I trust that you will find that you have bestowed it on one who fully appreciates its value.

Believe me to remain, my dear Sir Frederick,
Yr. ever grateful & affectionate
Louisa.

Sunday night

If you do not arrive very late this evening & are not too
tired we are alone & shall be most happy to see you.

Louisa spent her last unmarried winter at Brighton with
Mrs. Fitz. This must have been a cheerful time for the Smythe
family, with the prospect of Louisa's wedding ahead of them in
the spring. Frederick's military duties prevented him from being
with them except for an occasional short visit, but he sent
Louisa a watch and chain for Christmas. The Smythes were all
invited by the King and Queen to the Pavilion on various occasions, but when it was a question of dancing, only Cou apparently
obeyed the Royal command, escorted no doubt by Mama, as
Louisa evidently felt that her status as Frederick's *fiancée* pre-
cluded the possibility of dancing with other men. Louisa's
letters to Frederick were full of kind messages from her family.
Mrs. Fitz 'never ceases praising you'. 'Georgina begs me to tell
you with her love that she hopes you will not forget the Valtzes
you were so kind as to promise her.' When the Smythes returned in February to Cumberland Place, Frederick was
stationed at Chatham; he then went down to Clarendon to make
ready his house for Louisa, putting up at the White Hart at
Salisbury. 'Mama desires me to tell you with her love that the
house is so dreadfully quiet since your departure that she can
hear her spectacles fall; and even Cou, who you teaze so much,
is very anxious for your return. . . . I hope you found all the
grates well put in.' Both Louisa and Frederick were painted by
James Holmes in the early months of 1832, and Louisa wrote:
'Holmes is still convinced yours is to be the most splendid he
ever did. . . .'

Louisa Smythe was married to Frederick Hervey-Bathurst at
St. George's Church, Hanover Square, on May 14, 1832.

PART TWO

THE JOURNAL OF GEORGINA SMYTHE
1832–1833

1

THE LONDON SEASON

Cou's début – Mr. Trotter's coldness – Lord Hillsborough the favourite – Parties at Chiswick, Wimbledon, Fulham, Campden Hill and Regent's Park – Meeting with Augustus Craven at Greenwich – Hopes and fears – Cou's eighteenth birthday – First parting from Augustus.

With Louisa married, London was open to Cou. It is curious that Louisa's story should have ended so neatly at St. George's only three days before the seventeen-year-old Cou was due to make her début; with the result that the journals of the two sisters lead straight from one into the other.

We can tell, however, from the date on the first page of Cou's note-book that she did not start to write it in its present form until September 3, 1832, after the Season was over. (She had probably made notes of the earlier part.) It was undertaken as a distraction for her when separated from the man she was in love with. Later, when she is in a state of great emotional stress, she clearly pours out her feelings in the journal day by day.

Holmes's miniature, painted some time during the previous year, gives us an idea of how Cou looked at seventeen. She was shorter and darker than Louisa, with her hair elaborately waved and falling on either side of her face in the bunches of ringlets which were then fashionable. Her face, unless Holmes flattered her, was a perfect oval, her nose small but slightly curved; her eyes were large and mischievous, with a suggestion of wantonness. She was certainly more excitable and vivacious than her elder sister, full of chaff and fun; with a keener appetite for life and a greater capacity for doing harm to herself and others.

Georgina Charlotte Harriet Smythe was presented at Court on May 17, 1832, and wore, according to the *Morning Post*, 'a white tulle dress, trimmed with bouquets of flowers and silver lama; train of white satin, trimmed with silver lama. Head-dress, white ostrich feathers'.

Her earliest *penchant*—if we except Flavigny, for we do not know if his 'devotion' was returned—seems to have been for John Trotter, a handsome but aloof young officer in the Life Guards, who had been one of her sister's partners in previous years. She had been struck with him at Chillingham during her stay there in September, 1830, and had danced with him at Brighton during the winter of '31–'32. He seems, however, to have felt the need of marrying a more substantial heiress, and sought to avoid committing himself. 'Franco' Seymour, who is another of the first people she mentions, was less a beau than a friend of the family. He was Minney's nephew and an officer in the Scots Guards—or Third Fusilier Guards, as they were then called.

Until near the end of her first season it is clear that Cou thought more of Lord Hillsborough, whom she called 'Mountain', than of anyone else. Three years older than herself, he was a big, wild, moody young man, a Life Guardsman, and incidentally a great match. His father, the third Marquess of Downshire, was one of the richest landowners in Ireland; his grandmother Lady Downshire, Baroness Sandys in her own right, had for years been one of Mrs. Fitzherbert's closest friends; his uncles, Lord Arthur and Lord Marcus Hill, were old friends of the Smythe family.

Thursday, May 17, 1832

After Louisa's marriage, which took place on Monday, May the 14th, I made my Début. I had already been out during the winter at Brighton, but since my return to London in February my health had obliged me to renounce for a short time to late hours—& I never went but to two or three dances at Princess Lieven's & the Duchesse de Dino's—& I then knew so few people that I cannot say I amused myself much. Mama presented me on Thursday the 17th. of May. Everything was new to me, & I was in a state of enchantment. The same night, we went to a little dance at Lady Peyton's, which I liked *pretty well*. Franco & Mr. Trotter were there; two resistless inducements to make me like it. The latter is certainly cold in his manner to me, & Dieu sait! who has been *goodnatured* enough to influence him against me—for after all his unremitting attentions at Brighton his conduct appears inconceivable in my eyes. Franco, at present, is the same charming person as ever.

Wednesday, May 23, 1832
   The next Wednesday I made my first appearance at Almack's. The novelty of the spectacle enchanted me; the rooms are so beautiful & the music so perfect. Ld. Hillsborough, whose acquaintance I made at Louisa's marriage was there. I rather think I shall like him—he is so open & frank in his manner. However, all my *penchants* of this season will be *des frivolités*.

May–June 1832
   From that time I went to several Balls at Devonshire House, all charming. Ld. Hillsborough is my constant partner. Ld. Kerry is also an agreeable person—but he is *too* ugly. I know it is very wrong to be prejudiced by outward appearances, but I think one cannot help being prepossessed by agreeable ones. Captn. Macdonald is a nice, lively youth, & rather de mon goût.

Cou describes how she passed the time at a party of the Duke of Devonshire's at Chiswick: 'On the 18th. of June, we went to a Déjeuné at Chiswick. We took Ld. Hillsborough down; & on arriving there I was much amused at being handed out of the carriage by Mr. Trotter. The weather was lovely, & the scene of the most lively & varied description. Ld. Hillsborough was much annoyed at being obliged to return to Town for dinner—but was to come back in the evening. I talked a great deal that

71

day to Mr. Trotter; & we discovered ourselves to be in many respects totally different to the opinion we had of each other. Even during this conversation I could not help remarking that he was distant & cautious in his manner. The very certainty of this causes me a pang—but I must drive away the thought. I am angry with myself for not being diplomate enough to disguise the pleasure his conversation gives me—& I always think him the most agreeable & sensible of any of my friends. We danced till two in the morning. To my surprise Lord Hillsborough returned; but in a sulky, morose temper. I danced with him, & I found out that he had had some battle with a hackney coach-man—which sort of adventures, I fear, too often occur to him. I led the Cotillon with the Duke [of Devonshire], who was all amiability to me. We brought Lionel Ashley, & Ld. H . . .gh home. Poor Mama caught such a bad cold after this that we were unable to go to Almack's [on the following Wednesday], which I bore with all Christian fortitude.'

The *Morning Post* reported as follows: 'The Gentlemen principally dressed in blue frock-coats, with white trousers and white waistcoats (the flowered ones are out). The Ladies were superb, in flowered muslins with the new small silk hat or bonnet *à la Maradan*. At half-past six o'clock the *déjeuné à la jourchette* . . . was announced by a bell from the portico of Augustus. Tables were laid in the Grecian and Etruscan draw-ing rooms, and also in the summer apartments below. During this period the band of the Royal Horse Guards (Blue) played martial music under the umbrageous arms of a singularly fine exotic tree. About half-past seven the promenades commenced, whilst a proportion of the juveniles were amusing themselves on the swing and see-saw. There were others rowing themselves in punts or the four-oared cutter on the beautiful Serpentine Lake. The view here terminates with a Roman Temple, sur-rounded by the thickest foilage [*sic*] and birds of the most brilliant plumage. Whilst the aquatic parties were silently moving over the expanse of water, they were agreeably surprised by the most divine sounds issuing from one of the thickets; it was a party of female warblers singing Italian airs to the echo. An attempt was made to discover them, but alas! they had fled. At nine o'clock the table being cleared the dancing commenced to WEIPPERT's Music, and about midnight the scene of festivity closed.'

A clue to Hillsborough's headstrong nature, which evidently worried Cou, is afforded by a report in a newspaper of two years before. 'The gentleman who was concerned in the affray at Eton a week or two since, was Lord Hillsborough, son of the Marquess of Downshire. His Lordship, who is one of the finest young men at the College, was crossing Eton-Bridge, when he was insulted by a labouring man who, we are informed, applied to his Lordship very foul language. The consequence was that in a few seconds the labourer measured his length on the ground. Another labourer who came to his comrade's assistance was treated in a similar way; and although they made a most determined resistance, his Lordship proved too much for them. His Lordship has since settled the dispute by presenting them with 5l each. His Lordship, it will be recollected, saved, about a year ago, two boys from being drowned in the Thames.'

The summer of 1832 was exceptionally fine, and a number of brilliant parties were given out-of-doors. All those fortunate people who had houses with large gardens, or suburban 'villas', such as the Duke of Devonshire's beautiful Chiswick House, mentioned above, took advantage of the splendid weather. The Duke and Duchess of Somerset lived at Wimbledon Park. This wooded estate, with its lake, still exists today, though divided up into Municipal Gardens, golf links, sports grounds and the famous Tennis Courts where the International Tennis Tournaments are held.

Cou, who at fourteen had been adored by Flavigny, seemed destined to attract the admiration of foreigners, who perhaps saw in her a quintessence of English beauty, allied to an ease and vivacity in society which were more French. At this time the visiting Prince Adalbert of Prussia and his attendant Count Groeben seem to have singled her out for attention.

Monday, June 25, 1832

We went to a Royal Déjeuné at the Duke of Somerset's lovely place at Wimbledon. We went with the Ailesburys. The grounds are beautiful & very extensive. Comte Groeben handed me in to dinner. The crowd was so excessive that I got separated from Mama, & found myself placed between Ld. Hillsborough and *L'Etranger* [Groeben]. I should be very wrong to say I *disliked* my quarters, but I was in a dreadful fidget to get back to Mama. Dancing began early in a tent on the grass. I valsed with Ld. Hillsborough & Galloped with Prince Adalbert, of Prussia. Ld. Boringdon was one of my partners. I think him amazingly improved in manner since last year. About 10 o'clock, we danced in the house till past 12. Mr. Macdonald did not dance with me, but seemed to watch my movements; & in the course of the day prophesied to Elizabeth that I should become Lady H . . . I do not exactly know whether to wish for the accomplishment of this prediction or not. We brought Lord H . . . home.

Lady Elizabeth Brudenell-Bruce, youngest daughter of the elderly Lord Ailesbury, was Cou's most intimate girl friend, as Georgiana Elphinstone had been Louisa's.

Tuesday, June 26, 1832

There was a Review in the morning for the Prince of Prussia, but Mama would not allow me to encounter the fatigues of it, knowing what we were to go through in the evening. I had, however, the *satisfaction* of seeing the *Life Guards* pass—& one *helmet* [Hillsborough's] was doffed as it passed my windows. John Stanley arrived in Town, & paid us a visit. Lady Egerton also called, & was particularly horrified at seeing me looking so pale & ill. This evening was to take place the Grand Royal Ball at Apsley House. Minney strongly advised me not to wear Feathers; I therefore was coiffée'd by Nardin [the hairdresser] with a rose & my Blond Lappets. It was *du dernier Gout*! But I could not

74

help reflecting, as we were nearly annihilated by the crowd, how dearly pleasure is bought. The heat amounted to suffocation.

The *Morning Post* recorded: 'At midnight great impatience was expressed at the non-arrival of the KING and QUEEN, particularly among the people assembled at Hyde Park Corner, the crowd being immense. . . . However, at a quarter before one, a general cheer announced the approach of Royalty, the carriage lamps being seen like glow-worms in the distant shrubberies lining the Constitution Hill. Six of the Royal equipages preceded the one occupied by the KING and QUEEN. Their MAJESTIES were well received; in fact the shouts were enthusiastic. At the top of the lower flight of stairs stood the illustrious Host, in his full Marshal's uniform, and wearing all his orders. His Grace assisted the KING and QUEEN to alight, and conducted their MAJESTIES into the presence of the company.'

The King & Queen [wrote Cou] did not arrive till one o'clock! The first person I met was *Mountain* [Hillsborough], in such a Court dress—! I never saw anything look so ridiculous. I walked about with Mr. Bruce, & waded through the crowd at the imminent risk of having one's gown torn off one's back. In one of the rooms I met Mr. Trotter, & we sat down for a short time to talk. He *said* he regretted much not having found us at home the preceding day. But he is so totally different towards me now that I must no longer think of him but as a formal acquaintance. Some flitting image of a *Paget* or a *Ryder* [unmarried daughters of Lords Anglesey and Harrowby] soon passed before his eyes, & he seized that moment to quit me. I danced very little, as the crowd & heat had quite overcome me. The Prince of Prussia valsed with me; & I danced with Mr. Oliver & Mountain, with whom I led the Cotillon—into which we introduced the Mazurka, which Mr. Trotter (to my surprise) would dance with me; & at six in the morning I took leave of Mountain

75

for a week, as he was going to a Yeomanry Review in Kent. I like him malgré moi—but he is much too young to think of marrying.

Thursday, June 28, 1832

I went with Frederick in his cab to Breakfast with Louisa. They were going to the Hampton Races & wished me to be of the party, but I refused, thinking the Duchess of Bedford's Déjeuné would be more agreeable. But poor Mama was so unwell towards the middle of the day that we sent for Holland who said she was to remain at home for some days—& also would pronounce me to be looking ill, & unable any longer to bear dissipation. This was one of my low spirited days. Minney could not take me to Lady Jersey's & I staid quietly at home.

Saturday, June 30, 1832

I went with Louisa to Miss Jervis's Music—which was rather dull. This little thing gives herself great airs now, & I hardly ever give myself the trouble to speak to her.

Sunday, July 1, 1832

Dear Mama was a great deal better, & we all dined with Aunt Fitz. A regular family reunion of Damers, Jerninghams, Bathursts, Smythes & Frederick Seymour. I went away early with Aunt Cha to Portland Place, where we found Comte Groeben, of whom we took leave, as he was going off to Scotland the following day with his Prince.

Monday, July 2, 1832

I rode in the morning with the Ailesburys; & Elizabeth & I amused ourselves with conjectures as to whether Mountain would return for their Ball that evening. When we arrived at the Ailesburys', he was the first person I beheld, with his Mother. He soon came up to me, but seemed in a bad humor. I danced two or three times with him, & he promised to call the next day. We got home about 5 o'clock.

76

'The prettiest girl in England'
Georgina Smythe ('Cou')
From the miniature by James Holmes

John Trotter
Detail from a painting by an
unknown artist

Lord George Hervey
Detail from a water-colour by
Richard Dighton

Mrs. Smythe was having her usual money troubles, this time with her son-in-law and his family, probably relating to Louisa's marriage settlement. The first sentence of the following entry is only one of several which refer slightingly to the Fremantles and Sir Frederick. One cannot, though, resist the assumption that if anyone was behaving unreasonably it was Mama. Cou, of course, took her side.

Wednesday, July 4, 1832

The Fremantles called pour prendre congé, & were, of course, very coldly received. I drove out with Mary, & met Mountain in the park—looking so ill. At last he owned that, on returning from the Cricket Ground, his horse had bit him in the side, and that it pained him dreadfully. I will not express how truly unhappy this made me, as I knew he would not take care of himself. In the evening we went to Almacks where I found him dancing away & looking like a Ghost. I saw that it was no use to expostulate with him, but I half determined in my own mind that I would not be one of his partners. However, he over-persuaded me to take a tour de Valse with him, which I did, but very soon left off, & went & sat down by Miss Kerr, who, when I told her of his accident, actually shed tears. She certainly is rather innamorata with him, but I do not think I need *dread* her, so much as Anna Bolena did Jane Seymour—'Tu, mia rivale . . . tu . . . Seymour!' Out of spite he danced without ceasing the whole evening & I afterwards repented having shewn so much interest when I saw how perverse he was. Mama would take him home—but I was determined not to say another word to him.

Thursday, July 5, 1832

Mary Robinson was married this morn. to Mr. Vyner. Minney insisted on my going to the Haymarket with her to see 'The Lamb and the Wolf'. The party consisted of Mrs. Morier, Ldy. Georgina Wortley, Mr. Fitzroy & Frederick Seymour. The two latter, flirted the [whole] evening with

Lady Georgina—I never was so bored in my life. Mais avec ces jeunes coquettes femmes mariées les jeunes filles courent une mauvaise chance.

Friday, July 6, 1832

I rode early with Ld. Munster, after having waited in vain in hopes Mountain would call. However, par instinct, we took it into our heads that he had arrived after our departure —upon which we rode back under some pretence or other, et *l'on* y'était. He immediately came down, *vaulted* into his saddle, & came with us. We went to join the Bathursts, & had a charming ride, ce qui n'était pas fort étonnant. The Stanleys & Bathursts were going to have a large Party to Vauxhall in the Evening, & afterwards a Supper at Errington's. My Cousins actually went on their knees to persuade us to go, but without success; & William revint à la charge at 11 o'clock—but in vain. Mama foresaw it would be rather a lacking party, & therefore wisely thought it better that I should keep out of it—& I had not one inducement to go there.

'Lacking' presumably means lacking in decorum. It is odd to see the seventeen-year-old Cou being superior to her cousins' jolly family party.

Saturday, July 7, 1832

We did not see the Stanleys all day, but heard from Louisa that they were very indignant at our not going to them. I dined with the Bathursts, to go afterwards to the Opera. But after waiting Sir Frederick's return for ages, he came home at half past 9—bringing with him Mountain. Que j'étais heureuse! et que ce plaisir était inattendu! We persuaded him to dine with us, & after that Sir Fredk. lent him a *Coat*, & he came to the Opera—not, however, without the fear of being well *scolded* on his return. No one else came into our Box, & I had it my own way the whole evening. He certainly *seems* very *happy*, when in my society, but he is so young & so much sought after, that one does not dare think his affections will fix for some years.

Sunday, July 8, 1832

The day was so bad that we could not go to the Zoological Gardens. Franco Seymour called. How he is altered; I will, however, say one thing for him—as he is in love—but with *such a girl*! Lady Louisa Ryder. Je lui en souhaite bien du plaisir! . . .

Percy's Cross, Lord Ravensworth's 'suburban' house, to which Louisa had often been invited in previous years, stood in extensive gardens behind a high wall between Walham Green and Parson's Green. The Fulham Road then led through a peaceful landscape, in which there were a few old houses, such as Percy's Cross, and market gardens.

Monday, July 9, 1832

The Breakfast at Percy's Cross. We took down Lionel Ashley & John. The 1st person I saw was Mountain, who seemed hardly to dare speak to me, as he had been awfully rowed—& said that his Parents watched him narrowly. The Bathursts were there, & Louisa looked so pretty. I walked about chiefly with Miss Kerr, which I afterwards found was blamed as being *Missish*. However, I was not happy at finding Ld. Hillsborough was only allowed to notice me when his Family was not present. In the course of the day I met Ld. George Hervey for the first time since his illness. He talked to me for a short time, but I suppose I was not very agreeable, as he complained to Lady Isabella Fitzgibbon that the world had altered me much. I suppose my avoiding people was remarked, as no one asked me to dance. I know I looked miserable—& not until Ld. & Lady Downshire went away did I feel happier. At the same instant he was by my side—evidently as pleased at his liberty as I was at enjoying his society. He talked of my approaching Birthday, & how much he should wish to give me a souvenir, if he did not think it would be returned. He muttered something about having been congratulated that day on an event which he did not dare look forward to. I, of course, did not ask for an explanation. We danced together, but he was certainly not in spirits. I valsed with Franco, who was more like he used to be today, & to my astonishment Mr. Trotter asked me to dance. The former congratulated me on my reported marriage with Ld. Hi . . . gh. The latter merely said "Do you intend to give up dancing next year, like yr. sister?" I suppose these on dits, were again confirmed by Mountain saying at supper "I shall come home with you as *usual*"— which he did. I made acquaintance this day with Rowley's friend, Ld. Albert Conyngham. I have never been very anxious to know him, as I always thought he looked very conceited & *grand*. We shall see how I like him on further acquaintance.

Lady Downshire, a daughter of Lord Plymouth, thought Georgina Smythe was not nearly good enough for her son.

Wednesday, July 11, 1832
We went to a stupid Royal Party at Lady Salisbury's. Mountain hardly spoke to me. I thought at least he would be *quit* of his Mother at Almack's, but she even Chaperoned him there. I never saw him appear in so savage a humour. His brow was contracted, he bit his lips, & looked as if he could murder every one who approached him. I danced with M. Tolstoy, Paul Lieven, Mr. Macdonald, etc. but *he* never asked me till the end of the evening—& then I could not get a word out of him, & he left the room before the Ball [ended], which is quite unusual for him.

Cou began to get rather impatient about this time, with one of her more serious admirers, Lord George Hervey, a younger son of Lord Bristol. Poor Lord George, who looks charming in Dighton's water-colour, had debts, diseases and illegitimate children: he died young.

Thursday, July 12, 1832

I had a great wish to go to the Duchess of Bedford's Déjeuné but as Mama was very tired I did not say anything about it. Minney wrote to offer her chaperonage, & when the note arrived my perverse nature led me to refuse it—but on 2nd thoughts, Mama advised me to go, & I went. The first person I saw riding down there was Mountain. He hardly uttered to me at the beginning of the day, & I appeared not to seek him, & gladly accepted Ld. Kerry's arm. I met M. in the garden, walking alone with his Mother. Mr. Trotter talked to me for a few moments, as also Franco; but the arrival of the Harrowby tribe soon attracted their attentions. Ld. George Hervey was there with his sisters. When Ldy. Downshire was gone Mountain came & walked round the Gardens with me. I would not consent to go tête-à-tête, & made Lady Isabella follow with Ld. George. He complained much of the order he was kept in, and how he longed to be of age, pour secouer le joug. How far he has the power of doing this remains to be proved. He was obliged to run off very early to attend an Irish dinner *at home*. A dreadful thunderstorm came on; & I got into the house with Lady Isabella & Lord George. The latter was much agitated & could hardly speak. I ascertained from Ldy. Isabella, for the first time, that he really is very much attached to me. I never had been willing to believe this before, but now his very manner betrayed him. She has the greatest possible regard for him, & entreated I would not trifle with his feelings or give him any encouragement if I did not like him. I assured her that I had not the slightest preference for him, & certainly never *would* or *could* marry him. I came home about 8 o'clock as we were going to a Ball at Lady Kerrison's, which I thought might be pleasant; but in this I was sadly mistaken, as I hardly knew 3 men in the room. We came home very early, much disgusted.

Saturday, July 14, 1832

The day of Lady Mansfield's Déjeuné. We were not asked;

but I received a most comical note from Minney, saying how sorry she was that her going in Lady Clanricarde's carriage prevented her taking me. I afterwards discovered that this was the result of an appeal Ld. George had made to her to take me. He, in consequence, did not go. We drove in the Park, I dined with Louisa—as also William. We afterwards went to the Opera in Lady Fremantle's Box. Mr. Macdonald & Ld. George were our only visitors. William was quite disgusted at the latter because he remained the whole time, & actually would not let me be handed out by him—which amused me much. We returned to the Hotel to have some tea.

Sunday, July 15, 1832

Ld. Hillsborough called, & found [his uncle] Ld. Arthur sitting with us. We all three looked very foolish, & I did not know what to say. In short, I know I looked dreadfully guilty, & I am sure I do not know why. Mr. Armstrong called—& I could not help reflecting on the great change that one short year makes in the opinions & tastes of a girl of 17. I had nothing to say to this wretched individual, & I am sure he went away little edified by his visit. I went to the Zoological Gardens with the Bathursts. We met Franco, who walked with us for a short time, as also Ld. Boringdon. The Cravens [Lady Craven and Lady Louisa] were there. That dear, pretty Ldy. Louisa came to ask me if Mama & I would come to a Party on Board her Brother's Yacht, the Menai, at Greenwich on the following Friday. I was sure Mama was disengaged, & therefore accepted it. I by this means affronted that most *huffy* being, Sir Fredk., who had proposed a Water Party for the same day. However, I had a pressentiment that the 'Menai' would bring forth something agreeable—& en celà je ne me suis point trompée. We dined a family Party in Tilney Street, as also William & John. The former, who had never dined there before, was determined to obtain Aunt Fitz's Good Graces. He completely succeeded in winning her heart by his petits soins. We all

adjourned in the even (with the exception of Mama &
Ma Tante) to Mrs. Petre's, to raffle for a Watch—which
Miss Spalding won after all. Ld. Marcus Hill conducted the
thing, & did it in a very comical manner. There were a good
many agreeable men there—Paul Lieven amongst the
number. But Capn. Rous I could well have dispensed with—
& William amused himself by always contriving that he
should follow me.

Monday, July 16, 1832

I drove with Louisa, & we all, with Rowley, dined with
her; but owing to Sir Frederick being, as usual, playing at
Cricket, we waited dinner till near 10 o'clock—as Louisa
evidently did not dare order it until his return. When he did
arrive, the wine got into his head so completely that he became prosy & quarrelsome. I thought Rowley & I should
have died of laughing at hearing him working himself into a
great rage at any one saying he was not the *finest cricketer*,
& the *best husband*. He always gets into some dispute with
Mama, which quite provokes me.

The next day Cou went to a party given by the immensely
rich Lord Hertford, who was the original of Lord Steyne in
Thackeray's *Vanity Fair*. This voluptuous, but now decrepit,
nobleman had three London houses: Dorchester House, Park
Lane, Manchester House, Manchester Square and a villa in
Regent's Park, near Hanover Gate. It was at the last of these
that he gave the Fête on the 17th. The newspaper describes 'a
tasteful illumination on the lawn and among the shrubberies
down to the lake, all of which was arranged in the Parisian style.
The clock and tower of St. Dunstan's were lighted up with
globular lamps of a golden colour. . . . About half-past ten there
was a grand display of Bengal lights, so extremely vivid that the
whole place was as brilliant as noonday. . . . Soon after three
o'clock country dances and Scotch reels commenced. . . .
Throughout the evening a band, stationed on the lawn, in
Turkish costume, played marches and other airs.'

Tuesday, July 17, 1832

The heat of this day was quite intolerable. Sir Fredk. fetched me in his cab: to Breakfast with Louisa, & we went afterwards to chuse a Piano Forte for Clarendon, in consequence of which I got a dreadful headache. Isidor [hairdresser] kept me waiting till near twelve o'clock, therefore we got to Ld. Hertford's long after the dancing had begun. The first person I beheld was poor Edward Harris, arm in arm with Mary Anne [Jervis]; he looked very foolish & said very little. I danced two or three times with Ld. Hillsborough, & during some part of the Evening we sat together & talked, which I daresay was remarked. Miss Kerr looked very miserable, & I thought was once in tears when she saw him so attentive to me. I valsed once with Edward Harris, who certainly has not made any progress in that art. I led the Cotillon with Mountain, & Galopped in it with Mr. Trotter. Miss Bentinck brought us home at near 6 o'clock.

Wednesday, July 18, 1832

Mountain came at one o'clock to meet Tamburini, who, after all, never arrived. He staid a long time. Mr. Rochfort would call, to join my riding party, with Elizabeth. Ld. Hillsborough rode with us for a few moments, but soon set off in a great hurry to dine at Caen Wood. It was the last Almacks, & went off brilliantly; I could not help feeling a little triste at the winding up of these nice Balls, & can only live in hopes that the ensuing year will find us assembled there. Mountain was in high good humor, & we danced & talked a great deal together.

The Duchess of Bedford's party on the following day sounds, from the account in the *Morning Post*, to have been an exceptionally attractive one. The Duchess, a daughter of the Duke of Gordon, was considered fast. Her villa was on Campden Hill, near Holland House. 'Except at Vauxhall, there perhaps never was exhibited so general an illumination as the grounds in that Garden of Eden presented at ten o'clock; for every tree and shrub were lighted up by variegated lamps, resembling in form tulips and jonquilles; also the cascade and other fountains. To finish the coup d'oeil, the whole line of a spacious meadow was as light as day, from the effect of triumphal arches twenty-five in number, also composed of coloured lamps. . . . In the midst of all this magnificence were erected two superb marquees: one for the dance, the other for conversation, and in the latter were Persian carpets and ottomans. There were likewise chairs, sofas, and carpets scattered all over the grounds for the comfort of the distinguished visitants, a sort of luxury seldom seen. It was quite delightful to sit in an alcove distant from the gay scene and listen to the warblings of the nightingale—At half-past five there was a déjeuné à la fourchette; at half-past eight the quadrilles commenced to the music of WEIPPERT's band; at the hour of ten tea, coffee, ices, lemonade, orgeat, and cherry-water were served out in the hermitage and in the orangerie. In the conservatory were Liqueurs, Wines and fruits. Thus the time passed till one o'clock, and then there was a hot supper . . . served up on plate and china in four saloons in the Chateau. . . .'

Thursday, July 19, 1832

We went to the Duchess of Bedford's Déjeuné with the Ailesburys. Everybody was there, as it was to be kept up very late, being her last. The first thing that amused me was to see La Montagne [Hillsborough] walking off to dinner with an old dowager on each arm. Louisa was there senza lo Sposo! Qual miracolo! There was one of my acquaintances, Mr. Rochfort, that she had a great horror of knowing, &, I suppose, struck by her looks & manners, he asked me to introduce him to her, which I was obliged to do—& he handed her into dinner. Ld. Boringdon escorted me. He was very agreeable, & we afterwards walked about with him for some time. Ld. Albert Conyngham, who I then knew very little, talked with me. Ld. George Hervey walked with me a little. When the dancing began I was rather surprised at Ld. Albert's asking me for a Quadrille, as I never saw him dance before. I, for a wonder, danced almost all the Galopps. Poor

Mountain could not valse a bit, as the tent was not at all even, & several people fell. The reels & country dances were very numerous. The former amuse me very much. The Duchess of Bedford danced them till she fainted away. The whole thing was kept up till near 3 o'clock. We brought Ld. Hillsborough home. I was quite *done up* with the awful quantity of dissipation I had gone through the whole week. But with the anticipation of the Menai Fête the next day, I was determined to keep my fatigue to myself.

On the following momentous day Cou was to meet the entire Craven family. This consisted of Lady Craven, a widow, who, under her maiden name of Louisa Brunton, had been a famous actress, and her four children, Lord Craven, Augustus, Frederick and Louisa, aged respectively twenty-three, twenty-two, twenty and eighteen, none of whom was as yet married.

Louisa Brunton, whose great role had been Beatrice in *Much Ado About Nothing*, was not the only actress of her period to marry into a noble family. At that time both the Duchess of St. Albans, whose parties Louisa had attended, and Lady Harrington, whose husband, the celebrated Lord Petersham of the snuff-boxes, had recently succeeded to the earldom, had been on the stage; and the wife Lord Derby had lost three years before was the beautiful Eliza Farren, whom Gainsborough painted.

Lady Craven was a charming and virtuous woman, a good deal more respectable than her late husband, of whom the courtesan Harriette Wilson wrote in the effective opening sentence of her memoirs, 'I shall not say why and how I became, at the age of fifteen, the mistress of the Earl of Craven.' People liked Lady Craven, even if her grandfather had sold soap in Norwich. Cou and her second son, Augustus, fell in love at first sight. She described him as 'tall, dark and interesting'. There was something wild and dashing about Augustus: he was a romantic hero, a Rochester or Heathcliff, and bore a resemblance to his ancestor, King Charles II. His passion was hunting.

The *Morning Post* had something to say about the party on

the *Menai*, which it described as 'Lord Craven's Aquatic Fête'. 'The Company began to arrive about six o'clock and boats were in attendance to convey the Noble Visitors on board. The watermen had the badges of the House of Craven on the arms. . . . A temporary room of 35 feet square was erected on three barges moored for the purpose, and fitted up with rare and beautiful exotics, and the illuminations were very splendid. At seven o'clock the company partook of a sumptuous déjeuné, after which dancing took place to W E I P P E R T ' s band on board the yacht, which was fitted up as a ball-room, 80 feet long, and decorated with flags and signals of the various nations. . . . The shipping on the River hoisted their various colours in honour of the *Fete*.'

Friday, July 20, 1832

This day was lovely, & I may say que c'était un *jour* de *gloire*! I cannot imagine why I felt so convinced that this day would be the happiest of the year. When we arrived at Greenwich we found the Piazza before the hospital open to receive the carriages, & a smart boat to convey us on Board the Yacht. I *then* knew neither Ld. Craven nor Augustus. The former most civilly accompanied us on Board the Menai, which was fitted up beautifully for the occasion; & two Coal Barges lashed together at the side of the Yacht, where the dinner was served up. Lady Craven and Lupo received us— the latter, dear little thing, acted the part of Bouquetière to the Company. We then made acquaintance with Augustus Craven, the owner of the Yacht, who is tall, dark & interesting, with a very pretty figure and *thorough bred* manners. The Party was composed of the nicest people as Mr. Craven said he would only have the prettiest girls in London. Mountain had engaged himself to skull the Farquhars down, & therefore they arrived very late, & their *rower* a great *figure*. Everyone laughed at them, as it was evidently done to make up to the *heir-apparent*, & they followed him about all day. I was determined to amuse myself de mon côté, & made up my mind not to dance with him if he only asked me at the end of the evening. When the daylight closed in the Vessel was illuminated with coloured lamps [which] formed the initials of 'Louisa Craven'. The first Quadrille we danced without gentlemen, & laughed like *des Folles*. Augustus Craven placed himself by my side for the whole Evening, & although he hates dancing he would dance 2 Quadrilles with me. A *sudden impulse* made me form a favourable opinion of him. We made acquaintance with Lord Douglas, who is a very handsome Youth & dances beautifully. He Valsed and Galopped with me, & appears totally divested of affectations. I danced, as usual, with Ld. Boringdon, Frederick Craven, Mr. Rochfort, Mr. Macdonald etc. Towards *one o'clock* as I foresaw, Mountain approached me, (looking at the same time very foolish) & asked me to Valse. I felt piqued, & boldly asserted that I was engaged. Young Macdonald came up at that moment, & I was *impudent* enough to go & Valse with him directly. Mountain was, however, not repulsed, for he came a second time. But then I *really* was engaged—to Ld. Douglas —which made it still more *amusing*, as he never seemed to wish that I should know him. He then, I suppose, got into such a bad humor that he went away directly with the Farquhars, qui ne le lâchait pas de prise. It was so unlike him to leave so gay a Fete before the end. We kept it up till near 3 o'clock, & the Cravens would make us stay to go on shore with them. I never saw any family appear so amiable & united. I returned home with the feeling that it had been the happiest day of the Season—& I own I already felt a little penchant for the owner of the dear Menai. Yet how hurt I should have been if any previous day I had found myself neglected by Mountain. I cannot say the caprice was begun on my side, but certainly I was vexed to see the Farquhars trying (& apparently not without success) to get possession of him—at least for that day. Miss Farquhar is so pretty, clever & agreeable, that she might easily turn his head. But I could not help seeing with pleasure that people laughed at them. I own it was not a very amiable feeling—but it did not last long. At any rate, I shall not have to reproach myself

88

with having made up to him, nor have I ever felt so much pleasure in his society since I discovered that his Parents did not approve of it.

Saturday, July 21, 1832

A gloomy, miserable day, which seemed even to forbid one's thoughts being lively. Louisa was not well, therefore Sir Frederick came alone to ride with me. We met Mr. Craven, who joined us and appeared to me as charming as the day before. Yet I felt sorry to have made his acquaintance at the end of the Season when everybody was leaving Town. He was thinking of sailing the Monday following for Bordeaux, whither he was most generously going to conduct Harry Scott & his two daughters—one of them a lovely girl, in the last stage of a consumption. The Doctors here declared that the air of Bordeaux was the only thing that might give her a chance of recovery. Her father had been the intimate friend of the old Lord Craven, and his Son acted most nobly in giving up his own pleasure & offering to convey them on board his Yacht. Such a trait might perhaps be overlooked, or considered by indifferent people as a very natural action, but I think there are few young men who, in the present age, would sacrifice anything for duty, & it shows that he has been brought up in the *right path*. He told me he hoped to be able to go to Lady Farquhar's Breakfast on Monday, as he did not think the wind would be fair for sailing that day. Aunt Haggerston called to announce that Maria Stanley [her grand-daughter] was to come up next week to be married from her house.

Sunday, July 22, 1832

A wretched, dull cold day. We heard that poor Mrs. Robert Smith was attacked with the Cholera. Mama dined with the Bathursts. Errington dined with Aunt Cha & I, which was very cosy. I do not know when I ever felt so wretched. This Cholera seemed to fill one's thoughts with nothing but the image of Death. We heard in the evening that the poor sufferer was a little better. We went to drink tea with the Bathursts. Aunt Fitzherbert & the Jerninghams dined there. The latter were to leave Town the next morning for Cossey. But I could dwell on nothing but the Cravens, & I was in dread that Mama should not go to the Farquhars, & that Augustus would sail the same day.

Mama, however, did go to Sir Thomas and Lady Farquhar's déjeuné at Greenwood Lodge, Roehampton, and Augustus Craven was there, together with several other of Cou's admirers.

Monday, July 23, 1832

A cloudy dismal day. Mama, however, consented to go, & just as we were starting we heard the dreadful news of poor Mrs. Smith's death, as also of Harry Scott's: both decided Cholera. I felt quite chilled from hearing of this so suddenly, & we arrived at Roehampton with nothing but dismal & horrid ideas. The weather seemed perfectly in unison with one's feelings. A stillness & melancholy seemed to have possessed the whole company when we arrived, & there was a great scarcity of men. In short, it did not at all promise to be lively. Poor Lionel Ashley was there, & had been in the house the whole day during her illness, & had been her most intimate friend for ages. I must own, this does disgust one of the World, & the soi-disant Friends we make there: as one cannot exactly reconcile oneself to the idea that one's dearest Friend should enter a scene of dissipation ere one's ashes are cold, or consigned to the Tomb. However, we must not erroneously imagine that, though the fate of others, it will not be ours, as no one bore a higher character than poor Mrs. Smith or (who) as she believed, possessed more real friends. The only true & sincere one was Lady Isabella Fitzgibbon, who from excess of grief fell dangerously ill & ever since has appeared an altered being. On account of Harry Scott's death I feared the Cravens would not come—but at all events I felt that *he* would be obliged to remain in England now. The

Herveys arrived soon after us, & I dreaded lest Ld. George should affiché himself to me; therefore I contrived to be always *earnestly* engaged in conversation. Mr. Rochfort took us into dinner, during which time I talked a little to Mr. Trotter, & owned to him how much I thought Franco altered. He tried to assure me that I must be mistaken, as he knew what a regard he had for me—etc. I, however, remained in my own opinion. Mountain passed at this moment, but only asked me how I was. I cannot say that his appearance gave me much satisfaction, as it was another's arrival I was anxiously awaiting. Just as we returned to the lawn the first person I encountered was Augustus. I felt the color rising in my cheeks, but endeavoured not to show too much *empressement* in my manner. All the family was arrived, & Lupo was looking prettier than ever. We remained all together the whole day. I walked about with Lupo & Augustus—passed Mountain several times—& could hardly keep myself from laughing at seeing him *trying* to make himself *comfortable* on a *raised bed* of *brier roses*—and affecting perfect *insouciance* to the scene around him, when I plainly saw by his very countenance that he was merely playing a part to conceal his own vexation. After all, il se l'est attiré, therefore I cannot pity him— as he was such a universal flirt that I had never any reason to think he favored me more than others. Whilst we were walking we met Lady Strachan, who said to me "You must come to a little Déjeuné Ld. Hertford gives next Thursday, as one *cannot get on without you*"—upon which Augustus said "Yes, certainly Miss Smythe *must go*, or *I* cannot *think* of being of the party". This made us all laugh, & I daresay Lady Strachan will not have failed to make a good story of this. In the evening I danced the first Quadrille with Augustus, & was not a little diverted by seeing Mountain opening the *Ball* with Miss Farquhar. Lupo & I devised the scheme that whenever he should ask her to dance her Brother & I should be their vis-à-vis. The moment arrived to put this plan into execution. When the Quadrille began I saw she was teazing Mountain à toute force: for as he passed Augustus in the

Eté, he said "I hope you *like* your *Partner*". Lupo told me afterwards that she had been praising me but always found that Mountain surpassed her & that she had told him that her Brother was very much épris with me, & that they hoped it would be a *match*. Upon which he said "*I hope it may prosper*". I never saw anyone so little aquerri in concealing his vexation. He asked me to Valse, but was in very sulky humour the whole time. My hair came down, & I was obliged to go upstairs with Miss Farquhar. Augustus persuaded Mama & I to join their family reunion the next day, to eat White Bait at Greenwich. He was to drive us down in his Calèche & four. He asked Ld. Hillsborough to come, but he *declined*, as we expected. I danced again with Mr. Craven which I heard was remarked. He held my shawl, Boa etc. the whole evening, & while I was dancing sat by Mama. Lady Craven & Lupo went away early, but *he* staid almost to the end—but the Cotillon, which I danced with Ld. Edward Thynne, lasted so long that his patience was exhausted & he took leave of me, saying he should call for us the next day at ½ past 5. I never took Mountain out in the Cotillon, who was dancing with Miss Kerr, & during the greatest part of the time was sitting down talking to her. Lord Douglas selected me to Valse the figure of 8 with him, & we were the only couple who accomplished it. After all the events of the day Mountain found himself reduced to ask Mama to take him home. He was so sulky that he slept the whole way. But as he was getting out of the carriage he offered to *skull us* down to Greenwich. But we refused, saying that we could not *think* of throwing over Mr. Craven, who had made such a *point* of *driving* us down. It merely proved that pique & jealousy were his only motives for refusing to be of the Party.

Mrs. Smythe was so 'harrassed and worried about Law Business' next day that they were nearly obliged to back out of the Greenwich party. It was two months since Louisa's marriage and Cou could write, evidently echoing Mama, 'It really makes me distracted to think that all this anxiety proceeds from a

Above L.)   Lord Albert Conyngham. From a drawing by an unknown artist

Above R.)   Lord Hillsborough. From a miniature by an unknown artist

Below L.)   The Duke of Orleans. From the portrait by Ary Scheffer

Below R.)   Lord Ossulston. Marble bust by an unknown artist

Combe Abbey from the south-west. From an engraving by Louisa Craven

Hyde Park in 1828. From an engraving by W. Wallis after Thomas H. Shephe

horrid brutish Lawyer Sir Frederick employs. He, like a great fool, declares it is not *his* fault, as if, at 25, his Lawyer would dare act without his sanction. In short, this marriage, far from being as we thought a comfort to us, has brought nothing but trouble and expense.'

While Mrs. Smythe had money troubles, Cou was already running into the first obstacles placed between herself and Augustus. Her Stanley cousins did not like him. This is slightly sinister, as William and Rowland should have had every opportunity, being like Augustus keen members of the Melton hunt, of knowing him well. All three were rich young men, William being three years and Rowland one year older than Augustus; and it seems unlikely that William at least, being wild and extravagant himself, should find the same characteristics deplorable in his cousin's admirer. Did they know something more against him?

A passage in Harriette Wilson's memoirs may hold a clue to this mystery. 'The members of the Melton Club', she wrote, 'led what I considered a very stupid sort of life. They were off at six in the morning . . . and came back to dinner at six. While they sat at table, it was the constant habit of a few wretched, squalid prostitutes to come and tap at their windows, when those who were not too sleepy were seen to sneak out of the room. The rest snored and drunk till ten, and went to bed till hunting time again. The evening hunt dress is red, lined with white, and the buttons and the whole style of it, are very becoming. I could not help remarking that these gentlemen never looked half so handsome, anywhere in the world, as when, glowing with health, they took their seats at dinner in the dress of the Melton Hunt; and when the signal of those horrible dirty prostitutes was slyly attended to, by either Mildmay, Lord Herbert or Berkeley Craven, I could not help saying, Mon Dieu! Quel dommage!'

Harriette Wilson was writing of a time twenty-five years earlier; but it is possible to suppose that, in this as in other respects, Augustus took after his uncle Berkeley Craven, who will be met later in the journal. This is only a supposition; but one can imagine William Stanley and Rowland Errington being less ready to condone in a man who might marry their beloved cousin some fault which would seem trivial or ludicrous in the majority of their friends.

Tuesday, July 24, 1832

It was a showery day, but we had settled that *wind* & weather should not alter our plans. . . . William called & he remained to see us start, as he declared Augustus was the *worst whip* in England. It is very odd that neither of my Cousins can bear him, particularly William, & in this respect I think it is mutual, as Mr. Craven does not seem to bestow much affection on him—but I must say, does not say the illnatured things about him that William fails not to débiter, when speaking of *him*. After [we had been] waiting a long time, a very smart four-in-hand drove up to the door. The carriage to our surprise was empty, and *Fatty* Craven with his Brother on the Box. Fatty was sent up to tell us that on account of the rain Ldy. Craven and Lupo would follow in their own carriage. Sir Richard Bulkeley was with us when we started, looking much more like a man condemned to be *hung*, than to be *married*. I thought Augustus looked rather annoyed at seeing William. He drove us down admirably. Que j'étais heureuse. Ldy. Craven & Lupo arrived at Greenwich as soon as we did. We were completely a Family Party: & only missed Ld. Craven, who was obliged to attend the House. Augustus was so nice & attentive—he amuses me much by his quiet way of going on. He owned to me he was *épris*, & begged I would consent to become Lupo's *sister-in-law*. I took this, as it was meant, in joke, & he then was much annoyed that he could not make me listen *seriously* to him: & declares he can make nothing out of me. God knows, I should be willing enough to listen to him seriously if I could for one moment entertain a hope that his affection for me would be lasting! But we are both so young that I need not despair—& I honestly confess that of all the young men I have known this year he is the one to whom I give an entire preference. Lupo is the most charming, unaffected girl I ever met with, & appears clever & agreeable. The perfect union & happiness that reigns in this family would almost make me long to become a member of it. We laughed immensely, talking over poor Mountain—but not without doing justice to his amiable qualities. Nothing could be more kind than Lady Craven was to me, hoping I should become her Daughter's friend. At 10 o'clock we were obliged to ask Mr. Craven to drive us home, as we were anxious to go to Aunt Fitzherbert's, who, from fear of the Cholera, was to start the next morning for Brighton. On arriving at her door we took leave of our amiable conductor, who was most anxious to know whether I should ride the following day—which plan I had previously settled with Elizabeth. The Damers, Munster & Bruce came to Aunt F's a short time after we got there. I did not think she was *particularly* cordial to us, & dwelt on nothing but the awful dissipated lives we lead; but after all, is *rather* annoyed at our knowing everybody without *her* aid. I had been so truly happy all day that I never had time to feel my fatigue, but when I arrived in my bedroom I thought I could hardly have had strength to go to bed.

It is clear that the men in Cou's family all had ideas of their own as to whom she should marry. Frederick Hervey-Bathurst favoured Lord Hillsborough, who was certainly the greatest match; while William Stanley and his brother Rowland Errington were prepared to advance the claims of their friend Lord Albert Conyngham, second son of George IV's last favourite.

Wednesday, July 25, 1832
   The day was lovely, & I longed for 5 o'clock to arrive, which was the hour fixed for our riding. William called in the morning to know how our Greenwich Party went off, & just before I started he returned, bringing Lord Albert Conyngham with him. I soon discovered that his *real* motive for doing this was that he might ride with me & keep *off*

Augustus. Just as I was going to mount, I found Ld. Hillsborough at the door, on foot, looking very triste. I offered him my Groom's horse, but in vain. Could he have been transported in that moment dans le Palais de la Verité, I am sure he would have confessed his vexation at seeing me setting out with so numerous an *escort*. He went up to pay Mama a visit. After we had ridden a short time Ld. Albert left us, thinking, I suppose, that I was not *very* agreeable—which was true—for I saw Augustus riding with Mr. Macdonald & was *dying* for them to join us—which they did the instant Ld. Albert left us. Mr. Macdonald engrossed Elizabeth's attention, & I was *devoted* d'un autre côté. We are most pressingly invited to spend Christmas at Combe Abbey.* Such happiness I hardly dare rely on as coming within my reach. Every day & hour I see more of Mr. Craven I become more charmed with him. He is so agreeable, & appears so kindhearted & affectionate towards his Mother & Sister. He says I bear so strong a resemblance to the latter in manner & apparently in disposition, that on shutting his eyes he could fancy it was his sister's voice. Mr. Macdonald has not had much *difficulty* in discovering our little flirtation, & does nothing but torment us mutually. *He* escorted me home, & we then parted, to meet again at Lady Sefton's in the evening. When we arrived in Arlington Street the party was small & formal. I found *him* in the outer room, & after having been to speak to Lady Sefton, we returned, bringing Lupo with us, & sat hors de la société, en coterie, with the addition of Mr. Macdonald. We talked & laughed de si bon coeur, that I am sure we must have attracted every one's attention. Some of our friends hovered round our little circle, but we gave them no encouragement to join it. In the course of the evening Lupo & I exchanged Bracelets, that we might have some *more fun* with Mountain the next day. She lent me one of Augustus's hair, which he had given to her in the Spring. He *of course* said he hoped I should keep it as a Birthday present. How I wish there were not so many *prudish* rules in this Country,

* Lord Craven's house near Coventry.

as abroad there is not half the consequence attached to a *Cadeau d' Amitié.* As soon as the clock struck 12 they all went on one knee pour me baiser la main, & to wish me joy on attaining my 18th year! Mr. Macdonald & Francis Gordon muttered joy for *something else—on ne dit pas quoi....* All the company excepting us were going to Lady Codrington's Ball, but I had not the least wish to go, as I had a shocking migraine & was looking wretchedly ill.

On July 26 Cou went to Lord Hertford's second garden-party, where there was a Russian Horn Band on the lawn and fireworks, and where people played 'the new French game with the party-coloured hoops thrown into the air and afterwards caught with a couple of slender sticks'.

The Lady Strachan who had pressed Cou to come to this party was a notorious character. (It will be remembered that Louisa mentioned her having gone to Court without an invitation at the time of William IV's accession. She had, in fact, once been kept by the King when he was Duke of Clarence.) She had been a foundling, and became lady's maid to her benefactress. Her beauty got her talked about; she was known as Clothilde, and she eventually married the old sailor, Sir Richard Strachan. One of Lord Hertford's innumerable mistresses, she retained her influence with him by managing his harem. Her three daughters married foreign noblemen, and Lord Hertford left them large sums of money. To Charlotte, whom Cou mentions, and who became Countess Emanuel Zichy on marrying the brother-in-law of Metternich in 1837, he left £86,000; to Matilda, Countess Berchtold he left £80,000; to Louisa, Princess Ruffo, £40,000. Everyone in society knew about Lord Hertford's orgies, but even respectable people went to his parties and were polite to Lady Strachan: he was a marquess and a millionaire.

Cou was eighteen on the day of the déjeuné in Regent's Park.

Thursday, July 26, 1832
  What was my surprise on receiving this morning a very

pretty Vinaigrette, with a note, from Mountain. It shewed that he still retains a *slight regard* for me, & I blamed myself for having endeavoured to vex him by flirting with Augustus. Not but what I felt the ascendancy the latter had gained over him in my heart—& when I thought what my feelings were a month ago, I could not help being provoked at my own fickleness. William, Rowley & Minney remembered the 26th & all presented me with very pretty little souvenirs. But I will not conceal to myself that I felt hurt that Louisa should not have remembered it. I did not expect a valuable present from her, as I know she has plenty to do with her money, but the slightest memento would have gratified me. About 5 o'clock we went with Miss Bentinck to Ld. Hertford's Déjeuné. Mama walked about at first with Paul Lieven, & I with Tolstoy. In one of the walks I met Mountain walking with Miss Armstrong. I merely shook his hand, but did not chuse to thank him publicly. How anxiously I awaited the arrival of the Cravens. As soon as they came Augustus hastened to join us. He told me that he had been quite miserable about me last night, as he thought I was looking so wretchedly ill, & entreated I would take more care of myself. All this time Hillsborough amused me much by parading about with Lady Craven & Lupo. We all went in to dinner together—Lupo & Mountain sat opposite to me. The latter was evidently in a fidget to see my attention so engrossed by *the person* next to me, & at last shouted out before them all "*Cou,* did you get my note this morning? I suppose by not acknowledging it you mean to return what I sent you". I could not help laughing at this, as he seemed to have been unable to contain himself any longer. After dinner we walked about in the same *order.* In the Conservatory Mr. Macdonald overtook us & as usual began laughing. Mama at last looked very much displeased at my walking with him [Augustus] so long. I was therefore obliged to withdraw my arm from his: he perceived Mama's look, & pretended to walk away—though in reality he never was 100 yds. from me. He owned to me that he was very ill that day, but he was not

98

the less agreeable, & I own I am blind to every passing object when talking to him. Ld. George Hervey was there, but finding me always occupied with the Cravens, he did not succeed in eliciting a word from me. About 9 o'clock Lupo & I went with Miss Strachan to take off our Bonnets, & we then adjourned to the Ball Room, where I was engaged to dance the first Quadrille with *him*. But l'aimable garçon got impatient at our remaining so long upstairs & had changed his place to look for me. The Quadrille began, & he did not appear. Lady Craven told me that he had left her in a great fuss. M. de Mareuil came up to ask me to dance, but I waited to receive the other's permission, which he gave me, as he declared he would not dance a half finished Quadrille. I then Valsed with Ld. Douglas, after which came ce Quadrille *tant desiré* which we danced opposite to Lupo & Mountain. The latter was put into a great fuss, about my Bracelet, & teazed me to death to know *whose* hair it was. But all in vain, I *could* not tell him. After this I valsed with this *persecuted* individual, & took pains to express my thanks for his aimable souvenir. He was particularly amiable, & told me he was to leave London the next day, not to return till the following season. I could not help feeling sorry, as I think he has a great deal of heart, & that his feelings are strong & deeply-rooted. I galopped with Tolstoy. Valsed with Paul Lieven. Danced another charming Quadrille with Mr. Craven. Reels without end with Frederick Craven & Mr. Macdonald & Lord Douglas. I never danced so much, or with such spirit, as I felt it was *my* last dying speech. At 3 in the morning I led the Cotillon with Ld. Douglas, which, however, was not a good one, as people were tired. The Cravens remained by us the whole night, & I am sure people must remark the way in which we *cluster* together. Poor Mountain came up several times to supplicate me to tell him the history of my Bracelet. It seemed *hard* to refuse him anything the last evening, but he would only have been jealous had I told him the truth, & a little mystery was much better. Augustus thought this would be our last meeting, as they were all going to Gorhambury the next day, from whence he was to proceed to Combe, & to sail on Monday or Tuesday. He expressed a wish to come & see us the next morning, ere he set out for the Country which I was obliged to second strongly, as he insisted on my declaring whether his visit would give me any pleasure. I could not be such a hypocrite as to deny the truth, & I assured him that I should feel much *hurt* if he did *not* come. Poor Mountain could hardly speak when he took leave of us. Bon Dieu! How awfully tired I was d'esprit et de corps. I had been so excited by different things that my spirits were quite exhausted. When I got home I was so nervous & low that I hardly dared think over the events of the day. I found a letter from Louisa reminding me that this was the first time we had been separated on my Birthday. This idea was succeeded by so many melancholy ones that I cried for some time. After which I felt relieved, & things appeared less dans le noir. I felt that the London pleasures were quite at an end—but what was worse, I fancied that all those I had liked & loved would forget me in their absence & that while everyone's autumn & winter plans were settled, we had none. I could not exactly make out whether Mr. Craven *really* preferred me to any others, or whether it was merely to *amuse* himself that he thus flirted with me. I endeavoured to drive away all these perplexing doubts & fears, & tried to compose myself to sleep.

Friday, July 27, 1832

I got up tired & agitated. I felt that if *he* did not come to call on us he did not care about me, & the very thought of this made me truely wretched. Inshort, I worked myself into such a nervous state that I was even paler than usual. I got dreadfully nervous when the clock struck 2, & Mama remarked how ill I was looking, & by the very question of wishing to know the cause she made me feel worse. At last a cab drove to the door, which was quickly succeeded by a knock, & in an instant he was with us. I wished myself then far away, for the agitation & pleasure I felt made me so foolish that I could not

100

speak for some moments. He said "Miss Smythe, I will not conceal from you that you are looking most wretchedly ill, & Lupo & myself were quite miserable last night to see you dance so much". He talked of our coming to Combe in the winter as of a thing quite settled. This, thought I, will be our last interview, & a sort of melancholy feeling came over me when I remembered that he was going to sea in a vessel considered very unsafe. Mais il y a un Dieu qui veille sur les vertueux! He begged I would accept a view of the Menai that he had ordered for me. On taking leave, he merely said in a hurried tone "For God's sake, take care of yourself". He held my hand some time while a sort of triste smile played on his countenance; & when he was gone I hurried up into my room before anyone could mention his name. I there felt so faint from weakness, fatigue & over-agitation that I remained for some moments unconscious of everything around me. I then rode with Elizabeth, & told her all my miseries—she quite feels for me & herself thinks that he really likes me. We had not been riding long before Ld. Albert Conyngham joined us. I was not at all disposed to make the agreeable, & I am sure he must have thought me very dull. I do not know *why*, but I have an idea that could he remove *obstacles* he would also wish to enlist himself amongst what are called *mes adorateurs.* *
For he seems perfectly aware of my *little Craven flirtation.*

In spite of her gloom over parting with Augustus, Cou had to go out to dinner. It was quite an extraordinary dinner party at which to find Mrs. Wat Smythe and her daughter, and one cannot help wondering what lay behind it, unless of course some other ladies had failed to turn up. The only other woman was Olivia de Roos, the sister of the host. The rest of the party was made up of eight men—wits, dandies and the most sought-after

* If Georgina Smythe really did not begin writing her journal until September 3 as the date on her title page seems to imply, that is, just after she had refused Lord Albert Conyngham, she may here, as in other places, be attributing to herself thoughts and feelings in the light of after events.

dinner guests in the town. There was the amusing good-natured Alvanley, an old friend of Aunt Fitz, noted among other things, for having a cold apricot tart on his sideboard every day of the year; old Luttrell whom Captain Gronow said was the most agreeable man he ever met, far more brilliant than Rogers—the last of the Conversationists; the irrepressible 'Poodle' Byng; handsome Frank Russell, who rallied his retreating regiment waving the bullet-riddled colours at the battle of the Pyrenees, and about whom Wellington commented, "There's nothing like blood"; James Fitzroy, who was to die two years later; Greville, nick-named 'Punch', everybody's confidant and author of the most rightly posthumous memoirs in English; and Henry Greville, his brother, in demand as an amateur actor, later to become the patron of the tenor Mario and of the young painter Frederick Leighton. Henry de Roos, it is less agreeable to re-call, was soon to be found out cheating at cards; nevertheless Punch Greville recorded his usefulness in purveying women for his friends. Olivia de Roos was to become Lady Cowley and British Ambassadress in Paris: but only two of the clever men at the party ever married—and that somewhat arcanely. Could the dandies have invited young Cou to dinner—with Mrs. Wat in inevitable attendance—because they thought she was the prettiest girl in London, and therefore as desirable an adjunct to a dinner-table as a cold apricot tart on a sideboard?

I was obliged to go in early, as we were to dine at Lord de Roos's, but I felt so low that nothing gave me pleasure. We arrived late at dinner in the Regent's Park. Olivia De Roos was the only other Lady. The Gentlemen were Ld. Alvanley, Ld. James Fitzroy, Mr. F. Russell, Mr. Luttrell, Mr. Byng & Charles & Henry Greville. Ld. Alvanley is always agree-able & also Ld. De Roos, though in a quieter way, so that his next neighbour is the only person who profits by it. I was that *lucky* individual, & he was particularly *facetious*. It went off very well, although they certainly wanted another Lady to take the lead more in the conversation. We thought as we were out we might as well '*do the civil thing*' & go for an hour to Lady Mildmay's Ball. My spirits were unusually depressed, & it seemed as if the very music made me worse, To hear the same Airs played, & such a blank in the society. Tolstoy was the only person who seemed to participate in my feelings, for he was not more charmed with the Ball than I was. We came home about one o'clock. I was worn out & disgusted. This was the last Ball I went to.

Sunday, July 29, 1832

Rowley brought Lord Albert Conyngham to see us, & made me sing to him which frightened me very much, as I felt so ill & weak. Lady Craven & Lupo came to take leave of us. They renewed their entreaties about Combe, the very idea of which puts me into a complete *flutter*. Lupo & I swore to be friends. She tells me that her Brother is *really very bad*, as she calls it. How sorry I was to see them go! Certainly "l'absence est le plus grand des maux". We all dined with my Cousins. Nothing can exceed their kindness to me, & we spent a very agreeable evening.

Monday, July 30, 1832

I rode with Elizabeth, not dreaming of *who* I should meet, as I felt that there remained nothing in London to interest me. Ld. Albert joined us immediately. His conversation not interesting me particularly, I was idly gazing around me when, like a shot, Augustus passed by me. He instantly joined me, & said he had come out with the faint hope of seeing me, which he hardly had dared to think would be realised. Ld. Albert left us as soon as the other arrived, & I afterwards saw him passing & repassing with William & Rowley, who seemed very much *displeased* that Mr. Craven should thus have le champ libre. He was to sail the next morning. How happy & miserable I was at this moment— happy in the enjoyment of his society, & miserable at the thoughts of losing sight of him for so many months. We kept in the rear of the Party, that was very large, & had plenty of conversation. He assured me how much his happiness depended on our coming to Combe—& tried to make me listen to his *vows of Love* & *devotion*. But I was *cruel* enough to *laugh* at him. I never saw him look so handsome. His large blue eyes seemed more expressive then ever, & I hardly trusted myself to look at him. I asked him to come to the French Play in the evening, where we were going with Minney. He accepted this invitation most joyfully; but after a moment's consideration, he seemed doubtful whether Lady Craven would not claim the whole of his last Evening to herself, but that he should use every means to be with us. Jemmy also rode with us & the whole Party accompanied me to my door, when Augustus rushed off his horse to help me, & as I was jumping down he pressed my hand violently. We then dined in haste & went to Covent Garden, where we found Minney in a dreadful dilemma, having made a mistake about the Duke of Devonshire's Box, & finding it occupied by the Master of the Rolls & old Rogers. The former received her apology by saying "What a fool the Boxkeeper must be", but Rogers endeavoured to be civil, as they could not venture to turn any of us out. It was altogether a most comical scene, & worthy the pencil of a caricaturist. I half doubted, half feared Augustus's arrival. The first person who arrived was Ld. George Hervey, who stationed himself completely the opposite side from me, which was a great relief. Mr. Byng came afterwards, mais tout ceci ne me touchait guère. What was my extasy when I soon heard a hurried step approach the door & *he* rushed in. Dieu, quel bonheur! We sat down in a corner of the Box & talked quietly the whole evening. Poor Ld. George looked more miserable & *astonished* than ever. The happiness I enjoyed this moment, was, I felt, to be of very short duration. We talked over his intended voyage, which he was to begin the next morning at four o'clock. I could not help entreating him not to be too rash & to remember those he left in England who were much interested in his fate. I do not know how I brought myself to say these last words, but I was determined he should hear them, & I hurried through in a very inarticulate manner. I never knew till now that the absence of one individual could make so material a change in my happiness. He was the first person who had ever really appeared interesting in my eyes, & yet I often have observed in him a sort of capriciousness that could hardly betoken constancy, particularly as I know he was quite lately very devoted to Lady Louisa Lascelles, & now he professes to have found her dull. It is hard, however, from this youthful conduct to declare that a man will never fix his affections. But I digress, & must return to our parting that evening. I was quite nervous by the time the Sylphide was over, & when he conducted me downstairs to go to the carriage we neither of us said much. But he turned to Mama, & for at least the 100th time, entreated her not to disappoint them about Combe, & made me miserable by saying that if we did not come there he should always consider it as my fault, knowing the influence that I had over Mama. I did not trust myself to repeat again my feelings on this subject. As he put me into the carriage I did not nor could I speak. He merely pressed my hand, & thus we parted to meet perhaps after the lapse of months, when his feelings may be quite altered & I shall find him cold & indifferent. This thought was thrilling, & on my return home my thoughts were all confusion. I was & am still afraid of ever praising him, for fear Mama should take the contrary tone. She at present likes him, & I shall never try to enhance her partiality for him, as I always think that our nature prompts us to act from opposition. I can only hope that I am not deceived in my present idea of him, & that she will some day think of him as I do.

Cou had spent an evening in a box with the celebrated banker-poet, Samuel Rogers, and she had seen the second performance in London of the first Romantic ballet, *La Sylphide*, in which Taglioni had her greatest role: but her only thoughts had been of Augustus, to whom she talked incessantly. In 1832 opera and ballet were a pleasant background for conversation: today we are not allowed to take our seats at Covent Garden after the curtain has gone up for fear we shatter the rapt illusions of our fellow-worshippers.

Tuesday, July 31, 1832

A wretched, rainy day. Brooke Greville called, but I had not spirits to be agreeable. We dined at Aunt Haggerston's, where Rowley questioned me much about Augustus, & did all he could to argue me out of the opinion I have of him. I foresee that should my fate ever call me to become his wife I should lose the entire affection of my dear Cousins. We went to the Opera in Ld. De Roos's Box. Our sole visitor was Ld. George Hervey but my thoughts carried me far away from the scene around me, & I afterwards reproached myself for not being able to master my feelings.

'I never knew till now that the absence of one individual could make so material a change in my happiness.' In the course of her first season Cou had been given the cold shoulder by John Trotter, she had been irritated by the attentions of George Hervey, and had conducted a serious flirtation with 'Mountain' Hillsborough: now she was in love, and for the first time in her life exposed to the infinite varieties of sorrow. It is almost a law of nature that difficulties should spring up in the path of passionate love. Cou knew that her cousins disliked Augustus, so that even if she discussed him with William and Rowland she probably refrained from revealing to them the full extent of her feelings—as she did, it seems, to Elizabeth Brudenell-Bruce. She knew, too, that if William and Rowland knew something against Augustus—that he was unreliable, ruthless, immoral or irresponsible, that he had debts or bastards—then others must know it and repeat it to Mama and Aunt Fitzherbert. Even at eighteen she had the wisdom to play a waiting game with her difficult mother, not to exert pressure or to reveal how far her heart was committed. How much Mrs. Smythe knew by instinct or observation we cannot tell. But if Cou was shrewd enough to keep her own counsel and plan her campaign, she was not, in the long run, a girl who would resist the impulses of her heart. If she found Augustus really loved her— and Cou was certain she loved *him*—and if then Mama withheld her consent, she would run off and marry him, no matter what the cost to her reputation.

106

How could she know that Augustus was not trifling with her, that he really loved her? It was certainly rather rakish the way he kept pressing her hand. She *could* not know until Christmas —and Mama must be induced without being urged to pay the half-promised visit to Combe. She must wait till then. It was very hard.

2

LONDON EMPTY

---

*Maria Stanley's marriage—The assiduities of Lord Albert
—Count Tolstoy's pretty, mournful, little voice—Poor Lord
George Hervey—Cou's first proposal—Franco Seymour and
the Scots Guards' ball at Windsor—Thoughts about marriage,
Mama, heredity and Destiny—Mama's delays—Departure
for Clarendon.*

The season was over, and London was rapidly emptying: but
the Smythes had no country house of their own, and Mrs. Wat
had decided for the moment not to accept any invitations.
Parties, which might have distracted Cou in the absence of
Augustus, grew fewer and fewer.

August, however, began with a family wedding. Maria
Stanley, the only sister of William, Rowland and John, was
married to Sir Richard Bulkeley, a great landowner from
Anglesey. Cou wrote in her journal that 'family reasons prevented any of us being present'. What these can have been it is
hard to guess. Maria was a Catholic marrying a Protestant, but
Cou, after all, was the child of a mixed marriage. Cou had no
closer men friends than Maria's brothers, who were continually
in and out of Great Cumberland Place. Mrs. Fitzherbert, it is
true, had not spoken to her younger sister, Lady Haggerston,
Maria's grandmother, for many years; but if she had never
raised any objection to Mrs. Wat and her daughters staying at
Hooton or entertaining the Stanley boys at home it would be
odd for her to object to their attending Maria's wedding. Perhaps she, as a devout Catholic, thought Maria should not have
married Bulkeley, and therefore prevented Mrs. Wat, Protestant as she was, from seeing her married. The most probable

explanation, one feels, is that Mrs. Wat had found some imaginary grievance, as was her habit, to provoke a quarrel with Lady Stanley. Cou, who would obviously have liked to be at the wedding, does not complain.

During the summer Cou was to be alternately flattered and annoyed, then finally upset, by the attentions of her new admirer, Lord Albert Conyngham.

Lord Albert (pronounced 'Orbert') was the third son of the third Baron and first Marquess Conyngham. His mother was the daughter of John Denison, a north-countryman who rose from nothing and made an immense fortune. Plump, fair, pretty and silly, Lady Conyngham had been the only person who made George IV feel comfortable and happy in his old age. Whether she was his mistress in more than title is doubtful, and the stories about her rapacity for Crown jewels and other treasures have been greatly exaggerated.

Sir Osbert Sitwell, in the early chapters of his delightful autobiography, has portrayed Lord Albert as an intellectual and a dilettante. He certainly, in later years, travelled in Greece, collected antiquities and wrote a book. Cou Smythe, however, thought him stupid. Perhaps he was stupid about people and clever about things. Would an intelligent, perceptive—though by no means *intellectual*—girl like Cou have overlooked the good side of a seriousness which made him heavy-going in society? Serious and perhaps old-maidish he was, with his gifts of watercolours and his anxiety to show Cou 'a letter from an old Irishwoman to the late King'. I think he must have been rather stupid even in his intellectual pursuits. We all know people who read interesting books, but who are boring to talk to about them because they seem to miss the point of every-thing. Lord Albert certainly had little sense of humour. Yet he fell in love with Cou.

So a typical picture from this part of the journal is that of Cou and her companion Mlle Delisle bowling through Hyde Park in an open carriage, with the tall, solemn Lord Albert Conyngham cantering alongside. In the background hover two romantic figures on horseback: the beautiful Count Alfred d'Orsay, who dressed so superbly, but who was not quite respectable, because, according to Charles Greville, 'the general notion was that Lord and Lady Blessington were equally in love with him', and Count Tolstoy, a kinsman of the great novelist, who was staying with his aunt, Princess Lieven, at the Russian Embassy.

Saturday, August 4, 1832

That dear little considerate Rowley had left orders with Ebers to send me an Opera Box for tonight, being the last of the Season . . . It was the 'Agnese'. Aunt Cha came with us. We had Tolstoy for ages, who surprised me more than I can express by informing me that Comte Groeben is married to a very young person of 16, who he made his wife about six weeks before his arrival in England. Lionel Ashley paid us a little visit, but Ld. Albert Conyngham remained with us during the whole Ballet. He was just returned from the Brighton Races, where he had been much provoked by the failure of the Mare he had intended to christen *Cou*. Lord George Hervey, Dieu merci! always found our Box too full to gain admittance, & in the room his plans were again frustrated by Lord Albert's handing me to the carriage.

Sunday, August 5, 1832

It was a rainy, dismal day. Ld. Albert called & made me sing for him. He certainly is not *clever*, but seems a very goodnatured, bon enfant. The Haggerstons & Ravenscrofts drank tea here. Aunt Haggerston was much disgusted with Constantia's [Ravenscroft] unrefined appearance & coarse manners, as she calls them, & said to me, "Yes, my dear, it is very aimable of you to try & shew her off as pretty, but she is only an excellent *foil* for you".

Monday, August 6, 1832

Ld. Albert came at one to hear Tamburini, & he actually staid till near four o'clock. Mama was completely tired of him, & I was left to make the agreeable to him. Elizabeth called to take leave of us, & invited us most pressingly to come to Tottenham Park.* . . .

Tuesday, August 7, 1832
. . . Mama & I drove in the Park. Ld. Albert affiché himself to our carriage the whole time. . . .

Wednesday, August 8, 1832
Ld. Albert called, but was not admitted. We met him afterwards in the Park, when he told me he had called to shew me a Mss. Book of his, & asked leave to bring it the next day. Niente nella sera.

Cou's cold-shouldering of Lord George Hervey did not prevent her getting on with his sisters.

Thursday, August 9, 1832
Tamburini gave me a lesson in the morning. Lady Sophia Hervey wrote to know whether I should be at home at three o'clock if she & Lady Georgina called. They came, & we sang for some time. Ld. Albert, as I expected, arrived in the middle; & remained after them till near five o'clock. We again met him in the Park.

Unexpected pleasures are always the sweetest, and the fact that Lady Elizabeth Brudenell-Bruce had been prevented by indisposition from leaving London enabled Cou to enjoy with her a heart-to-heart discussion of the former's various admirers. In the absence of Augustus, this was for Cou by far the pleasantest way of spending an afternoon.

Friday, August 10, 1832
Elizabeth wrote me a note this morning, which I was much astonished at receiving as I thought she had left Town. But she had been dreadfully ill, & wished much to see me if I would be charitable enough to go & see her about 5. I went, & we had a very delightful *cose*. We talked all my *little*

* The Ailesburys' house in Savernake Forest, near Marlborough.

111

affairs over, & she is quite decided in thinking **Augustus** by far superior to any of the others. I afterwards drove in the Park with Madelle Delisle. Lord Albert rode by the carriage a great while. We were to meet in the evening at Minney's, where I had invited him to go. Poor Lord George was driving in the Park with his sister, & cast every now & then a mournful glance at our carriage, & I, comme une vraie méchante, was *very* pleased that he should see Lord Albert's attentions. I found Minney's *Thé*, as I anticipated, very agreeable, excepting that they would make me sing, which made me very nervous. The Ravenscrofts were there, which I was charmed at, as they will now no longer be able to say that we prevent Minney asking them. Ld. Albert talked to me the whole evening, & amused me much by wanting to know at what time he might call the next day, but I told him Mama was to be *très occupée* the whole morning. This did not satisfy him. He heard me appointing M. Tellier to come on Sunday with M. Tolstoy to sing, upon which he urged me to name an hour that morning when I thought they would be gone. I never *before* heard that people fixed a common morning visit, as they would an Evening Party. I did not however give him any other answer than that he might call at any hour he chose. Lady Tankerville was particularly amicale to me, & we once more talked over Chillingham scenes; & she for the first time accused me of having then been *smitten* with my *companion de la Battue* [Trotter]. I never knew she had found this out. Lord George was there, as also the whole family, the marriage between Lady Augusta Hervey & Fredk. Seymour having been just announced. They have my sincerest wishes for their happiness & a long continuance of it. I do not know her at all, but believe her to be amiable & handsome. I must, however, defend myself as to having any *penchant* for Ld. Albert. We mutually talk—more from knowing him as the dearest friend of Rowley than from the remotest idea of flirting; & I am always finding myself drawing comparisons between Augustus & all my other friends—if such they can be called—& I must own the latter have not the advantage.

Saturday, August 11, 1832

We had no visitors this morning, but in the Park we found our *Preux Chevalier* [Lord Albert] waiting for us. Aunt Haggerston stopped to speak to us, & we introduced him to her. He never left the carriage, & when we attempted going round the Park, & [had] hopes of getting rid of him, we found him still cantering by our side. The Bulkeleys returned to Town, but we did not see them this even. . . .

Sunday, August 12, 1832

The heat was so great that we did not go to Church. We had a great collection of morning visitors. First of all Ld. Arthur, then Ld. Albert, Ld. George Hervey, Sir Richard & Lady Bulkeley. The latter is looking quite lovely. We introduced Lord Albert to her; & she very goodnaturedly asked him to drink with them in the evening. He was then going to dine at Greenwich with D'Orsay, which made me convinced that he would not make his appearance in the evening. M. Tellier & Count Tolstoy came, & we sang together for a long time. The latter has a pretty, mournful little voice, which I own touched me a little. There is such a melancholy expression in his countenance, & he at the same time appears so aimable, that it is impossible not to feel interested in him. Lord George Hervey would, I thought, never go, but his lengthened visit did not *secure* him an invitation for the evening. Hyde Villiers came late & made himself rather agreeable. When we arrived in Hill Street [the Bulkeleys' house] about 10 o'clock I confess my surprise was great on finding Lord Albert already established there. *Sir Dick* & Maria kept teazing me the whole evening about Augustus, & I did not think Lord Albert enjoyed la plaisanterie much—not that he cares the least about me, de cela je suis assurée—but because all men are so vain that they cannot bear to feel themselves rivalled, even were it in a quarter in which they took no interest. We parted that night, as *I hoped*, for some months; as he was to start the next morning for Goodwood Races. I merely *hoped* this was the

113

case, as I thought other people would of course set it down as a decided flirtation—no one ever having affichéd themselves to our carriage in such a marked manner before; & I could not exactly reconcile myself to the idea that Mr. Macdonald & Francis Gordon should go & proclaim me a heartless coquette when they had seen me so lately shew so decided a preference in another quarter.

Monday, August 13, 1832

Aunt Haggerston came to take leave of us. We did not see the Bulkeleys, who were to start tomorrow morning for Baron Hill [the Bulkeleys' house in Anglesey], where they are. I wrote to Lupo, & enclosed the Menai Valse* for Augustus. . . .

Tuesday, August 14, 1832

I went to sing with Lady Sophia Hervey, & was introduced to Frederick's Fiancée [Lady Augusta]. She is handsome, but looks ill & languid, which I am sorry to see, as he would have required a person of an active character. I afterwards drove with Minney, who took me again to the Bristols, at whose door I sat for at least an hour, & brought me down an invite to go there the next night to drink tea. But it seemed to me so rude, their not asking Mama, that I was sure she would not let me go. We were asked to Lady Clanricarde's, in the evening, but did not go, as we both agreed that those reunions of young married women were a great bore.

Wednesday, August 15, 1832

An excuse was, of course, sent through Minney to the Bristols. We drove in the Park, where we met Minney, who had just received a most absurd letter from Lord George Hervey about my more absurd invitation for the evening, at the mauvais ton of which he was particularly horrified.

* Georgina had evidently composed a waltz for Augustus.

114

Thursday, August 16, 1832

I went out early with Madelle Delisle to execute commissions for Louisa, & called on Minney, who made me return at 7 to drive her out—when she settled to come home & dine with us à l'impromptu. We tried to pick up some *refreshers* for the evening, & only succeeded in securing Lord Munster, Ld. George & Frederick Seymour. I was much ennuyéed, as Frederick is become more prosy than ever.

Friday, August 17, 1832

Miss Jervis *condescended* to call on us today, but was received very coldly. We drove in the Park. Ld. Munster brought up Lord Augustus FitzClarence to introduce him to me. We invited Tolstoy & Augustus Liddell to drink tea with us, as we expected the Ravenscrofts. The latter, however, failed, & we had nothing but Tolstoy, who made himself very agreeable, but, I fear, was much bored.

Saturday, August 18, 1832

About 3 o'clock today, we were surprised by a visit from Lord Albert, who was just returned from Goodwood Races. I went to execute some commissions for Maria, & we afterwards walked in Kensington Gardens & drove in the Park. He was there, but I prevented his talking to us for more than an instant, & I saw him shortly after *well beset* by all the Cadogans, who I hear are very anxious for him to marry one of them.

Sunday, August 19, 1832

Lord Albert called, but was not admitted, which I think is very right, as it really is too tiresome to be persecuted every day by the same person. Hyde Villiers called, & when we told him Ld. Albert was one of our Habitués he said "Good heavens, there is no such *Goose* on any *Man's Common*". We went to the Ravenscrofts in the evening, but found no one there. I sang till I was quite tired.

Monday, August 20, 1832

No one called in the morning. We drove in the Park, where Ld. Albert had stationed himself, and asked leave to bring some Water coloured drawings, for us to look at, in the evening. Mama consented to this request, & he came. All these drawings, which were very pretty, were intended for my Album, & he amused himself the whole evening by fixing them in. I could not help laughing when I reflected that he had seen the picture of the Menai, & seemed as if he would not be *outdone.* He made himself more agreeable than usual, talking over past times with Mama, which I listened to, without being able to take a part in the conversation. He staid till past 12, & appeared much disgusted at being obliged to go to the Canterbury Races the next day. I rather think that a pressing word de ma part would have made him give up the Races, but as I had no particular wish that he should remain, & above all, was determined not to give him the slightest encouragement, I was silent.

Tuesday, August 21, 1832

Lord George Hervey called, & we asked him to drink tea here. I drove in the Park, & asked Tolstoy & Paul de Lieven to come, but they were both engaged with a party to Vauxhall. So we had the Ravenscrofts, & only Lord George for our Beau, who certainly is a dead weight in Society.

Wednesday, August 22, 1832

We did nothing, nor saw no one.

Thursday, August 23, 1832

I drove out with Mad^elle Delisle, not in the least expecting to see un visage de connaissance, when who should ride up to the carriage but Lord Albert. He certainly looked rather foolish, for as the Canterbury Races were not over he was at a loss to give a rational reason for his return. When I told Mama of this, j'avoue qu'elle a fait la mine.

Friday, August 24, 1832

Lord Albert called, but was not admitted, for we knew we should meet him in the Park, & Mama thought that quite sufficient. To our astonishment le Comte de Groeben called on us to take leave. They [Prince Adalbert and Groeben] were just returned from Scotland, & were to leave England that night. He told us he meant to bring his wife over next year, & begged we would make his Château near Berlin our pied à terre, if ever we travelled that way. We drove in the Park, and *Longues jambes* [Lord Albert] never quitted the carriage. At last, pour nous en débarasser, Mama invited him to the Ravenscrofts in the evening, which he most readily accepted. When we arrived about 10 o'clock in Portland Place we found Mr. Kinloch & Captn. Fitzmaurice only. The latter, a brother of Lord Orkney's with a great pair of moustachios, & a ton de garnison. Notwithstanding all this, he is amongst the number of those *unfortunate* ones qui se meurent d'amour pour Constance. Lord Albert soon arrived, & unluckily devoted himself to me the whole evening—which, of course, made Aunt Emma proclaim it to be a *settled thing*. Had she known how little our conversation had approached to anything bordering on sentiment! He gave me a long account (without naming the parties) of a most distressing scene in which he was unwillingly made a principal actor, at the Ball at Apsley House this year, by a young lady chusing to make him the confidant of her amours —a most extraordinary thing to do in my idea!—& then bursting into tears, made a regular scena, which was putting him in a most awkward situation, as everyone, of course, thought that it concerned himself. Inshort, during the whole of the affair he found himself obliged to take a part. But it appears that the young lady acted with so little discretion that she drew upon herself the blame of all parties—being foolish enough to commit herself by writing letters. He swore he never would again be such a fool as to lend a *helping hand* in any affair of this sort. We also talked over Melton, which he is obliged to give up as his Uncle Denison considers it at least the entrance to the *Infernal Regions*. He remarked the perfect union that existed between Mama and me, & our *friendly* way of going on. Therefore our conversation was very rational.

Saturday, August 25, 1832

No one called in the morning. Mama & I walked in Kensington Gardens, where, to our surprise, Longues Jambes spied us out, & followed us. After this he rode by our carriage for some time, & at last began to praise the French custom of paying evening visits. Mama was so afraid, he shd. offer himself for that evening that she said she was going out. Upon this he looked, I thought, rather huffed, & although he was to leave Town the next morning for his Uncle's, he rode off without taking leave. Mr. Cosby, who is his intimate friend, talked to us for some time.

Sunday, August 26, 1832

Lord Munster called, pour prendre congé, as he was going to Petworth the next day. Mr. Byng, M. de Gersdorff & Tolstoy also called. We asked the two latter to drink tea with the Ravenscrofts in the evening. Our reunion there consisted of Captn. Fitzmaurice, Mr. Kinloch & the two I invited. I talked most to Tolstoy, who is charming & talks so agreeably in a quiet way. He is by no means deficient of esprit, et rien ne lui échappe. We persuaded Mama to be at home on Tuesday evening.

Monday, August 27, 1832

A wretched rainy day. We did nothing.

Tuesday, August 28, 1832

A wretched cold day. About 3 o'clock who should call but Lord Albert. He really is the greatest fidget in existence. Never stationary for 48 hours anywhere. It is exactly like a Faun. Today he takes a pathetic leave of one, & the next, there he is again. We, of course, invited him to come in the evening. We drove in the Park, & were completely perished. He rode by our carriage for some time. We afterwards met Lord George Hervey, who we also asked for la soirée. The *entire tribe* of Ravenscrofts came to us. Ld. George & Lord Albert arrived at the same moment, & neither of them appeared to be very glad to have met. Tolstoy also came. The evening went off very gaily, & I am afraid that poor Lord George was the only one qui n'avait pas à s'en vanter. Tolstoy settled to come & sing with me the next morning at 3 o'clock.

Wednesday, August 29, 1832

It rained all day. Poor Tolstoy was obliged to write me a very pretty note, full of regrets & excuses, at being obliged to give up [the] pleasure of taking a singing lesson from me this morning. Lord Albert called, but was denied, as it really is too absurd to receive him every day.

Thursday, August 30, 1832

After raining the whole morning, it cleared up a little in the afternoon, & I drove with Mad^{elle} Delisle, but did not meet a creature. We went to the Ravenscrofts in the evening, where I hardly thought Lord Albert would have remembered to come—but he did, & I never saw anyone look so wretched or so out of spirits. After some time Tolstoy arrived; & I fancied I perceived a sort of cloud of jealousy pass over Lord Albert's countenance, when he saw l'étranger engross my attention. But I have no doubt but that this was my fancy. When we began to sing Ld. Albert talked to Mama, & she told me he dwelt on nothing but his disgust to the world, & how he wondered that men could make up their minds to marry, as all girls became so artful when they had seen a great deal of the world. In short, poor man, I am afraid he was this evening rather haunted by the blue devils. When we were going away, Tolstoy & I, for fun, went on our knees to persuade Mama to be chez elle on Sunday; & when they both offered to hand me downstairs, I cut the matter short by not accepting either. At the door of the carriage Ld. Albert asked leave to call the next morning to bring us a letter from an old Irishwoman to the late King.

Friday, August 31, 1832

Mama gave us the carriage at 11 o'clock, & we walked the entire round of Kensington Gardens. Little did I think what would be the events of this day. Ld. Albert called & staid for ages. When we pressed him to come to us on Sunday evening he said that he had promised to go on that day with D'Orsay to Lord Lumley's, in Suffolk, for a week's shooting, but that our invitation he could not resist, & therefore should defer his departure until Monday. I afterwards drove out with Mad^{elle} Delisle. At first we only saw D'Orsay, Paul Lieven & Tolstoy. The latter came up to the carriage au désespoir at being obliged to take leave of me, as he was to start the next morning en courier for Paris—for 10 days. This vexed me, as he was a great loss for our Sunday's reunion. At last we saw Lord Albert galoping into the Park. He did not then join us, but we soon again met him with D'Orsay & some one else. He came to the carriage, & I was just going to inform him of Tolstoy's defection when he hurriedly said "Miss Smythe, I have got something for you, that I had not an opportunity to give you this morning." Upon which he threw a letter into my hand, & darted off! I remained stupidly looking at the direction, & when I was convinced it was for me the whole rushed to my mind in an instant. I trembled from head to foot, & as if the letter brought contagion to me I gave it to Mad^{elle} Delisle, saying that I should certainly not open it. I cannot describe my feelings at this moment, as I felt in a sort of stupor. We immediately came home, & after telling Mama all that had occurred, I opened the letter. It was indeed as I had guessed a declaration of his affections, saying how vitally his happiness depended on my decision, & how cruel a refusal was to a man's feelings. The letter seemed to imply that he had never calculated on being rejected. In-short, the whole thing left me in a state of unfeigned astonish-

ment. Never had I suspected that he entertained such sentiments for me, as never once had he given me to understand
that my society was in any way influential or more agreeable
to him than another's—& I had always imagined that he was
attached to Miss Bagot. Therefore this was indeed a painful
discovery. Had it not been for dear Mama I should never
have known how to extricate myself from this dilemma. I
positively wished to refuse him, but wished to express it in
terms that might conciliate him as a friend, without giving
him any hope for the future. I knew exactly *what* I *wished* to
say, but I should have been quite at a loss how to word it had
not dear Mama most goodnaturedly written me a copy of my
answer, stating the surprise & pain his letter had caused me.
That my youth & happiness had, as yet, prevented my ever
thinking of changing my state. But that I could not but feel
honored & flattered at the esteem he had for my character,
which I feared appeared always giddy & thoughtless. With
his permission, I hoped to be allowed to meet him again as a
Friend. Good heavens! how nervous I was the whole evening
after having despatched this Letter. I was sadly afraid his
pride would be wounded, & that he would hate & abuse me as
a cold hearted Coquette. I almost indulged a wish of having
an interview with him, when, in a very few words, I felt, I
could exculpate myself of any such like accusations. This was
my first proposal, & it agitated my whole frame so much that
I hardly slept at all.

Saturday, September 1, 1832
   I got up very early, as I felt convinced that he would write
to one of us. We went & walked in Kensington Gardens, but
found no letter on my return. It rained all the afternoon, so
that we could not go out. This was perhaps very lucky, as,
had I encountered him, he might well have said I had no
feeling. Could he however but have known the anxiety &
agitation I underwent all day, he never would have thought
this. I can say with the most perfect truth that I never once
meant to give him any encouragement—nor did it ever strike

me that he had any preference for me. It seemed natural
enough that he should frequent the society of the only remaining people in London; & from being so intimate a friend of
Errington's—that seemed another link to our friendship.

Sunday, September 2, 1832

About one o'clock we received a visit from Mr. Cosby.
Strange to say, although an intimate friend of Lord Albert's
he never mentioned his name. Of course I never alluded to
him. After he was gone it occurred to us that he might have
been sent as a Spy—to see whether I seemed to be at all
touchée'd. As I was then still in the same state of anxiety I
could not look gay. We had no one else all day. The Ravenscrofts drank tea here. I could not help remarking how
differently this evening went off to any of the others. All
my favorites were gone! & in their stead, we had nothing but
Constantia's suite—viz: Captn. Fitzmaurice, Major Hall,
Mr. Hook & Henry Hunter. During the course of the
evening Mama received a letter & I was longing to rid myself of the whole society, to discover whether it came from
Lord Albert. When we were in our bedrooms Mama called
me, & gave me a letter from him to her, enclosed in one from
Mr. Cosby. Poor Ld. Albert's was very flattering & affected
me much. He stated that till that moment he had not allowed
himself to acknowledge the dreadful blow my letter had been
to him, but that on reperusing it attentively he could not but
esteem me the more for it, as it contained so much tact &
good sense, very rarely to be met with in so young a person, &
that the honorable sentiments expressed in it did as much
credit to my mind as the amiable feelings that pervaded it did
honor to my heart, & that when he could calm his feelings &
have more command over himself, he should then be only too
happy to meet me again as a Friend—but that he felt for the
present that would be impossible. Mr. Cosby's letter confirmed our suspicions of the morning—namely, that he had
been entrusted with his friend's letter, but had not been able
to deliver it to Mama before me. He described the wretched

state Lord Albert was in, that as his most intimate friend he had been privy to everything that had occurred, & had seen my answer, which, he feared, left nothing to hope for the future. He said he had never known Lord Albert attached to anyone before he knew me, & that he thought it would take a very long time before he could recover [from] it. He praised his character most highly, & said he was sure that had I consented to become his, I should have always found in him a most devoted & amiable Husband. He had left Town that morning for a week. I own that all this made me for an instant regret having refused him; but when I considered my youth & frivolity of character I felt I had acted wisely, as knowing so little, myself, of his real character, it would indeed have been running great risks to have accepted him. Dear Mama left me throughout, entirely to my own decision, as she said she had no earthly objection to the match excepting his mother's reputation. I went to bed low & wretched, though by far in a more tranquil state of mind than I had been for the last 2 days.

Monday, September 3, 1832
  I received a letter from dear Rowley, saying he heard that his friend Albert & I were to be seen daily together in the Park. That will no more be said. Should he ever be informed of what has passed between Lord Albert & myself, it shall at least not be through me. We walked in Kensington Gardens. Lord George Hervey called, but I was unable to join in the conversation as I felt so unwell & so harassed that I had not spirits to talk. Mama answered Mr. Cosby's letter. I drove in the Park, disgusted with London & everything around me. We went to take leave of the Ravenscrofts in the evening, who were to start the next morning for Ramsgate. I could not help being glad of this, as in my present state of mind I shall be very glad to enjoy a little perfect tranquility.

Cou was now longing more than ever to leave London, but the awkward business transactions which had been going on between her mother and Sir Frederick made her unduly pessimistic over the prospects of enjoying her stay at Clarendon.

Tuesday, September 4, 1832

We drove a little in the afternoon. I felt low & miserable. I do not anticipate much pleasure at Clarendon as I feel how difficult it will be after all that has happened to restore perfect *amicable feelings*. I am quite angry with myself that I should have lived to discover in my Sister's husband a perfect coldness & indifference to Mama's affairs, when he knows that all the anxiety she has undergone, & still undergoes, is occasioned by his Lawyer.

Maria Stanley, now Lady Bulkeley, was evidently pleased with the first sight of her new home at Baron Hill in Anglesey, which commanded a view of the Menai Strait and the Welsh mountains, for the letter Cou received from her next day, was 'all happiness and extasy'. That afternoon in the Park the Smythes met Cecil Forester, whom Louisa used to call 'le beau Cecile', and whose beautiful sister Mrs. Robert Smith had died of cholera six weeks before. Cou thought he was 'looking so handsome in deep mourning'.

Then at last there came a letter from Louisa Craven, with news of Augustus.

Thursday, September 6, 1832

My long expected letter from Lupo arrived. They are now at Hamstead [Hamstead Marshall near Newbury], having for the last three weeks been remaining at Ryde in the most painful state of anxiety on poor Augustus's account, as they knew he had left Bordeaux a fortnight ago, & therefore ought certainly to have been arrived. At last Ld. Craven joined them, & finding his mother very ill from constant anxiety of mind, he hurried her away from Ryde—where she never remained off the shore for an instant—& on Tuesday, thank God! they received a letter from Augustus from the mouth of the Gironde, where he had been wind-bound for a week. How much this relieved my mind, & how more than thankful one ought to be to that all-powerful Being who thus watches over & preserves his meanest creatures.

Suddenly cheerful, Cou no longer felt so bored with the routine of London life out of season.

I drove in the afternoon, & walked in Kensington Gardens. This quiet, regular life, suits me very well, & I should feel perfectly happy if I was not constantly tormented with the idea that my innocent conduct may have been considered by Lord Albert as encouragement, & that, in his own heart, he may fancy himself ill-used. Little disposed as I should feel to marry him, I would on no account let him think that I have played a Coquette's part, for I *esteem* him, though I could not *love* him—& all men confer an honor by expressing such sentiments for one. Lord Arthur Hill came in, quite unexpectedly, in the evening.

Friday, September 7, 1832
No one called. We walked & drove in the afternoon. Although I do not expect him to be so soon returned to Town, yet I always feel nervous on entering the Park & dread the sound of a horse.

Saturday, September 8, 1832
Ld. Arthur & Lord George Hervey called in the morning. I drove with Mama. Mr. Cosby passed us—mais voilà tout!

Sunday, September 9, 1832
We drove with Lord Arthur down to Roehampton. The day passed rather pleasantly. They are all so kind to us. Ld. Marcus was to start the next morning for Subbourne. I heard that poor Mountain had met with a bad accident from a thrust of a Buck's horn, which broke an artery in his hand, & they were afraid he would have bled to death. Poor fellow! He seems fated to come to an untimely end.

Monday, September 10, 1832

In the afternoon I went with Mad^elle Delisle to walk in Kensington Gardens, after which we drove in the park. I will not endeavour to describe what were my feelings, when all of a sudden, Ld. Albert passed the carriage. I trembled from head to foot. Mad^elle Delisle said that D'Orsay was with him— but I saw nothing, as my head felt quite giddy. I did not know what I should do if he were to come & speak to me. He passed us again in the midst of a large group of men, who, as Mad^elle Delisle told me, were all looking earnestly at me. The third time I encountered him, to my horror, he rode up to the carriage. I never ventured to look at him, but kept my veil down the whole time. As far as I could see he held his horse back, that his agitation should not be perceived; but it shewed itself enough, in his voice, which trembled dreadfully. He merely asked how Mama was—when we left Town—to which I answered "Next week, I believe". He then merely expressed his pleasure at having seen me, & hurried off. I was so truely agitated that I felt my manner was both cold & formal. I fancy D'Orsay urged him to speak to me, & per- haps, although very distressing for both parties, it was as well, & broke the ice for the future. Mad^elle D. tells me that he was perfectly scarlet while speaking to me. I was some time recovering [from] this scene on my return home— which had agitated my whole frame.

Tuesday, September 11, 1832

Mama thought it best to give orders not to admit him (if) in case he called—which, however, he did not. . . .

From now on Lord Albert disappears from the picture. The Park was empty—not even D'Orsay to be seen. Tolstoy was in Paris. Only the despised Lord George Hervey remained in London for his sister's wedding to Frederick Seymour. There was nothing to keep the Smythes in London, and yet Mama continued to delay her departure.

Mlle Delisle, Cou's devoted ex-governess, her companion

126

and *confidante*, whom, she wrote, 'has always acted as my best Friend', was leaving the Smythes for 'a Mrs. Knox'. It is a curious reminder of nineteenth-century customs to find that this educated Swiss lady of whom her charge could write 'I shall miss her in every action of my life', was specially asked to dine with her employers, perhaps for the first time, on the Sunday before she left them. The dinner table at least was one place where she would not be missed.

Minney Dawson-Damer came up to London for her brother, Frederick Seymour's wedding; and she had a gossip with Cou about the latter's admirers—a subject, it appeared, on which Aunt Fitzherbert kept herself surprisingly well informed.

Monday, September 17, 1832
... About six o'clock we called on Minney, who came up to town today for Frederick's Wedding, which takes place tomorrow. She and *little* George are in high force & good humour. Minney began to attack me about Lord Albert, saying she had been told that I had used him *very ill*. I pretended not to understand her, & said that I was not at all aware of having been to blame. She says he is gone to Doncaster, very much *affronted*. I suppose, these are the *on-dits* of the world. I did not expect to escape censure, but I shd. indeed be much hurt if I for a moment thought that all this came from him. I certainly shall find this out by some means. It appears that Lord George Hervey's visits at Hampton Court were to entertain Minney about me—& by this means the Gossips then set about the report that Mrs. Damer flirted while her husband was absent. One day she accused him of being *jealous* of Ld. Albert—which suspicion made him very indignant. What astonishes me more than all is that Aunt Fitzherbert should have told Frederick Seymour that as for Ld. George & Ld. Albert, I only amused myself with *them*; but that Augustus Craven was my *decided* Favorite. How she ever found this out is to me an enigma—as never once have I named Augustus to her, & certainly I should not have shewn so little tact as to praise a Conyngham to her.

127

But one's actions & words never fail to be observed & construed in a thousand different ways. I am quite disgusted with the gossip & tracasseries of the world. Why they cannot leave one so insignificant alone is surprising to me. I find that Frederick had expressed a great wish that I should be one of the Bridesmaids, but it appears that the idea was given up, as Lord George opposed it most strongly—stating that it would be very *impertinent* to ask me to *condescend* to be Bridesmaid to a person I hardly knew. I am so fond of Frederick, & have such a regard for him, that I would willingly have done this to oblige him. We took George Damer to Crockfords to dinner, where we met Mr. Cosby, who came up in the most cordial manner to us, & I thought would never have done shaking my hand—therefore I cannot infer from him, that as a friend of Ld. A's my conduct has been reprehensible, as he would then be very wrong in shewing so much empressment towards me. I wrote to Elizabeth, & expect to hear of him from her. Minney paid us a visit, after we were undressed.

Another Seymour, Minney's nephew and Cou's old friend, Franco (who was many years later to succeed his cousin as fifth Marquess of Hertford), also appeared in London. Franco was Adjutant to the Scots Guards—or Third Fusilier Guards, as they were then usually called—stationed this year at Windsor; and the regiment were to give a dance. Franco 'promised a good Ball, and named *Hillsborough* and *Trotter* who are going'. 'Although neither of these are *the Favorite*', wrote Cou, 'yet my affections are not as yet so firmly fixed but what a Ball is still a great temptation'. News came that Uncle Hayman, Fanny's father, had suffered a bad hunting accident at Rudge, and Cou was on tenterhooks that he would die and prevent her going to the Ball. No fatal message came, however: and, in point of fact, Mr. Hayman subsequently recovered.

Tuesday, September 18, 1832
Dieu merci! we received no intelligence from Rudge, & are therefore going to the Ball. Minney called after the

Wedding, which she said went off admirably—& without tears. The Bride looked very handsome & was very composed, but poor Frederick was rather agitated. We started at four o'clock & arrived at Windsor about six. I felt very happy. Franco had ordered our rooms for us, & we ordered dinner immediately. We were told that all the Officers were to come & dine at the Inn at seven o'clock, but we had hardly begun our little repas before l'aimable Adjutant [Franco] walked in & begged to share it with us. I cannot describe his delight that we should really have come. He made himself, as usual, most charming, & we laughed & talked till near 9 o'clock, when I adjourned to dress, & he went to see his brother officers. Just before I had quite finished my toilette, Mama came in to tell me that Mountain had been sitting with her for ages, & was very anxious to see me. I knew he was to come, & hastened downstairs. How charmed I was to see him again! But he cd. hardly recover his surprise at finding us there. Mama went to dress, & we were left tête-à-tête for some time. We talked the season over, & when he asked me about the Cravens I felt quite *honteuse* when I recollect the way in which I had behaved to him latterly. However, I can only say that I do not deserve his friendship—& I see that all my faults & misdemeanours are forgotten by him, & that he (I think) me prefère toujours un peu. I am angry with myself for not having a more decided preference for him, but at present I am so entirely prévenue d'un autre côté that it will take some time ere I can alter—& why should I alter? Should Augustus have quite forgotten me, & be really cold & in-different towards me when next we meet—it will then be time enough for me to change my sentiments. We arrived at the Barracks about 11 o'clock. I never saw anything so perfect as the whole thing. The illuminations outside the building were beautiful, & a whole suite of temporary pas-sages, lined with Soldiers, led to the Ball room. The military Band was playing, & the whole sight was splendid. The ball room was hung with colors & trophies that had been taken in different victories, & each chandelier was surrounded with a

129

perpendicular circular column of bayonets—which produced a most military coup-d'oeil. Weippert's band was stationed at the top of the room within a railing made of crossed swords & guns. All the Seftons, Maryboroughs, Burghershs, Bagots & Cowleys, were there. Miss Bagot looking more lovely than ever, although grown very fat. I do not know why, but she is always associated in my mind together with Ld. Albert. I danced with Francis Molyneux, Franco, Ld. Hillsborough, Ld. Alfred Paget, Mr. Riversdale Grenfell, two German friends of Franco's, whose names I never could make out, & Mr. Knox. But I danced at least seven or eight times with Franco, which I believe I should have avoided. But I felt that we had come down on purpose to please him, & as I love him of all things, I wd. not refuse him. I know that poor Mountain was much annoyed at this, but ill luck attends me when he is there, as I always find myself acting in a manner calculated to estrange him quite from me—but his good heart prevails, & he forgives & forgets. During the evening I had a great deal of conversation with Franco. We, of course, reverted to the old subject abt. Mr. Trotter, & I pleased him much by saying that I entertained a higher opinion of him than I did of anyone. He has had, poor fellow, a most violent attack of Cholera, & although recovered from it, he has so constantly relapses that the Doctors think very badly of him. When Franco told him, Monday, that we had promised to come down, he said that should he feel well enough that alone would make him put on resolution to come. But as he did not make his appearance I fear he is ill again. Franco told me that I must never judge of him by his conduct, for as he could not yet marry he never liked to know people too well—inshort, his principles are too noble, almost, for this world. We talked about marriage, & he gave me a little good advice on that subject. I did the Mazurka with him, & I own it distressed me a little to see Mountain's miserable countenance as he sat by Mama, a silent spectator. Franco saw it, & spoke to me on the subject. He reminded [me] of the reports that circulated during the Summer, & surprised me much by telling me that

130

my conduct at the 'Menai' had not escaped him. He did not exactly blame me, but merely cautioned me against trifling thus with other people's feelings, lest I should at last trifle with my own without intending it. At six in the morning we left the Ball & I took leave of Mountain, to meet again, as I hope, at Combe. I heard this evening of the safe return of Augustus. What pleasure this gave me! I liked my Ball very much, but should have felt much happier if dear Mama had not been so unwell. She made this exertion entirely to please me, & it was too great for her. She was dreadfully ill on her return from the Ball, & I felt miserable to see her in this state. I never was so tired in my life, from having been so much out of the habit of keeping such late hours. I went to bed too much agitated & excited to be able to go to sleep, & it was not till near 8 o'clock that I closed my eyes.

Wednesday, September 19, 1832

Franco was to come about two o'clock to walk with us & lionize us, but dear Mama expressed a great wish to start as soon as possible, & we therefore set out for London at one o'clock, & arrived here about four. I was low & wretched the whole way home. Mama was so ill & so low about herself, & I was then alone with her for the first time in my life. Even dear Madelle. Delisle was gone, & on our return the house looked as still as if Death had entered its threshold. I could hardly keep up my spirits. My head throbbed with the most violent pain, but I endeavoured to master all my feelings for dear Mama's sake. The scene of the preceding day seemed to have passed before my eyes like a dream, & I reproached myself for not having been more empressée to Mountain. But I have such a horror that it should be thought I sought him for his title, that I always am much more distant to him in society. He is grown much more handsomer, & looks thin & pale since his accident. I almost feel a pressentiment that it will be my fate to become his wife, but when I think of Augustus this idea is very painful. I spent a wretched evening, & we went to bed very early.

Thursday, September 20, 1832

I got up feeling better, but dear Mama was not much improved. Uncle Hunter called, & Miss Delisle came & spent the day here. I drove out with her. We saw D'Orsay, Ld. George Hervey, Mr. Cosby, & Clement Hill. The latter got so *dead drunk* at the Ball that he was obliged to be turned out. He staggered up to me in the supper room, when I was with Franco, but I seized hold of his arm, & dragged him away, as I got dreadfully alarmed. He forced himself again into the Ball Room, & came up to Mama to ask her whether she had had *good sport*, & killed *many birds*.

Friday, September 21, 1832

Dear Mama is little better, but we shall not leave Town before Sunday night or Monday morning. I feel as if we never should leave it, but hate it more every day. Dear Franco wrote me a few lines to enquire after Mama, & stated that had it not been for me he shd. have thought it a bad Ball, but as it was he had liked it of all things. I feel he *really* is one of those few I may call my friends, & I have the greatest esteem for him. . . .

Apart from her longing to leave London, Cou's one desire now was that Mama should accept the invitation for Christmas at Combe. Yet at the thought that Augustus Craven might propose to her, Cou became distraught. She knew—or she thought she knew—that she loved him: nevertheless, she realised that there were reasons against the marriage.

. . . I wrote yesterday to Lupo, & long to hear from her now that *he* is returned. Combe is constantly in my thoughts, & I have now a faint hope that we actually shall go there. What will be the result of that visit? Should I have courage to answer Augustus as I did Ld. Albert? I doubt this excessively, but I am, thank God, not forced by this visit to marry him. I only fear that it will increase my attachment for him, & I doubt whether Mama wd. approve of the connexion, as I fear the Berkeleys & Cravens are not very good blood— & I am told, he is dreadfully extravagant. But it is of no use conjecturing thus upon things that must take their own course—for I am sure there is no possibility of altering one's destiny. . . .

Cou's remark about the Berkeleys and Cravens brings up the interesting question of what, in fact, constitutes a good marriage. On the continent in those days, and to a certain extent today, the answer would be simple: each partner in a marriage must have at least the *seize quartiers de noblesse*, that is to say that their sixteen great-great-grandparents should all have had the right to bear arms. Cou Smythe, for all her background of dim country squires, may probably have been able to boast this: Augustus Craven, with his actress mother, worthy woman as she undoubtedly was, could not. Yet he was the younger son of a peer and took precedence, for instance, of the better-born Frederick Hervey-Bathurst. To probe further, Augustus's grandfather, the sixth Lord Craven, came into his barony in the most devious way: he was very remotely related to the first Lord Craven who had befriended the Queen of Bohemia in her exile—and even this gallant old soldier had merely been the son of a rich Lord Mayor.

The last two Lord Cravens had both been promiscuous in their affairs with women: but the Berkeleys were even more notorious. Augustus's grandmother, born Lady Elizabeth Berkeley, after being turned away by her first husband, Lord Craven, for resorting with her lover to a house of ill-fame in Covent Garden, travelled abroad and seduced the elderly Margrave of Anspach, Brandenburg and Bayreuth. When their respective consorts were dead, she married him, made him sell his principality to his uncle, Frederick the Great, and brought him back proudly to England. Queen Charlotte refused to receive her at Court with the honours due to a Serene Highness, so the Margravine had to content herself with driving her carriage and six in that part of the Park reserved for Royalty, and with writing and acting the principal role in a series of plays at her private theatre by the river at Brandenburg House. Once more a widow, she moved to Naples, took furiously to gardening, turned Catholic, and was made Princess Berkeley by the Pope. She was a lively and attractive, if headstrong and conceited woman, whom her own pompous and somewhat empty memoirs present in the least attractive light. The fact that the Margravine's brother, the fifth Earl of Berkeley, had several children by his mistress before marrying her led to a case in the House of Lords and the separation of the Earldom from the Berkeley estates. Her eldest illegitimate nephew Colonel Berkeley, later Lord Segrave and Earl FitzHardinge, acted on the stage at Cheltenham and was described by Charles Greville as 'an arrant blackguard'. The Margravine's great-grand-father was that noted rake the first Duke of Richmond, child of Louise de Kéroalle by King Charles II.

The Berkeleys were at least an interesting family to marry into, though it is understandable that Mrs. Smythe may have had qualms. Yet who can prophesy which strain will emerge? Their recent history might be lurid, but Berkeleys had fought at Poitiers and Flodden: they were among the oldest and noblest families in the kingdom.

Another question which Cou took into consideration when she thought about getting married was her mother's financial affairs: these were no better than they had ever been.

Charles Smythe, Mrs. Wat's last surviving brother-in-law, had persistently avoided paying her the money due from his brother Jack Smythe's estate. This we know from a letter Mrs. Fitzherbert wrote to Colonel Gurwood a few months before, apropos of a visit from Charles Smythe's daughter, Mrs. McNotty. 'She says his temper and his penury increases every hour. . . . The only thing now on his mind is a thorough deter-mination of never paying Mrs. Smythe a farthing. . . . There is sad work going on with Smart and the lawyers disputing every-thing and keeping poor Mrs. Smythe in the greatest degree of poverty and distress not having as yet paid her a farthing of what was due to her at my brother's [Jack's] death, nor anything as yet settled with regard to the property at Brambridge. . . .'

Under the circumstances it was natural that Cou should occasionally feel an obligation to find a well-to-do husband as soon as possible.

... Mama talked seriously to me about the situation of her affairs. Dieu sait! what will become of us next year. I have strongly advised her to break up her establishment, get this house off her hands & go abroad for a year or two. And yet this would indeed be a melancholy thing for me—to leave all my friends just as I am entering on the world. I often ask myself what I should do if I had a wish to marry? I should feel so cruel at leaving Mama, & yet she is now most anxious that I should be established, seeing as she does how perfectly impossible it will be for us to live as we have done. I consider all this as nothing for myself, who may make a good marriage; but for Mama, who has been accustomed to live in luxury, it is a severe blow to be forced to separate yourself from your comforts at an age when you have lost your love for dissipation & pleasure. I certainly feel that Louisa reaped all the benefits of an extravagant house, & that I suffer severely for it. However, this may hereafter be of service to me.

More delays over leaving London.

Saturday, September 22, 1832
Our departure is now really fixed for Monday, & I trust that we shall not remain an hour longer in Town. I am so sick of it & so disgusted with it that I feel as if I never should like it again ...

Sunday, September 23, 1832
... Before I went to bed I perceived Mama was again fluctuating as to her departure—& I really felt so cross that I could hardly contain myself, as it is nothing but laziness; &

I am sure she has no wish to leave Town, although she makes so many protestations abt. it.

Another outburst against Mama, and a resolution to marry *anyone* in order to escape from her procrastinations, was swiftly followed by repentance.

Monday, September 24, 1832

As I foresaw, our departure is again postponed. She says we are to start at seven tomorrow morning, but I know she will do nothing today, & we shall be still here for days. She has now the excuse of a swelled face, which will, I daresay, last her for some time. However, it is only for a time that I shall have to lead this sort of life, as I am quite determined to think of marrying as soon as I can. I wd. almost accept Ld. Albert from ennui of my present condition. I am resolved that I will be another's before a twelvemonth has passed over my head. Not having a soul to go out with, I was forced to remain in the house the whole of this lovely day—but before it was over I repented what my cross humour had made me rashly write in the morning. Mama is really not well enough to undertake a journey, & she is so kind to me in being sorry for the dullness of the life I lead, that I reproached myself most bitterly for having thus given way to my temper. I trust, through God's assistance, to have more command over it in future; as I feel that my thoughts are not half sufficiently engrossed with religious principles—& without these, our nature is too frail to overcome worldly temptations . . .

Meanwhile there came news of Louisa's old admirer.

. . . Tolstoy called on us, & was, as usual, very agreeable. He told us that he had seen Charles de Mornay at Paris, who has got great moustachios, & is grown much fatter. Il ne doit donc pas être beau. I shd. very much like to see this fascinating individual again, but his carrière diplomatique will, I fear, carry him far away from England—& Dieu sait! if I shall ever go to Paris. . . .

Cou's reading reminded her of Lord Albert.

. . . Whilst reading the Memoirs of James Ist today, I cd.
not help applying a passage in them to poor Ld. Albert. It
was on the occasion of the King's asking Bacon (when prime
minister) what he thought of a French Ambassador, lately
arrived at the English Court. "I think him, Sir, a tall proper
man." "But what think you of his head-piece?" rejoined
James. "Why, Sir, tall men are like houses of four or five
stories, wherein the uppermost room is the worst furnished."
But this is rather a *severe appliqué*, though I fear a just one.
We are *not* going tomorrow. This evening passed like the
rest.

The long-postponed departure was preceded by a fit of
misgivings over life with Louisa at Clarendon.

Tuesday, September 25, 1832
This day was lovely, like yesterday. Henry Hunter called
on us, & spoke in rapturous terms of Clarendon. I wish I may
be as agreeably surprised, for though most anxious to leave
Town & arrive there, yet I cannot help feeling that I shall not
be happy there, as there are always jealousies when Louisa &
I are together, & Mama is so much more amiable towards
me when away from her—& my spirit will not submit to that
sort of thing, as I *cannot* help being aware that the comparison
would not prove against me. I drove out . . . Tolstoy came to
speak to me for a few moments, & he afterwards passed by us
accompanied by D'Orsay, who, as usual, eyed me well. I
would give worlds to know whether he corresponds with Ld.
Albert & what remarks he makes upon me.

On September 26 the Smythes left London.

AUTUMN AT CLARENDON

Leaving London in their carriage at four o'clock, Mrs. Smythe
and Cou slept the night at Egham; they arrived at Clarendon
Park near Salisbury between five and six on the following day.
One or two lady's-maids presumably travelled with them,
besides their coachman and groom, but it is a curious fact that
in her journal Cou hardly ever alludes to servants, food or
interior decoration. Even clothes she barely mentions, though
an exceptional *coiffure* by Nardin or Isidor is once or twice
briefly referred to. All the appurtenances of what modern
fashion papers call 'gracious living', the local colour which
would occupy so large a part in a novel, letter or journal written
today, Cou took for granted. She was interested in people, and
the people she was most interested in were men.

Sir Frederick Hervey-Bathurst's house, Clarendon, was a
plain and handsome grey stone building dating from the end of
the seventeenth century. The ruins of a medieval Royal Palace
stood on the property, and the estate must be almost unique in
Great Britain, not for remaining in the same family, which it
has not, but for retaining its same boundaries since the Middle
Ages: a deep ditch, nine and a half miles long, still surrounds it.
In 1357 four Kings, Edward III, David of Scotland and the
captive John of France and Philip of Navarre had hunted

together at Clarendon. Sir Frederick's house (which, with some early Victorian additions made by himself, remains much the same today) stood on a green plateau, to the north of which huge woods stretched out in the direction of Salisbury, and which to the south-east dipped down to a lake. The living-rooms on the ground floor were panelled.

Thursday, September 27, 1832
We . . . found them all looking most flourishing, & charmed to see us. Nothing can be nicer than the House, which is entirely furnished, excepting the drawing room & Louisa's Boudoir. Aunt Cha is quite at home, & will, I hope, remain here some time longer.

Now began for Cou two and a half months of idle country life, enlivened only by the advent of an occasional visitor. As it would not have been proper for Augustus to write to her, the most she could look forward to for the time being was a letter, now and again, from Lupo. The autumn stretched ahead of her like a desert: but she felt that if she dealt tactfully with Mama and did not show an unbecoming degree of enthusiasm, she might come at last to the enchanted oasis of Christmas at Combe.
One day was much like another, except for the weather.

Friday, September 28, 1832
A lovely warm day. . . . We took a charming walk in the woods, which are beautiful.

Saturday, September 29, 1832
The day began rather showery, but I rode in the afternoon with Sir Frederick through the woods & round home by the Downs. The old grey went beautifully, & I was not frightened. The evenings pass very merrily, as Sir Fred. & Louisa are all amiability towards me, & everything has gone on smoothly—no recurrence to past events.

Sunday, September 30, 1832

We did not go to church, but Sir Frederick acted *parson*. It was not fine enough to walk.

The expected visit of her favourite cousin, Rowland Errington, though welcome to Cou, alarmed her somewhat, as she feared what reports he might have had of her behaviour to his friend Albert Conyngham.

We half expected Errington to arrive, but were disappointed. I rather dread his coming, as I feel sure that he is aware of what has passed between his Friend & me; & as I have studiously avoided mentioning so much as his name here it would make me feel very awkward if Rowley were to laugh at me on the subject. I have not the slightest doubt, however, but what Mama has published the fact [of Lord Albert's proposal] to Louisa, as it is very difficult for her to keep a thing secret. I forgot to mark having received a most charming letter yesterday from my dear Lupo, written on Board the Menai. It is full of Augustus, but her tact shews itself in not having communicated any direct message from him, merely kind remembrances from *all* her Brothers—who are going to Jersey & Guernsey, while Ldy. Craven & Lupo remain at Hamstead. The more I think of Augustus, the more I feel how attached I am to him—& yet why should *I* expect greater constancy from him than he has shewn to others? Should I go to Combe & find him unaltered, I fear no remonstrances from my Family would induce me to abandon the prize I had won; but should it be decreed otherwise I trust to have strength of mind enough to banish from my thoughts one so unworthy of my affections. I received also yesterday a very kind letter from Elizabeth. After all, she could give me no tidings of Ld. Albert save that he was at Doncaster, for she was not well enough to attend the Races, & does not seem at all *au fait* as to the issue of our acquaintance. I wrote to her immediately to beg she would write me all the details she could muster concerning his plans & those

140

of *others*—for she is going to Harewood, where she intends spreading Augustus's *penchant* for me.

Before he met Cou, Augustus Craven's name had been linked with that of Louisa Lascelles, Lord Harewood's youngest daughter.

Monday, October 1, 1832

A disagreeable, showery, cold day. Louisa & I drove a little way on the Southampton Road, which is beautiful. The damp gave me a sore throat & the Rheumatism all over me.

Tuesday, October 2, 1832

I rode with le beau-frère to Salisbury, & came home over the Downs, where I chose to get rather alarmed. In the middle of the woods, by moonlight, we fell in with the rest of the family. Mama had been *floored* in a most ignominious way, Balaam having laid down with her. I never saw so lovely an evening—not a cloud to be seen. To see the setting sun on the Downs was really a splendid coup-d'oeil. Inshort, I am perfectly happy here, as now all society is alike to me, & I would much rather enjoy as I do now the union of a small family party. My thoughts are always reverting to the past, & trying to unveil the future; the present occupies but a small portion of my attention. They are all here anxious that *Mountain* shd. conquer, & that the Menai should fail. I let them talk, as it is time enough to await events.

Wednesday, October 3, 1832

A wretched damp day. My Rheumatism was so bad, & also my sore throat, that Louisa ordered a fire in my dressing room, & there I staid. I felt low & triste & was glad to be alone to indulge my thoughts.

When Cou was bored, or deprived of male society, she tended to grow slightly hysterical. Her feelings, suppressed no doubt in the presence of her family, were vented on her diary in the form of capricious underlining (shown here in italics).

Thursday, October 4, 1832

  . . . Louisa & I drove to see an *old woman* at Farley. It rained torrents as we came home.

Hillsborough had been invited to stay for shooting, but could not come.

Friday, October 5, 1832

  A wretched rainy day, & to make it *still more pleasant*, Mountain sent an excuse, without even a distant hope of his coming. I was troubled with the *blue devils* all day, although I am very angry with myself for caring about him.

Two days later Rowland Errington arrived to enliven the party.

Sunday, October 7, 1832

  Louisa & I got up early & went to Morning Service at the Cathedral. I was enchanted with it, so like a Catholic Service. Errington arrived, which I am quite delighted at. We laughed immensely all evening. I shewed him the Drawings Ld. Albert had given me, which he was much surprised to see in my possession, knowing how much he valued them. But he evidently *knows nothing*.

Monday, October 8, 1832

  The *men* went out shooting, & Lou & I walked in the woods. Nothing particular passed this day.

Tuesday, October 9, 1832

  We took the Luncheon to our Beaux at *Piper's Barn*, & followed them shooting for some time, & came home tired.

Wednesday, October 10, 1832

  We lunched at *Elkin's*, & Lou & I got wet through coming home. We were *rather* lively in the evening.

Thursday, October 11, 1832

  I did not go out the whole day, & felt low & ill.

Friday, October 12, 1832

Cha & I went in the carriage to *Locke's*, but were obliged to walk part of the way there as it was impossible to get the carriage down the chalk hills. We arrived there very late, found our Beaux very cross, having lunched. We staid a short time with them & then set out to walk home—lost our road, were caught in the rain, & made it about 5 miles, instead of two or three. How tired I was!

Saturday, October 13, 1832

The Gentlemen went out cub-hunting & returned about 4 o'clock to walk with us. We went down to the Water, which I had never seen before. It is very pretty; & the evening was so fine & clear that it reminded me of Chillingham! I felt low & could have cried willingly. Not a day passes but I dwell for hours on my future life, conjecturing *what* will be my fate, & whether Augustus will remain constant. Sometimes I feel he will, at other moments I ask myself *why* I *shd. think* so, & what particular reason I have to imagine that he *ever* seriously liked me, or that I should be the *one* to whom he will shew the first symptom of constancy. All this makes me miserable, & I then picture to myself what I should do were Ld. Albert to persevere. In point of *circumstances* he is amazingly above the other, but how could I attach myself or look up to a person of so weak a mind? I believe him to possess a thorough good heart & amiable disposition, but I can fancy nothing so dreadful as feeling that you were guided by a fool. I think constantly of Combe, & put everything in the most disagreeable light. Should *he* propose, & the match be disapproved of—que faire alors? I certainly might affirm with verity that I never came there with the intention of making up to him—although one should feel rather awkward, having to refuse a person in his own House. I really must endeavour not to fret & worry myself so much, as I am sure none of my family, Mama perhaps excepted, wd. approve. Not that I would ever be foolish enough to be influenced by my Family.

Sunday, October 14, 1832

We, that is to say, Louisa, *Rowley*, Sir Frederick & myself, went to Evening Church. After which Rowley wrote to Ld. Albert, & he amused me much by using my name several times in the Letter, little aware of what had passed between us. I must own I feel a curiosity to see his answer.

Monday, October 15, 1832

Nothing particular happened this day, excepting that Rowley & I rode out together, which amused us much, considering how we used to get scolded for even speaking to each other. However, now everything goes on so well that it appears a dream. There certainly can be no *danger* on *my* side.

Tuesday, October 16, 1832

Nothing *qui vaille* happened today. The Gentlemen went out Shooting, et voila tout.

Wednesday, October 17, 1832

Rowley & I again rode to Salisbury. The evening was lovely, & we were very agreeable. We all felt low after dinner, as poor Cha was to leave us the next day.

Thursday, October 18, 1832

Aunt Cha started very early. It was a dull, miserable day. We did not go out at all. Everything looked so melancholy that I was seized with a fit of *les Blues*.

Two days later came news of the death of the last Smythe brother, Cou's uncle Charles. He died at Brambridge, the family house in Hampshire which was only 20 miles away from Clarendon, and which was to become Cou's home after her marriage.

Charles Smythe had been a miser; neither Mrs. Wat nor her daughters had any reason to regret his death. In the previous December Mrs. Fitzherbert had written to Minney

144

describing the plight the Smythes were in on account of his behaviour. 'She cannot get Charles to pay her a penny and really I don't know how they can exist. The girls have written to him to say his not paying any of them deprives them of the necessaries of life. If he takes no notice they must somehow or other adopt more violent measures for they cannot go on. He owes them now nearly two thousand pounds.'

Henceforward Mrs. Wat and her daughters would enjoy the whole of what remained of the Smythe estate.

Mrs. Fitzherbert and Lady Haggerston were now the only surviving children of the first Walter Smythe.

Frederick rode over to Brambridge, and Cou's cousin Henry Hunter arrived to stay; but to her by far the most important event of the day was a letter from Lupo Craven.

Saturday, October 20, 1832
. . . This morning I received a most charming letter from Lupo, entreating us to pay them a little visit at Hamstead on our road to London—which Mama says she will do. It was full of *pretty* things from *August*—ah! que je suis heureuse! They seem to have settled everything for our going to Combe. What extacies I shall be in if I find myself there at Christmas! Not a day passes but I dwell constantly on him, & the more I think of him the more convinced am I of my attachment to him.

Sunday, October 21, 1832
Mama was dreadfully low & unwell all day. Sir Fredk. started for Brambridge before Breakfast. Rowley & Henry Hunter rode to Church. We did not go, of course.

Monday, October 22, 1832
Rowland received a long letter from Ld. Albert. He is at Slane Castle [the Conynghams' house in Ireland]. Speaking of us he says "Mrs. Smythe is one of the most agreeable persons, I know—& as for 'Cou', she is a darling little creature, so unaffected & goodhumoured." Not a syllable did he mention of anything else, & I have the satisfaction of

145

feeling that he does not *abuse* me at least. Lou & I walked to Alderbury. The Gentlemen went out shooting. . . .

Mrs. Smythe became seriously ill, and it is significant that when the doctor was fetched he put her on a diet which excluded wine.

. . . In the evening Mama was so very ill that she quite alarmed us, & there was a long consultation as to whether Sir Fredh. shd. ride over to Salisbury in the middle of the night to fetch Dr. Fowler. It was at last decided that they should wait until the next morning. However some of the party sat up till near four o'clock with us. Sir Frederick's anxiety about her made me love him twice as much as I ever did before, & dear Rowley's kind & affectionate attention about her is something too charming! I will not describe my feelings when I reverted to the possibility of my losing such an angel of a Mother & being left an Orphan so young! But there is a Heavenly Protector, who watches over us all & who never forgets any of his creatures.

Tuesday, October 23, 1832
A wretched, melancholy day! Mama was not better. Dr. Fowler came to see her, & has put her on quite a new regime. To leave off wine *entirely*, to drink Bath Waters, Burton's Ale, Chocolate, Baume de Vie, etc. It has taken a complete weight off one's mind now that she has seen him.

Wednesday, October 24, 1832
The day begun gloomily. Rowley & I settled to ride, & in the afternoon the weather was lovely. We rode by Farley, Winterslow, over the Downs to Pitton, & so by Locke's, home through the Woods. I got nervous on the Downs, but otherwise we had a charming ride. Henry Hunter (who) went out shooting with Sir Fredk. & taking poor little Dash for a Cat shot twice at him. He, however, was not much hurt, but poor Henry was very miserable abt. it.

Thursday, October 25, 1832

Henry went away very early in the morning, & Sir Fred: & Errington started at 10 o'clock to attend Uncle Charles's Funeral. It altogether reminded me so much of the last scene at Brambridge, being about the same time of the year, that I felt wretched all day. We hardly went out at all. They returned abt. 7 o'clock & satisfied us much by saying it had all been remarkably well managed.

Friday, October 26, 1832

We remained out in the Garden all morning. After Luncheon Mama & I drove to Salisbury, & the Gentlemen went out to shoot. Poor dear Rowley came home in a most deplorable state, having really shot poor little Dash dead. He was much too wretched abt. it himself to admit of anyone's saying anything to him.

Saturday, October 27, 1832

They went out shooting for the whole day. Lou & I drove out, & went a very pretty road. I caught a cough & pain in my chest from remaining so long yesterday in the garden without a bonnet.

Frederick was constant in his opposition to the Cravens.

Sunday, October 28, 1832

A shocking, rainy day. We amused ourselves all morning with Billiards & Battledore, & when all these failed I went to my room & wrote to dear Lupo accepting their invitation to Hamstead. But I am continually in a fidget relative to Combe, as Sir Fred. is decidedly averse to our going there, & whenever the Cravens are mentioned he immediately begins abusing them & saying that I shall get into a scrape there etc. All this annoys me tremendously, as I cannot brook a disappointment in that quarter.

Monday, October 29, 1832

This day really was a wretched one, as my dear Rowley

left us. He has made himself such a treasure that I am quite miserable. In short, I believe that he is better than the Generality of the world, or else I see with *prejudiced eyes*; for I do not think I know anyone with such a truly affectionate heart. Lou & I drove to Salisbury in the afternoon, but I never was so tormented with the *Blue Devils*. The day corresponded perfectly with my feelings, & I cd. not rally during any part of the even. If I could only feel any *certainty* in our plans—but no! everything seems dans le vague, & I have a sort of pressentiment that things will not turn out as I could wish. I begin really to think that it was a misfortune for me to become acquainted with Augustus Craven, as nothing gives me *real* pleasure but the thoughts of seeing him again. But then! Shall I find him altered? become cold & strange? Heaven forbid! I must endeavour to drive away these thoughts that I know I *ought* not to indulge in. I spent a most wretched evening.

A letter from the old family friend, Lord Arthur Hill, introduces the idea of yet another possible marriage for Cou, namely one with her cousin Rowland.

Tuesday, October 30, 1832

I was very unwell all day, & did not go out. I received a long letter from Ld. Arthur, who is at Hillsborough. He *strongly advises* me to *share Rowley's fate* & become Mrs. Errington. I certainly could not meet with a more indulgent Husband. I also heard from Elizabeth, who is just returned to Tottenham & wishes us very much to go there tomorrow or Thursday. But Mama is certainly not well enough to move at present. Therefore I wrote to say that we must delay the pleasure of seeing them for some little time longer.

The family were now called upon by a somewhat notorious lady, Mrs. Lane-Fox (called by Cou 'Mrs. Fox-Lane'), who was staying at Longford nearby. It is singular that of four 'notorieties' of the period stigmatised in her journal by the

148

Duke of Wellington's friend, Mrs. Arbuthnot, the Smythes were on friendly terms with three. 'I must say', this virtuous lady had written on September 15, 1829, 'I think it will be rather a good thing if the ladies will *pull up* a little and set their faces against the sort of barefaced liaisons that are becoming the fashion. It is bad enough Lady Strachan living with Lord Hertford, tho' he is such a miserable cripple that any real impropriety is out of the question, but Mrs. Fox and Lord Chesterfield is too bad. It is all the King's fault; he has let down the royal dignity, has received at his Court the Duchess of St. Albans and Mrs. Manners Sutton, both *des femmes entretenues*, and now one is laughed at if one objects to receiving any woman, however atrocious her conduct.' The Duchess of St. Albans had been the actress Harriot Mellon, and Mrs. Manners Sutton, wife of the Speaker, was sister to D'Orsay's friend, Lady Blessington.

Lord Chesterfield, who for years had been passionately in love with Mrs. Lane-Fox, and who stayed everywhere at country houses with her, suddenly proposed to, and was accepted by, Anne Forester, eldest sister of 'le beau Cecile', in October 1830, and sent Charles Greville to break the news to his deserted mistress.

The Radnors at Longford were the Hervey-Bathursts' nearest neighbours, and Mrs. Lane-Fox's brother, Edward Pery Buckley, had married Lord Radnor's daughter by his first wife.

... Mrs. Fox-Lane, her Father & Brother called here today, & were much charmed with the place. Mrs. Fox told us that Ld. Marcus intended coming here. How I wish this may be true. Rowley wrote a few lines to Mama this morning. I did not think him in spirits by what he said. I wrote him a long letter, & endeavoured to express how truly we miss him. I trust I shall hear tomorrow from Elizabeth. I was very unwell in the evening, & went to bed early.

Friday, November 2, 1832
I had the Rheumatism in my head all day, & my cough was

very bad. It was a rainy day, & moreover I had no letters.
Mama received a letter from Aunt Cha, who says Aunt
Fitzt. is affronted with me because I never wrote to her abt.
Charles Smythe's Death. She may recover her *huff*, for I am
too ill to write today.

Saturday, November 3, 1832
   . . . I had this morning a nice, long letter from Rowley.

Sunday, November 4, 1832
   I was not well enough to go to Church, where Louisa &
Sir Fredk. went in the afternoon. I had a few lines from
Aunt Cha & Rowley, making enquiries after my health.
Another conversation occured after dinner relative to
Augustus Craven. Of course Sir Fredk. abused him. I kept
my *temper* & held my *tongue*. My conduct towards Lord
George Hervey did not either escape his censure.

George Hervey, of course, was Frederick's third cousin.

Monday, November 5, 1832
   Sir Frederick with his Agent went over to Brambridge
early. Dr. Fowler came to see me. It was awfully cold, but we
walked out a little. Mr. Baring Wall wrote to say he would
dine & sleep here tomorrow, which put Sir Fred. & Louisa
in a fuss, & they wrote off immediately to invite the Longford party. The latter however refused, upon which an invitation was issued to a *Mr. Baker*, the member for Salisbury!
and the *Brute* is *coming*. Mr. Garnier also arrives tomorrow
to stay two days. How I do hate the idea of this stupid dinner
tomorrow.

Tuesday, November 6, 1832
   I received a letter from Aunt Cha & from Elizabeth. The
former scolds me for encouraging Rowley unfairly. Aunt
Fitzherbert asked her whether we were coming to Brighton
this year. I wish she may invite us for *after* Christmas.
Elizabeth's letter gave me the greatest satisfaction, as she

tells me of a most satisfactory conversation she had just had with a Lady Pollen, relative to Augustus. This Lady is a relation of theirs, & has known them all since they were children. She praised *him* most highly in every respect, & said his only fault was *changing* often. She told Elizabeth that she knew all *abt. me*, & wished to know whether I *really liked him*, as she thought it would be such a very nice match. How much have I lost by our not going to Tottenham, as she was going to ask him to meet us. Now we cannot go there at all this year, as they are going to Paris very soon. When she expresses in her letter a fear that I shall be angry with her for dwelling so much on that subject she little thinks how nearest it is my heart, & what pleasure it would cause me could I know for certain that he has not forgotten me. But I feel my ill-luck in everything, & I dare not think on the probability of our going to Hamstead or to Combe. Well, the dinner took place, & went off very stupidly. Baring Wall seems such an effeminate man, & Mr. Baker would not let anyone talk but himself. They made me sing a little in the evening, but long before it was over I was quite dead tired.

Baring Wall left Clarendon 'before anyone made their appearance' next morning; and it is interesting to find, after Cou's comment on his effeminate manner, that he was charged, in the following February, with indecent assault on John Palmer, a policeman. In May, however, he was acquitted by the Court of the King's Bench.

Thursday, November 8, 1832
    In the midst of the rain Louisa & I drove over to Long-ford. The weather certainly contributed to make the place look dismal, but I never can fancy its being pretty. The park is a perfect swamp, & the house an old castellated mass of buildings, half unfinished, & without any prospect of seeing the termination of it. We found Lady Radnor & Mrs. Fox-Lane at home. The latter leaves this county on Saturday for London, *regretting* much not having *seen more* of my *sister & I.*

I could not help laughing, considering I had never seen so *much* of her in my life, & did not *much wish* to *associate* with a person like her. I never in my life beheld anything so wretched as the country looked this evening, & I cannot help being low when I see all surrounding objects looking so mournful.

Cou gave vent to her boredom in an outburst of underlining. The news that Aunt Fitz had been expressing her views on Cou's potential husbands was a further source of irritation.

Friday, November 9, 1832

Mr. Page came to inspect the progress of their Garden. Dr. Fowler called & ordered me to ride everyday, & as the Baronet is bored at leaving his digging I commenced this afternoon by riding alone with the *Coachman* as Groom. I did not dislike it, although it is *not gay.* I did not *think,* when I came here, that *man*-kind would be at such a low *ebb.* However, in one respect I am *not* sorry that I shd. lead such a very tranquil life, as it will probably *excite* Mama to *repay* me in the *Winter*—& she knows how amply it is in her power to do so. Nous verrons! I rather imagine that our visit to Combe is counted upon with so much *certainty* that an *overthrow* will not be received with a *good grace.* Aunt Cha wrote me a word that Aunt Fitz. & her had been discussing the *pro* & *con* of an alliance with Rowley—that it had been decided by them that it would *not do.* After which the *Emperor Augustus* had been *talked over,* but was decidedly *rejected* on account of the *theatrical* connexion. There are many *connexions* I should *despise* much more than that one, for no individual can say one word *against* Lady Craven. At any rate, I should much wish people not to trouble themselves about me, as no one's opinion save Mama's in *those* things shall ever influence me—*talk* they may, & to *little* purpose. Since *these* are Mrs. Fitz.'s *opinions,* I most heartily trust she may have *left* London ere *we* reach it, as Mama, I fear, is *easily* made to *believe ill* of people.

Saturday, November 10, 1832

It never ceased pouring the whole day. I was far from well, & sat in my own little room alone the best part of the day. In the evening I amused myself playing at Chess with Sir Frederick.

Sunday, November 11, 1832

The day was fine. I was much disappointed at not receiving any letters. Lou & I went to the Cathedral in the afternoon, & were much charmed with the Anthem. Mr. Baker escorted us from Church to the White Hart, where our carriage was. We met Ldy. Radnor, who informed Lou with great *glee* that Ld. Marcus had written to her to say he shd. be with *her* on Wednesday, previous to his visit at Clarendon. Dr. Fowler dined with us, & was remarkably agreeable.

Monday, November 12, 1832

Mr. Baker, Mr. Jacobs & Mr. Brodie breakfasted with us. Three Salisbury men, & the two last far from being gentlemanlike. They afterwards went out to shoot with Sir Frederick. I rode out alone about 2 o'clock, & rather liked indulging my own thoughts. In the evening I wrote to ask Elizabeth here for a day, which Sir Frederick is to be the Bearer of tomorrow, when he intends *hunting* with *Tom Smith's* Hounds.

Tuesday, November 13, 1832

In the morning, there was a dreadful fog, notwithstanding which Sir. Fred. went out very early to Hunt, having 25 miles to go to Cover. In the afternoon Louisa & I drove to *Mr. Cove's*, the Gardener, & were passed on our way home by a carriage going at a furious rate—evidently run away with. Sir Fred. came home at the same time we did, having met Elizabeth, but having completely forgotten my letter. I forwarded it by this evening's post. I received a long & charming letter from dear Lupo, begging that the day for our going to Hamstead may be fixed in my next letter—with a message from Ld. Craven saying "Tell Miss Smythe that if she does not remain some time at Combe, you will never forgive her". Augustus is now at Melton, but spends the whole winter with them at Combe; therefore I must make up my mind not to see him before Christmas. At Hamstead Ld. Craven will be. Therefore, who knows if *he* will not *endeavour* to *supersede* his younger Brother. I do not *imagine* his having *much* success, as, to my taste, he looks so anything but *thorough bred*—et voila *le tout* à mes yeux. The Cravens have all been in Town for a day to chuse silks etc. for Ld. C's house in Charles St., which he is going to fit up in the Louis 14ze. style. Aunt Cha wrote word to Louisa that Madme. Bathyany is spreading the report everywhere of my approaching marriage with Tolstoy! Bon Dieu! que de bêtises!

Wednesday, November 14, 1832

The day was piteous—the rain never ceased for one instant. We were all to dine at Longford, but Mama pleaded the excuse of not being well enough, & Lou having been taken *suddenly* sick the evening before, she also thought it *wiser not* to go. Ainsi, there they plantéd Sir Frederick & I, who felt ourselves obliged to go. I never felt less disposed to leave home, the weather was so dreadful, & I knew I shd. find it so dull. We arrived there safely about 7 o'clock, & found the party to consist only of Lady Radnor, Mrs. & Miss Bouverie & Ld. Marcus, Ld. Radnor & his Brothers having been obliged to dine at Salisbury. It would have been much more agreeable had we only found Ld. Marcus & the amiable Hostess, as the *female* Bouveries were dull & heavy beyond description. Ldy. Radnor was very *amusing* at dinner, but rather *astonished* me by her *manner* of talking. Ld. Radnor & *two stupid* Mr. Bouveries arrived before the end of the evening. I had never before seen his *Lordship*, & was particularly diverted at his imperturbable gravity & *matter of fact* manner—such a complete contrast to his Wife. They settled to dine with us on Friday. Sir Fredk. & I were certainly not sorry to find ourselves again at home. I was much shocked to hear from Lady Radnor that Louisa Hardy is in a rapid decline, & they are going to take her directly to Malta, without however much hopes of her recovery. Should she die, her Mother may well have to reproach herself with having destroyed her Daughter's health by excess of dissipation.

Thursday, November 15, 1832

The day did not prove much more prosperous than yesterday, & we were unable to go out during the whole day. I had a letter from Aunt Cha, who leaves Town today. She mentions poor Lady Stafford being at the point of death at Brighton. She will be a great loss to her family. Nothing particular happened today, & I was low all day.

Friday, November 16, 1832

Ld. Marcus came this morn. for Breakfast, after which he & Sir Fredk. went out shooting for the day. The Radnors, after all, cannot dine here today. About two o'clock I set out on horseback for Longford with a note to invite them to dine here tomorrow, but when I arrived there I did not find Lady Radnor at home, therefore contented myself with cantering to the *approach*—for from Clarendon there is no road but through the Park, which is a complete *swamp*. I came very fast, & alltogether enjoyed my ride of all things, as I find myself much less of a *Coward* when riding alone, & also much less fatigued. I remained in my dressing-room en robe de chambre till dinner time, as I thought it much too fatiguing to dress twice. I heard from Rowley this morning, who leaves London on Monday. He tells me that Ld. Albert is still in Ireland, & old Ld. Conyngham dying—& (by way of news) informed me that *August* is gone to Melton— no *remarks* upon *him*—*of course*. Ld. Marcus made himself remarkably agreeable at dinner, & the evening went off à merveille.

Saturday, November 17, 1832

A lovely day. The Gentlemen went out shooting immediately after Breakfast. About 10 o'clock Lady Radnor came to bring her excuses, not being well enough to dine out. She therefore has fixed to come tomorrow. Shortly after her departure Ld. Radnor arrived & amused us much by his quaint, odd manner. Lou & I took a long drive & did not get home till late, when it was very cold. Dr. Fowler dined with us & made himself very agreeable. We heard of poor Lady Stafford's death, which shocked us all much. She will be the greatest possible loss to her whole family, as she had the management of everything. Almost all her children were with her at Brighton at the time of her decease.

Sunday, November 18, 1832

A dismal cold day. We, however, went to the Cathedral in the afternoon, & on our return found an excuse from Lady Radnor, who said she really was too unwell to come out. She expressed a wish that Lord Marcus and *I* would *dine* and *sleep* at Longford tomorrow. Quelle idée! Elle se dit être une si *excellente chaperone*. Quel aveuglement! We endeavoured to beguile away the evening as well as we could senza la *bella* Contessa. We had a *few words* about the Cravens; & the Baronet, comme de coûtume, was *sharp* & not *very civil* on the subject. Ld. Marcus looks all astonishment at his brusque manners to Mama & I sometimes—so different to what *he* is accustomed to see.

Monday, November 19, 1832

Sir Fredk. went out hunting early, & Ld. Marcus went shooting alone. The day was rainy & disagreeable. However, in the afternoon Mama & I succeeded in driving to Longford, which really did look most wretched. Lady Radnor was at home, & we went to see the Gallery of Pictures. The Collection is very fine. The first one that struck me as being beautiful is a Madonna's head by Guido; Jupiter & Europa by the same; two Claude's, very beautiful—& many others too numerous to name. In short the whole collection is very fine, & I wish I understood them better. Ld. Marcus dined there, & on his return I found I had not lost much as he said the party was very dull. They go to Coleshill [their other house in Wiltshire] on Wednesday, where they have much pressed us to spend a few days.

Tuesday, November 20, 1832

I received a long letter from Elizabeth, expressing a thousand regrets at not being able to come here, as the Duke of Gloucester is going to them. I also received a few lines from Minney, who is at Gorhambury, where they are busy preparing Tableaux which are to be acted at Hatfield the first week in January. The Cravens were much pressed to be of the party, but declined, saying *they* had a party at Combe at Christmas. Ld. Hillsborough takes the part of Richard Coeur de Lion in the Talisman, & Ld. Craven the *Pretender*. The Gentlemen went out shooting, but the day was too bad for us & we remained at Home the whole day. We took leave of Ld. Marcus, when we went to bed, as he was to start at 7 in the morning. I am very sorry he is going as he is so agreeable. I shd. much like to know what he *really* thought of his visit, as he seemed every now & then much surprised at Sir Fredk.'s manner.

Wednesday, November 21, 1832

The day was dull & gloomy. I, however, rode a little way, & for the first time felt how much I should appreciate the company of some very agreeable person. How happy should I be were I able to transport myself to dear Lupo's side. Mais patience!

Frederick Hervey-Bathurst was not only surly and outspoken in his speech to Louisa's family (perhaps he found Mrs. Wat exasperating), he seemed to neglect the most elementary forms of politeness. The visit of two of his Regimental friends called forth fresh criticism from Cou.

Thursday, November 22, 1832

Two young Guardsmen, friends of Sir Frederick, arrived for Breakfast. One is a Mr. Leveson Gower, & the other Mr. Wright, the *Surgeon* of the Regiment. These are *his only* sort of *friends*! They went out shooting the whole day. Although the day was lovely I gave up riding & took a long drive with Louisa. On my return I wished to write to Lupo, but Mama begged I would not, as she cd. not fix the day for going there, & therefore wished me to defer writing for a few days. If in that time she will *really* name a day, why, then I have no objection to defer anything. My whole thoughts are engrossed by that Family, & the more Christmas approaches the more nervous I become as to Combe. I daily strive to compose my mind for the worst, & await patiently the issue of events. Mama has never really said she should *not* go, therefore I have still great hopes. The young men were *rather* agreeable during dinner, but in the evening when they joined us in the Drawing room Mr. Leveson Gower was anything but *sober*, & annoyed Sir Fredk. very much—who, when we were gone to bed, *rowed* him most amazingly. They made me sing, mais cela m'ennuyait! I should not think they are *much* accustomed to Ladies' society. Sir Fredk. does not either, shew much *usage*, for when Mama came down to dinner he never introduced his friends to her, or waited to hand her in. It is in these sort of little attentions one distinguishes l'homme du monde, & I think refined manners are so very charming in every one that unless they degenerate into effeminacy they cannot be too studied in men.

Friday, November 23, 1832

They were out shooting all day. I intended to have ridden, but the weather looked so stormy that I drove with Lou to Salisbury instead. Mr. Baring Wall has invited them to meet the Jerseys at his house on the 2nd. of December. I would give anything if Mama would take that opportunity of paying our little visit to Hamstead. The evening went off like the previous one, but I perceived that neither of the young Gentlemen had much conversation. Mr. Leveson Gower is rather an oddity, but the other hardly ever opens his lips. In short they have not made themselves agreeable enough to leave a blank in their absence.

Saturday, November 24, 1832
I was prevented again by the weather from riding. This was one of my *Blue Devil* days, & I as usual thought of nothing but absent Friends. I am really worn out with conjecturing, & am now becoming seriously impatient. Hamstead would make everything *clear*, for although *he* will not be there yet I know that I shall require a very short time to see clearly through things. Lupo is too franche not to speak of her *favourite* Brother. Sir Frederick's friends left us this evening immediately after dinner. The Baronet drove them into Salisbury, & did not return till past eleven.

At last it seemed certain that Mama would go both to Hamstead Marshall and to Combe. Cou felt able to congratulate herself on her restraint in talking of the Cravens and on having concealed her anxiety that their invitations should be accepted. She even gave her mother the credit for having deliberately avoided discussing them in front of Frederick and Louisa.

Sunday, November 25, 1832
Aunt Cha wrote to Mama, & forwarded an invitation to us to go to Rudge after Combe, which is only 40 miles distant. The day was lovely, & Mama came with us to the Cathedral. On our return I told her I was going to write to Lupo, & wished to know what I was to say relative to Hamstead. What was my delight when she told me to say that she had strong intentions of offering herself some day next week, if she felt well enough & they were disengaged. How happy I was!—particularly as I found how well my plan had answered in never questioning her about her intentions. She made me doubly happy by saying "But I fear they will

159

think us very troublesome, going to *Hamstead* as *well* as to *Combe*." I was determined, however, not to shew too much joy on the subject. I wrote a long letter to my dear Friend, & am most anxiously awaiting her answer. I think Mama is so right not to talk of her winter plans here, where she sees the *"green eyed monster"* prevail so much.

Monday, November 26, 1832

As the weather was very fine I resolved to ride, & set out about half past two. I first went on the Southampton Road, & then, finding the clouds were gathering fast around me, I turned off towards West Grinstead. The road was so heavy that I could not canter, & it was not until I saw that a violent storm would burst in a few moments that I set off full gallop; but, however, was nearly drenched ere I reached home. In the evening I began Mrs. Trollope's 'Refugee in America'. It seems written, if possible, in stronger terms of contempt for the Americans then even her first work, & from her account, if it is correct, I am sure I should hate them most cordially, as I never could brook with common patience their contempt for the "old country"—as they term England.

Mrs. Trollope's book and a life of James I are the only two books Cou mentions reading during the year 1832.

Tuesday, November 27, 1832

It was a wretched rainy day. At one o'clock I adjourned to my *Boudoir*, where I amused myself in various ways until dinner time. I prefer solitude so infinitely to undergoing the same every-day routine of conversation.

Now arrived at Clarendon Harry Smythe, whom Cou had never met before. Nothing is known about Henry Smythe, the fourth brother to Wat, Jack and Charles. The Harry who now appears on the scene must have been his son, and presumably illegitimate or he would have inherited Brambridge. The fact that the births and deaths of Roman Catholics were not recorded in the registers of parish churches, as those of Protestants have been for centuries, makes it hard to trace the history of a family such as the Smythes. Wat Smythe is the only one of Mrs. Fitzherbert's brothers the date of whose birth we know.

Wednesday, November 28, 1832

The day, altho' stormy, proved fine enough in the afternoon for us to walk. My *new* cousin, Henry Smythe, who was to arrive today, overtook us in our walk. I had never seen him & from the slight glimpse I could catch of his face he appears *tolerably* good looking. One cannot help pitying him, being left so destitute. In the evening they played at Whist, which spared us the trouble of making *l'aimable* to him.

Thursday, November 29, 1832

Mr. Wyndham's Hounds met here, & the Gentlemen went out with them. Lou & I drove out pour passer le temps . . .

Friday, November 30, 1832

This was a wretched rainy day. I heard from Rowland, who says Augustus has asked *him* to Combe! We remained at home all day.

Saturday, December 1, 1832

I heard from Lupo, who says that next week will be perfectly convenient to them. Poor Auguste has had a very bad fall out Hunting. I also heard that poor *Mountain* had had a very narrow escape in the same way. This is the beginning of a month that will in all probability be fruitful in events. I expect *much* pleasure & happiness in this short month, & *even beyond* it! Any one reading these lines might readily imagine that some great *change* was going to take place in my life.

Sunday, December 2, 1832

The Bathursts were engaged for today & tomorrow to Baring Wall's, but this morning's Post brought Sir Fred.

such an alarming account of Lionel that he set out for London immediately. Harry Smythe also left us in the afternoon, & we found our *female* Trio rather *triste*.

Monday, December 3, 1832
The wind was so high that we remd. at home all day. Lou was fidgetty & low without her Marito.

This was the first time Frederick had been away from Louisa since their marriage; and the letter she wrote him has been preserved:

Clarendon, Monday,
December 4, 1832

My very dearest,
This letter I trust will not reach you as living upon the hopes of seeing you tomorrow; but I must write in case you should be detained beyond the hour that the letters come in. How melancholy we all are without you, dearest Frederick, & what a gloom your absence has cast over us all . . . This is the first time we have been separated & were it often to occur it would make me by far too miserable, but you will be with us again, my own dearest, & I shall then be happier than ever. These two days have appeared longer than a fortnight at any other time. . . . Mr. H. Smythe went away after lunch looking very sorrowful. I asked him what report he should make to Mrs. Fitz of Clarendon; he said he shall tell her it was perfect Paradise. He told us a story which will I think amuse you, but I shall keep it for tomorrow. Though I am not like Mrs. F. in thinking him quick or handsome, I think he has a great deal of good feeling in speaking of Uncle Charles. . . . Mama & Cou send very much love. . . . If you have time, will you get me a pretty manuscript music book.

It is impossible not to sympathise with Harry Smythe, whom Mrs. Fitzherbert considered lucky to get through her a post at £200 a year. He disappeared forthwith from history, causing, presumably, no more trouble to his rich relations.

Much as she was always complaining about his bad manners and bossy behaviour, Cou missed Frederick and was glad of his return. He brought an uncle with him.

Tuesday, December 4, 1832
   Dieu merci! Sir Fred. wrote to say he shd. be back late tonight. The day was very fine, & I rode. It was one [of] my *very nervous* days, & I was much frightened at meeting some oxen driven by some tipsy men. My hope of going to Hamstead this week has quite vanished—Mais il faut toujours espérer. Sir Frederick was to pick up Mr. Hervey on his way—& they did not arrive till one in the morning.

Wednesday, December 5, 1832
   Sir Fred. gives a most deplorable account of poor Lionel. I sadly fear he will not get over it. Lou & I took a very long drive, & came home quite frozen. Mr. Hervey was remarkably agreeable the whole evening. He is "pazzo per la Musica", & I sang a great deal for him. This was *one* of the *most agreeable* evenings I have passed here, as Mr. Hervey is so remarkably clever & well-informed.

Thursday, December 6, 1832
   I forgot to mention in my account of yesterday that I heard from Elizabeth, who has made acquaintance with Lupo & is more than enchanted with her. Mama also made me write to Lupo to say that we *positively* shall be with them at Hamstead on Thursday next! Oh! Gioja! The evening passed very agreeably. I sang a great deal.

Friday, December 7, 1832
   Lou & I walked, malgré le brouillard *affreux*. I had to sing & play the whole evening to my vieux galant, who goes away tomorrow morning. How very unlucky that there should be *une chère moitié** already!

* This is one of the few places in her journal where Georgina is coy and facetious about her flirtations.

Sunday, December 9, 1832

I received an answer from Lupo, who joyfully accepts our offer for Thursday. Augustus is with them, having been obliged to leave Melton from having injured his foot in his fall. She does not say how long he remains, but I cannot help hoping that he will be gone ere we get there. I went to the Cathedral & took the Maids, as Lou wd. not go.

Monday, December 10, 1832

This was a rainy day, & we remained au logis.

Tuesday, December 11, 1832

The day was lovely, & Lou & I drove to Salisbury. I have been in a continual fidget of late to go to Hamstead, & now that the time of our departure is so near I am more nervous than it is possible to imagine. I am in reality very sorry to leave Clarendon, as I am not as yet at all accustomed to being separated from my dear Sister.

The next day there arrived news of the death of one of Louisa's old admirers.

Wednesday, December 12, 1832

We received this morning the particulars of poor dear Hyde Villiers' death. It was occasioned by effusion of water on the brain, caused from a tooth that had been extracted seven years ago! Poor fellow! he passed from six hours sleep into Eternity! I can hardly bring myself to believe his Death—he was such a true friend of ours. I only pray that he was in a fit state to die. I hear that Lady Maria Conyngham is going to marry an Irish Mr. Somerville. I suppose we shall find the gentle Albert in Town. This time tomorrow I shall be with Lupo! Yet I feel that the moment is too near, & if *he* is there—Bon Dieu! I shall be too nervous to speak. However, I will not fill my mind with imaginary désagrémens.

164

The journey from Clarendon to Hamstead Marshall near Newbury took the Smythes six hours in their carriage, including a stop in Andover.

The old mansion of Hamstead Marshall had been burnt down in the eighteenth century, and the medium-sized house subsequently built in another part of the park was given as a dower-house to the actress Lady Craven, Ashdown Lodge and Combe Abbey being her eldest son's principal seats. The two latter houses have now passed out of the family, but Hamstead Marshall is probably much as it was in the days of Cou Smythe's visit. The Hayter portrait [see illustration facing p. 204] of the second Earl, which Cou admired, still hangs in the house, but the water-colour of Augustus by Heath has unfortunately disappeared.

Thursday, December 13, 1832

The day was lovely, & although we had intended starting early we did not get off before 12. I was far from well during the whole journey, & nervous as possible. The distance was greater than we had expected, & we were obliged to take four horses from Andover. We were obliged to stop on the road to light the lamps, & after a most tedious & hilly stage we did not arrive there till six o'clock. As the carriage drove up to the door I will not endeavour to describe the various sensations that came over me. We were hardly out of the carriage before dear Lupo rushed into my arms. She received us in the most charming manner possible; she said the Gentlemen were just come in from shooting. I asked not a question, & we proceeded to the drawingroom. They were all standing up to receive us, & I dared not look round the room, but went straight up to Lady Craven, who was all amiability. In the same moment *that* voice, so deeply impressed in my memory, sounded in my ears; I turned round —& encountered the being who alone has occupied my thoughts for the last six months. But how altered in looks— so ghastly, so thin, & seemingly so depressed in spirits from illhealth. How shocked I was! But, thank God! his manner towards me was the same as ever. He spoke but little, & I talked to Lupo while we remained in the drawingroom—not knowing exactly what to say to *him*. We soon proceeded to dress, & when our toilette was finished, Lupo came to fetch us. The party in the house consisted chiefly of the family— Ld. Craven, their Uncle Berkeley, & two young men, a Capn. Wodehouse & a Mr. Popham. Ld. Craven handed Mama in to dinner, & Augustus took me. I was dreadfully ill the whole time, as much from agitation as anything else. He talked a great deal at dinner, & he is the same as ever. The attention of the whole party to Mama were indeed charming, & gave me the greatest satisfaction. The evening passed delightfully. I sung a little, & then we talked. Poor Augustus! he owns he is very ill & out of spirits from having been confined to the house for the last ten days, & yet, weak as he is, he is determined to return to Melton on Monday. Ld. Craven appears quiet & remarkably gentlemanlike in his manners. How completely do I retract my former opinion of him! The devotion of all of them to Lady Craven is truly delightful. She seems a charming person, & inshort we felt quite *at home* for they put one so completely at one's ease. I saw that Mama had a favourable impression of the whole family, & I knew that this visit would greatly influence our going to Combe . . .

Uncle Berkeley, eldest surviving son of the irrepressible Margravine, was a typical Craven, devoted to women, horses and every expensive pleasure, high-spirited, reckless, attractive and amusing.

. . . Berkeley Craven, altho' a very *mauvais sujet*, is very amusing. He told me an anecdote of Ld. Albert Conyngham that made me laugh. He once travelled sixty miles with him, sometime in July or August. He was very absent & at last, after musing for a long time, said "I am very much in love with *Cou* Smythe—she is very handsome, clever and agreeable. I know my Father wd. like it, & I am sure my Mother

166

wd. be enchanted." "Well", says Berkeley, "why the *devil* don't you propose?" Augustus was by me when he said this, & I pretended to be much surprised & not to know much of the gentle Albert. But, however, *they* seemed to know a *great deal* about him & me.

Friday, December 14, 1832

Lupo came into my room, *dressed*, before 9 o'clock, & sat on my bed for an hour, talking & laughing. Then she took a long *run* before breakfast. Inshort, I never saw anyone so active, both in body & mind. We were all assembled at Breakfast about 11, after which all the Gentlemen excepting *August* went out shooting. Lupo & I adjourned to the Drawingroom, where we played Duetts on the Harp & Piano Forte. I never saw anyone so clever as she is. She plays extremely [well] on both the abovementioned instruments, draws most beautifully in every style, & speaks five or six languages fluently. Lady Craven, Augustus & Mama remained in the Library. There is a magnificent picture of Ld. Craven by Hayter—the most striking likeness I ever saw. But I was struck immediately with a very pretty, water colored drawing of Augustus by Heath. He is on horseback in all his military accoutrements, & looks *brigand* like himself. This idea amused Lupo of all things. Poor Mr. Craven was more *seedy* than ever today, & hardly spoke all morning. After Luncheon we 4 Ladies went out walking. The gardens are beautiful, & the Park very extensive, & all of wild ground. Inshort the whole place is lovely. When Mama was quite tired she went in, & I continued my walk with them & went to the Fishery, which is very pretty. The river Kennet passes through their grounds. On our return home we found Mama *flirting* with Mr. [Berkeley] Craven. In the evening they tried to persuade us to stay another day, but we would not consent to it as we should not then be able to be at Combe on the 24th—& *what* will I not give up for *that*. Tomorrow Augustus attains his 22d. year, & we sat up till past twelve o'clock to wish him a thousand happinesses. I really *never* saw anyone so completely charming as he is, & may he ever remain as he is! is my most sincere prayer.

Saturday, December 15, 1832

Although we had [told] them not to get up for us in the morning, both Ld. Craven & Augustus were down, as well as Lupo. This was the prettiest little attention possible, & it will not be difficult to believe that it gave me the greatest pleasure. I was very sorry to go, as I ever shall feel some misgivings about Combe until I actually find myself there. We were off by ten, & after a most dreary, rainy journey, we arrived in Town, by 5. Oh! how I hate the sight of London! We went in the even. to the Ravenscrofts, & found them all very well. But I was much too tired & low to talk.

Sunday, December 16, 1832

A wretched foggy day. We did not go to Church. Madelle Delisle came to see us, & thought me looking very ill, & in fact I know I worry myself to death. Elizabeth called on us. I was charmed to see her. She talked of nothing but the delights of the Craven family. Charles Gore also called—of all *bores* in the world.

CHRISTMAS AND NEW YEAR AT COMBE

In reading the journal of Georgina Smythe it is hard not to keep comparing her with one or other of Jane Austen's heroines. She moved in more worldly circles than Elizabeth Bennett and Fanny Price, but she moved, so to speak, along the same lines.

There was nothing for a well-brought up girl to do in those days except to find a husband. Cou was not taught to cook, and never even ordered a meal in her life; she knew nothing about politics and was only vaguely conscious of the lower classes. She spoke French and Italian, sang well, played the piano, and sketched—probably rather badly. Life centred round *men* (the italics are Cou's). If a girl danced prettily, had good manners, listened well and had a talent for 'making the agreeable', she secured a husband.

Like one of Miss Austen's heroines, Cou goes through a period of depression, doubt and separation from her lover. In the background, 'Mama' is ever present, a slightly ogrish, slightly comic, and perhaps even—like Mrs. Bennett—a slightly embarrassing dowager, on whom so much depends. At last Cou comes, like Catherine Elliott in *Northanger Abbey*, to the mysterious great house, the hero proposes, and after another short period of tribulation, fortune smiles.

On the whole young people of the upper class do not marry for love: when a couple like Cou and Augustus fall in love and want to get married there are bound to be difficulties to overcome. For one thing, a girl is not usually passionately attracted to a man by the qualities which are calculated to recommend him as a husband. It was the reckless, romantic brigand in Augustus that struck Cou at Greenwich, when 'a *sudden impulse*' made her 'form a favourable opinion of him'. In her calmer moments she did not need Mama to point out to her that Augustus was far from steady—or that he was a younger son. The story of Cou's stay at Combe Abbey was therefore destined to take on some of the excitement of a novel.

Sunday, December 23, 1832

At last all my fears are come to an end. We left Town at two o'clock on our journey to Combe—that place that has haunted my imagination by night & by day for the last six months. Oh! what a weight I felt off my heart! to think that tomorrow evening I shall be with all those I love. We only got as far as Dunstable, but, however, it was quite far enough, & I feel *so* happy that I hardly can contain myself.

Combe Abbey, standing in a great park at the end of a long and unusually wide avenue, is a building of several periods, which has grown and diminished with the years. At the end of the sixteenth century Lord Harrington incorporated three sides of the medieval cloister in a new house: a western wing was added to this in the early seventeenth century. In the seventeen-eighties the first Lord Craven built a splendid wing to the north and west of the old house. This classical block, which displays the Craven arms not only on its pediment but on the fine lead water-pipes, contains the great North Parlour and the panelled dining-room in which many of the scenes described by Cou took place. The western rooms, of which the dining-room was the central one, look out towards the shrubberies where Cou used to walk with Lupo and towards the lake.

Cou was greeted on her arrival by the familiar face of

Johnny, the Cravens' Negro footman. It is curious that Harriette
Wilson, the courtesan, mentions in her memoirs a black footman called John kept by the previous Lord Craven when she
lived with him at Brighton some thirty years before: if this
Johnny was the same person he would be at least forty-eight. His
referring to Augustus familiarly as 'Master Augustus' suggests
that he was an old family servant with whom the Cravens were
on affectionate terms.

Monday, December 24, 1832

I was dreadfully nervous as we got nearer to Combe, &
we arrived there at a little after 4. It was a very dull evening,
& the old Abbey did not look gay. How my heart beat!
However, *Johnny* reassured me by saying that Lady Craven
& Lupo were alone. When we arrived in the drawingroom
Lady Craven & Lupo received us à bras ouverts—they really
did seem charmed to see us. They told us that they were
quite alone in the House, but expected all the *Boys* to dinner.
We had been there a very short time when Augustus arrived
from Melton with Captn. Wodehouse. He had had another
fall on the same foot. He really is too unfortunate. We sat
down to dinner about 7, in the middle of which arrived Ld.
Craven & Freddy from London. In the eveng. August &
I talked very agreeably. I can hardly believe I am really at
Combe. My room opens into Mama's, & is delightful—inshort, we are treated en Princesses.

In 1832 the habit of Christmas present-giving was evidently
not so widespread as it is today: Cou mentions no Christmas
presents. Nor had Christmas cards been invented. Christmas
trees, of course, were introduced from Germany by the Prince
Consort a few years later.

Tuesday, December 25, Christmas Day, 1832

We were all down at Breakfast about half past 10, & all,
with the exception of Mama, went to Morning Church. After
that they took me all over the house, into the picture Gallery,

which is very fine, inshort, the whole place is immensely ancient. The stone cloisters go round the ground floor; but the size of the place makes it very difficult to find one's way. We went to the Tennis Court, which is charming, with a Gallery for Spectators. After Luncheon we all walked & went to see the Stables, which are very fine, & August's horses are very handsome. Ld. Craven has a splendid Stud, but he hates Hunting, & is rather bored at having to keep so many horses. His brother's Stud is at Melton. He has only got a few *pet ones* here. Grand Duke looks more *dear* then ever. We walked in the Shrubberies for a short time; but as I am supposed to be en petite santé Lady Craven would not let me stay out too long. *Mon Auguste* handed me into dinner today, which he will always do when there is no other Lady to *usurp* his services. In the evening, we sat in the North Parlour—a room of such a size! & such a fire place, on which actual *Trees* are thrown—& it is stirred with a large pitch fork. As it was Christmas Day we were determined to make a great *scindie* [shindy], which is not difficult in this family, for I never saw such spirits as Lupo & Freddie possess. They made me sing—chiefly English—after which we played a round game of cards. Bon Dieu! what cheating & laughing! Ld. C. more mad than any of them. Then we all adjourned into the Dining room & had some famous Snapdragon.* The sort of figures we all looked! We did not go to bed till half past one or two. When we got into our rooms Mama told me she was much displeased at my having talked so much to August. I feel that I shall have much to go through here, but I trust that things will end as I could wish. I dare not allow myself to think what my wishes are on the subject.

When Cou was excited, playing games or dancing, she naturally found it harder to conceal her preference for Augustus;

* Snapdragon was a dish of brandy with raisins in it. The lights were extinguished and the brandy was lit: then the fun was to pick the raisins out of the brandy without burning your fingers and finally to blow out the flame just before all the brandy had evaporated.

and Mama was already showing signs of the censorious mood which was almost to spoil their visit.

Next day, for the first time, Cou had qualms as to whether the attraction Augustus felt towards her was entirely disinterested: for she had inherited money and property, and was an heiress in a small way. These suspicions soon passed, never to recur.

Wednesday, December 26, 1832

Lupo & I got up by half past 9, & made Breakfast for the Gentlemen, who all went out Hunting. After having seen them start, driven by Augustus, we went & practised on the Harp & Piano Forte. Late in the afternoon Lady Craven, Lupo & I walked. It was a lovely evening, & I felt that Combe was in reality the seat of happiness. I cannot say my own mind was at rest—I felt nervous & as if this happy feel[ing] would soon be disturbed. I hardly know what to say of *his* affections. He shews himself devoted to me, but God only knows whether his views are not interested. They appear convinced that I am very rich, & I sometimes wish I was portionless. Lord Craven came in very early, as he had hurt his leg & gets very soon tired of Hunting. He walked with us for a short time, & then Lupo & I came in & practised. Ld. Villiers was expected to dinner, & as I had teased Lupo about wishing her to become Lady Villiers we had great fun in jumping up at every sound of the door bell. Five times did we rush into the cloisters—but in vain! I thought we must have died of laughing, for Johnny, who came into the North Parlour, said that *Master* Freddy was come in from Hunting—upon which I turned to Lupo & expressed my anxiety for fear August should have had a fall. Johnny then left the room—when a few moments afterwards another ring at the door bell excited our attention, & we were rushing to one of the doors when Johnny's black face appeared at another & he said "Only Mr. Trowton come to dinner, my Lady; perhaps you don't know that *Massa Augustus is* come in, *Miss*." When he was gone we both fell on the floor in a fit at the absurdity of the whole scene—& Johnny's *clever hit* in bringing *me* tidings of Augustus. At dinner we told him of all this & amused him much. They made me sing. 'We met' is become a great favourite of the whole family, particularly of the *Emperor's*. After this we danced. *He* made himself more agreeable than ever. I begin to think, & do firmly believe, that this visit will seal the happiness or unhappiness of my future life. When he is talking to me I feel spellbound—& have no eyes nor ears for anything.

When he felt he was not getting enough attention, or when he hoped he might provoke Cou into showing anxiety or affection, Augustus would bring up the subject of a projected trip to North America. (A hundred years later he would have threatened to go off and shoot big game in Africa.) The thought of this perilous voyage, presumably to be made in the *Menai*, was rightly calculated to fill Cou with alarm.

Thursday, December 27, 1832

Although the day did not seem very fine we were to have ridden, but it was discovered that there was only one side saddle, & although Lady Craven proposed my riding with Augustus by the side of their carriage, of course I declined until Lupo could ride too. He remained in the Music Room the greater part of the morning with us & after Luncheon Lady Craven, Lupo, August & I set out in a Phaeton & four with Postillions for Coventry, in search of a side saddle. Lupo went with her Brother in the back seat, & their conversation seemed eager to the greatest degree. On our return Ld. Craven joined us, & we walked in the Shrubberies for some time. Augustus said "I have been telling Lupo of all my future plans & wishes, Miss Smythe, & have also been talking of my voyage to North America." As the mention of this always alarms me I could not help saying that I hoped he would change his mind ere the time came. "There is only *one* circumstance that will change my plans, & I have been

174

telling it all to Lupo." Of course j'y voyais clair, but pretended not to have heard him. I own this speech has doubly increased my agitation. Lord Villiers arrived during dinner. I thought he looked rather surprised at seeing us here, particularly as they were only a family party. I never knew him before. He is very gentlemanlike, but I do not suppose that *I* shall get much acquainted with him, as my time is well *occupied*. He told us of Ld. Rivers' approaching marriage with Miss Leveson Gower. They made me sing a great deal. Ld. Villiers seemed pleased with my singing; but August always leans over the Piano Forte & seems immensely interested. After this we danced—the Quadrille, as usual, was August's —but Ld. Villiers galopped with me. We then sat down, & August & I entered into a very serious conversation about Melton making young men very selfish, which he owns, but says that were he once *settled* he should give it up, as he never would *oblige his* Wife to go there, as he thinks (that) the society & the way of life dull & anything but good for a young married woman. He expressed his horror of flirting married women. He then began talking of early marriages, which *he* decidedly *approves*. He says that the longer men remain single the more selfish they grow, & that as for girls, nothing he shd. dislike so much as marrying one who had been about in the world for several seasons, where from constant admiration she had become a heartless Coquette. He then touched on the subject of proposing to people. He said he thought *no* man wd. *ever* think of hazarding himself unless perfectly or nearly sure of his ground. This rather alarmed me. He also said that he never could believe that a man could be *really* attached twice—that, if you had been refused by her whom you really loved, you might certainly get over it & perhaps marry, but never with any feeling of *love* towards the person. I got very nervous & felt low. He seemed agitated I thought, altho' I hardly once looked at him. We both perceived that we were doing each other no good—& all of a sudden he said "Well, we must put our trust in Providence & take a *big drink*." This speech made us both laugh & turned

the *tide*. Ld. Villiers who was talking to Lupo at the other end
of the Sofa, was evidently watching us. I said this to Lupo,
who told me that at the end of the London Season he had
called in Queen St. to ask August whether he was going to
marry Miss Smythe. So that *now*, I think, I *must* make up my
mind to have it talked of. I know that it is very foolish in me
to talk so much to him—but I am not myself when in his
company.

Friday, December 28, 1832
  Altho' it was a wretched foggy cold day we resolved to
ride at 2 o'clock. I rather expressed a wish that Ld. Villiers
should be of the party, but, however, August did not seem to
agree, & I plainly saw that it was not his wish to have a
Coronet in the way. Freddy came with us. We were both
mounted on the Emperor's Hunters. He rode with me whilst
Lupo & Freddy went on before. My horse (Radical) went
beautifully, & I never felt so courageous. He was devoted,
& praised my seat immensely. Our conversation fell entirely
on the most commonplace subjects, which I could not help
admiring him for, when he had then every means of making
known his sentiments towards me. In the evening I sang,
after which we danced *as usual*. I tried the Mazurka with Ld.
Villiers. I talked to August during the remainder of the
evening, & every evening I am more & more fascinated by
him. Inshort, I am now quite aware that that sort of preference that I felt on first knowing him has now become
deeply rooted in my heart. All the Autumn whilst at Clarendon never was he absent from my thoughts—& now God
knows how it will end. I dread to think of *what may* be the
end of it. When we got to our rooms Mama spoke seriously
on the subject. I know her horror of early marriages, & I
sadly fear that she thinks him a great scamp. I know nothing
of his *real* character, as with me he may perhaps play a part.
I have not the slightest doubt of his being, at present,
extravagant, nay even wild,—but I cannot help thinking that
both those faults will be corrected by time.

Saturday, December 29, 1832

We had intended riding to Kenilworth, but the day proved so very rainy that we were forced to stay at home. Lupo & I practised a great deal, & we thought that of course Augustus would pay us a visit—Mais non! he never made his appearance. Lady Craven & us two walked in the picture Gallery for exercise, & they talked most agreeably of their travels. When we all assembled in the drawing room before dinner Augustus was there, & said that he had had the blue devils all day, & therefore had shut himself up in his own room. I could not help fancying that he looked annoyed with me. I am very innocent of the cause. He took me into dinner, & we talked a good deal. But in his manner I perceived a degree of embarrassment & indecision that puzzled me. In the evening I sang; & after that had a long conversation with him by the Piano Forte. He was endeavouring to persuade me how much he liked me, & how truly happy he was to see me his sister's friend. I said very little, for I *felt* too much. We then danced; & Lord Villiers took his departure at midnight. Of course he has every reason to set it down as *settled*—& would to God it were! I dread encountering the London gossiping & reports. My heart is won, & I feel as if nothing can change it.

At last Augustus spoke the fatal words.

Sunday, December 30, 1832

As church was not until half past two Lupo & I spent the intermediate time in looking over some prints that would do for Tableaux. We asked August's aid, & he selected one or two in which I shd. have to act alone with him. I do not think *that* will exactly *do*. We all went to Church with the exception of Mama, & I am much pleased with the reverent manner in which *he* attends to the Service. After that we all walked in the Shrubberies. Had I then foreseen what I was to go through in the evening—oh! what would I not have done to avoid it. He took me into dinner, but talked very little. In the evening, as usual, they made me sing—& *we three* afterwards talked together. I thought his manner hurried, & he left nearly all his sentences *unfinished*. Lupo & I accused him of this, & I said as it was Sunday he ought to *look up*. He appealed to his sister to know whether he had not from the first admired & liked me. She confirmed this, & I, laughing, told him that his admiration would certainly greatly diminish were he to know me better. He then asked me at least to *believe* what he said. My answer was that I never could bring myself to credit that anyone *really* was attached to me. This speech worried him, & I broke off the conversation & proceeded to another part of the room. He followed me, & asked me whether he was [to] consider my last words as *true*. I said "Yes, certainly". A little later in the evening I was sitting between him & Lupo; he was in a complete rêverie, looking ghastly pale & apparently perfectly unconscious of what was passing around him. Freddy contrived to engage Lupo's attention—& I had once resolved to leave my seat. God only knows how deeply I repented not having done so, for in a few minutes Augustus approached nearer to me & said "Your last speech, Miss Smythe, has had a great effect on me, & has nearly driven me distracted. I am now resolved that, whatever may be the reception I meet with from you, I will no longer disguise my feelings. From the first moment I saw you my admiration was very great—& since that I have become sincerely attached to you. I know that my feelings have carried me away, & that you will now hate me for this avowal—but although I have scarcely a hope of meeting with any return from you, yet I was resolved you should no longer remain ignorant that on you depends the happiness or misery of my Future life." It is difficult to describe the sensations that agitated me. I said that I trusted he would think better of it—that I did not & could not believe that his present sentiments would last, as I know my faults too well to think myself worthy of him. This seemed to drive him wild, & he worked himself into such a dreadful state of agitation that the tears were in his eyes, & he could scarce command his voice. He said that nothing *ever* would

178

alter his sentiments, but that if they annoyed me he would never again recur to them, & would endeavor to conceal the deep & ardent affection he felt for me. What would I have given to have been able to convey to him *my* feelings—but, alas! I am not able thus to dispose of my heart—or rather, I should say, my hand—for God knows, my *heart* is his! I told him that of course I should repeat our conversation to Mama tonight, & that her answer I would faithfully deliver to him tomorrow. He said "If Mrs. Smythe has any serious objection to me the subject shall never again be mentioned, & I shd. wish my family ever to remain ignorant of it. Should she object only to my youth, I would go abroad for any time— inshort, I would do anything to please her." I was aware that the whole party must have guessed the tenor of our conversation, & when I left my seat to join them I felt like a culprit. I was so nervously agitated that I scarcely knew what I was doing. Dear Lupo, as if aware of what was passing in my mind, was more kind & affectionate than ever; and it was with the greatest difficulty that I kept myself from crying. I saw in Mama's countenance how much I shd. have to go through ere the evening—or rather night—was over. Heaven only knows! I have been constantly placed in most difficult & awkward situations since I have been here—& should probably have acted more prudently if Mama had been more conciliating in her manner to me, & not so violent as never to hear reason. He had begged me not to mention the subject to Lupo, & I had promised this—which, however, I thought a hard case, as I knew how wrongly I should be judged by the rest of the family. When I got to my room I had the disagreeable task of explaining matters to Mama. She at first was very furious, & blamed my conduct immensely. However, I by dint of patience brought her to listen to me. When she asked me whether I wished to marry him or no, I felt as if I dared not say I did—knowing what an awful responsibility it is. I said I *certainly* did prefer him to *everyone* else, but that her opinion & advice were what I asked for—& also what answer I was to give him. She said

179

she thought him a *scamp*—& very extravagant; that he was almost too young to know his own mind, & she thought that such a marriage at present would prove far from happy. I cannot say that she in any way *positively* objected to it or *prohibited* it. She said she liked him very much, but did not as yet consider him at all qualified for a husband. I could not help feeling the truth of all this, as I know full well how little I am capable of *steadiness*, & how often—or at least *twice*—I had imagined myself in *love* during the one season I had been out [presumably with Trotter and Hillsborough]. When I spoke of an engagement she immediately said that she would never allow anything of the sort, as in Lou's case it had proved very detrimental to her; & therefore she would either have me marry him or else break it off entirely now, without giving him a hope for the future. I therefore was to tell him from her that, much surprised as she felt, yet, of course, I must feel flattered by the honour he had conferred on me; that she did not [wish me] nor was it my wish, to marry so young, knowing so little of the world or of my own feelings on the subject; that as for an engagement, she wd. never consent to one. Therefore she hoped he wd. still continue our friend, but that everything else would be at an end. I can hardly bring myself to describe the feelings that I experienced. I felt as if it was my death blow to dismiss him without any hope—& yet I had not the courage to show a resolute will to accept him. I tacitly consented to all Mama had said, the truth of which I felt, altho' I was unwilling at the moment to think her advice just or reasonable. But when she said that this event must oblige her to leave Combe before the end of the week—oh! God! I was half distracted. The very idea of it drove me mad. I burst into tears & entreated Mama not to think so. I promised to conduct myself quite differently if she would only remain a little longer. She said no more on the subject; & we parted friends, though both sorrowful. I went to bed—but certainly not to sleep, for nothing could exceed the dreadful agony of mind I was in. I placed the whole thing before my eyes. I felt that I could no longer be blind to the state of my affections; but also, strong as they may now appear, I trembled when I reflected how little I could depend on my own *stability*, when my vanity & love of admiration were excited. Also, how little I knew of him, when I thought of him as a Husband—& how much better it was to undergo my present misery than to find myself married to a man who might prove totally different to what I had imagined him to be. I was still considering over everything when the clock struck seven. I then tried to go to sleep.

Monday, December 31, 1832

When I woke about half past nine I saw dear Lupo by my bed side. She must have perceived how fagged & wretched I looked. She seemed grave, & brought me a beautiful bramah pen that August had desired her to shew me, & which he had just given to her. I own I was afraid he had meant it for me, & felt it quite a relief off my mind when she said it was hers. With what a heavy heart I dressed this morning. Lupo came to fetch me to go down to breakfast. I hazarded myself to ask her whether the Gentlemen were gone out hunting. She said "No", as there was a frost. This was indeed bad news to me. When we got down stairs Lady Craven received me as if she felt for me. August shook hands, but spoke not a word. He had breakfasted, therefore sat away from the table. No one hardly spoke, & Lady Craven remarked what a silent party we were. After this she proposed our proceeding to the Picture Gallery to settle about our Tableaux. I felt very averse to entering into any amusements of the kind in the present state of my spirits. However, I cannot say but what I thought *anything* preferable to remaining *quiet* that day. He followed us about all over the house, but I, of course, avoided him, as I could not *wish* to have to give him *Mama*'s answer. After this he went out riding, & came home just as we were going out walking, having had a fall. Ld. Craven was en petite santé today. I suppose he has not as yet spoken with his Brother on the subject. When we went to the Picture Gallery before dinner he [Augustus] said "I fear, Miss

Smythe, you have not done as you promised, in speaking to Mrs. Smythe." I said I had. "You then leave me in this horrid state of suspense, without giving me her answer?" I told [him] I would when I found an opportunity. All the family were then there, so that it was totally impossible for me to speak to him. Mama & I were dressed early today, & when we arrived in the drawing room we found no one but August, which was most distressing, as Mama did not speak a word, & we were both much *put to it* what to say to each other. Sir John Shelley arrived just before dinner. Ld. Craven was not well enough to dine with us, so that Augustus had to take Mama in. He did not take Ld. Craven's seat, so that I found myself next to him as usual. Lupo was on the other side of me; & I never underwent such a trial as endeavouring in anyway to keep up my spirits. The tears were in my eyes the whole time. Poor August—he was evidently struggling as much as myself against his feelings, & talked & made more noise than he ever does naturally. Then if he was quiet for a few moments, how absent & dejected he looked! We spoke very little to each other, & only on ordinary subjects. After dinner we went into the Picture Gallery to try the lights, but did not act. August having come out first, was left alone with Mama. I was in hopes he would have spoken to her. When the dancing was proposed, I danced with him—which I dreaded as I feared that it would lead to an explanation. However he begun the subject himself, & asked me whether I would forgive him for having been such a fool as to give way to his feelings which, he said, had last night been too strong for him to disguise them. He begged to know whether I would let things be as they were before. I said that my wishes were his upon the subject; that I feared it would prevent our remaining at Combe. This made him quite wretched, as he said he felt that he had destroyed the peace & comfort of our visit there. Lady Craven had spoken to him very seriously on the subject before dinner, &, as he said, called him a great fool for having thus acted. I, in consequence, did not give him Mama's answer—nor does he as yet know that *I like* him. He said he

182

once this morning had had serious thoughts of going to Melton, & had it not been for the persuasions of his own dear Mother he wd. certainly have gone there to drive away his misery in a constant state of excitement. As it is, he is determined to hunt every day, at whatever distance the Hounds may meet. He never closed his eyes all last night, & is looking more hagged than any one could conceive. This is my dear Mama's Birthday—but alas! to me it has been a day of misery! My New Year has not been ushered in with very cheering prospects. I wonder whether, if it pleases the Almighty to spare me till next New Years Eve, I shall find myself wedded to him I love alone on Earth! I had another very long conversation with Mama, & I went to bed feeling rather happier, but my heart was still heavy. Fatigue both of mind & body made me sleep sound & well. This is then really the last hour of 1832. How can I account for the way in which it was spent? I fear that *Vanity* has led me away, & I trust that (in) the ensueing year I shall, through the Grace of God, be enabled to amend my Life & to reflect often & seriously on the nonentity of all things here below. It has been my first trial of the world, & I can only say that even my slight & imperfect knowledge of it has far from improved the beau ideal I had conceived of it.

1833

Although she had promised Augustus not to mention his proposal to Lupo, when she read in Lupo's face that she knew all about it, Cou could no longer resist indulging in a confidential talk. How delicious to be able to tell the sister of her beloved— though it would have been improper for her to tell *him*—that she returned his affection! Lupo's sympathy, together with Lady Craven's kindness and good sense, went far to relieving Cou's feelings. Nevertheless, owing to a muddle over the *tableaux vivants*, which gave Mama a chance to express her disapproval in public, the first day of 1833 ended badly.

Tuesday, January 1, 1833

Lupo & I got up very early & were both dressed before ten—which was very alert, considering *I* had not got to bed before half past three. When we got down to make Breakfast for the Hunters, they were none of them come down. When they did arrive I wished them all a happy New Year— but when August came up to me I said I hoped every succeeding Year would bring him more & more happiness. He merely pressed my hand, but could not speak. I got up this morning in much better spirits & with the determination to keep my mind at ease on the first day of the Year. But how little do we know what we shall have to go through, even in a short day's span? I saw by my dear Lupo's manner that she knew all, & I could stand concealment no longer with her—& so I opened my heart to her. I even owned to her the preference & attachment I felt for her Brother. Poor girl! She cried dreadfully, & said "Poor dear August little thinks that you requite in any way his affection—& that is indeed very great—for you." We talked everything over together. August has not spoken to her since Sunday, but Lady Craven has talked it over with her; & when she told me what her Mother's sentiments were on the subject I found them to agree perfectly with Mama's. They both feel how young we are, & how slight our acquaintance has been, to enter into so serious an engagement. It may easily be conceived that neither of us felt very lively. We were obliged to engage ourselves in preparing for a Tableau we were to act in the evening, but I think there never were seen two people so little inclined to exert themselves. I told Lupo that I was most anxious to speak to Lady Craven; & she said that Lady C. had expressed to her the same wish. The day was too bad to go out, so that, whilst we were practising in the North Parlour, Lady Craven came in. I summoned up all my courage, & ventured to begin the subject myself. I said I feared that my conduct must have appeared to her very wrong towards her Son, but that could she only know what my feelings were, she would perhaps in some measure forgive me. Nothing could exceed her kindness & affectionate manner on this occasion. She embraced me & begged I would not for an instant imagine that she could attach any possible blame to me; that I had in no way acted unfairly by him; that altho' she knew he had always admired me immensely, yet that she had had no idea that he entertained such sentiments towards me; & that certainly she had been as much surprised as she was annoyed when she had discovered it in his manner. I told her exactly what Mama had said about it & she said that she perfectly coincided with her in every point; that nothing would annoy her so much as to see Augustus married at an age when he has had so little experience of the world, & was so unfit to make me happy. She said she had spoken very seriously to him, & that he had owned to her that his feelings had got the better of him, but that ever since he had avowed them to me he had never had a moment of peace— that the misery of his mind could not be described. This conversation naturally agitated me immensely, & it was impossible for me to express my sentiments either *clearly* or *calmly*. I said I should like her to speak to Mama, as I thought matters wd. in that case be so much better explained; & though the idea of doing so had never left her, yet she had never courage to begin. She therefore most amiably at my request promised to do so. I did not know the result of the conference before dinner. Ld. Craven was not well enough to leave his room the whole day. The Gentlemen came in late from Hunting, & August was obliged today to sit at the head of the table next to *Mama*. I pitied him, for I know he stands in *awe* of her. He was in the same forced spirits as yesterday, & I could not help every now & then looking at him to see how excited & feverish he seemed; & then I felt wretched when I reflected *who* it was who thus worried him. Gustavus Talbot arrived today: his alias here is *Boots*. After dinner we proceeded to dress for our Tableau, which was Sir Joshua Reynolds' Fortune Teller. Freddy was for tonight to do Lord Craven's part. Whilst we were dressing Dapper [Lady Craven] told me that Mama had been most kind—that of

185

course her feelings on the subject were too natural to be commented on. She told Lady Craven that she intended leaving Combe this week, but Lady Craven expressed her most heartfelt wishes that she would alter her mind, as she would answer for her Son acting just as she should direct him. Inshort, I think the next few days will decide whether we shall go away or not. They always have begged us to remain with them as long as they remain at Combe, but I fear that now I must give up that hope. When Lupo & I were dressed what was my surprise when, instead of Freddy, she sent for *August*. Lupo looked equally astonished. Whether in the moment she forgot all about it, or what was the reason of it, I have never been able to divine. Never was there so unlucky an occurence. Nervous & of course out of spirits, I was already quite unfit to act—& naturally his being in the Tableau made it ten times worse. He seemed very much perplexed, & as much surprised as we were. The agitation & excitement prevented our being able in any way to command our countenances. The whole thing went off shockingly. When Mama came up she hissed the performance, as naturally she was much annoyed. Oh! what a harassing, wretched evening this was! Would that I could forget it! When I got down into the North Parlour I dared not approach Mama. I felt like a culprit. I believe my costume of Fortune Teller became me very much—at least they all told me so—but how I hated myself for even *looking* well. I cared only to please *one* person, & he seemed afraid of looking or speaking. He sat down on the sofa with his face buried in his hands—& never moved. I, of course, did not approach him. But could he have known what my feelings were! Not knowing what to do, I proposed dancing. Freddy danced with me, but *he* never attempted to ask me. I am quite sure that he was wretched at having [been] made to act—& God knows! it was a most trying scene to both of us. What a New Years Day! I trust, that the misery I underwent will be rewarded.

Wednesday, January 2, 1833
It was a wretched, wet day, but the Gentlemen went out

186

Hunting. Ld. Grimston arrived. They did not come in till after we were gone to dress. August was not in the drawing-room when we arrived there, & Lupo told me that he had got a blow in his eye & had hurt his foot again. Poor fellow! What ill-luck he has! & how more than wretched it makes me when I consider that he Hunts in this violent manner to get *out* of *my way*. He forces high spirits, but it is easy to perceive what an exertion it is to him. In the evening Lupo & I acted "Meditation": it went off remarkably well. Ld. Craven came to see it. After this they made me sing, & August asked for '*We met*'. It was the first time I had sung it since the events of the few last days. I was so agitated that I could scarcely get through it. After this he danced a Quadrille with me, but I had no *conversation* with him, as he even effects gaiety with me, & seems quite fidgety if the conversation ceases for an instant—so afraid he appears that he should forget himself. I have not near so much command over myself, & cannot affect the spirits I do not feel—for never was I so harassed or so worried. My looks plainly show it. This morning I came down to Breakfast with my eyes swollen out of my head, owing to a most dreadful letter I found by my bedside from Mama when I awoke—& my constitution is really *not* strong enough to bear these shocks.

Thursday, January 3, 1833

This was a most lovely day, but still I felt too depressed to enjoy it. I never get to bed till past three in the morning from the long conversations I have with Mama, which leave me in such a nervous & excited state that I can with difficulty get any sleep from the palpitations at my heart, which almost prevent my laying down. August & Mr. Talbot went out Hunting very early. Mama received a note from Lord Arthur [Hill], who is at Coventry, to say that he shall ride over & see us in the course of the morning, & expresses a *wish* to get an invite to *dinner*. Both Uffy [Lord Craven] & Lady Craven begged she would insist on his dining & sleeping at Combe. In the afternoon Lady Craven, Lupo & I walked out, & on our return Ld. Arthur was arrived. He did not know any of the family & therefore we had to introduce him. Whilst we all [were] talking in the drawingroom before dressing time the *Hunters* returned, & we laughed famously at them for never having been able to find their *horses*, & having been the whole day after the Hounds in the *Dog-Cart*. I cannot say I regretted this circumstance for dear August's sake, as I am perfectly miserable whenever I now look at him. I hardly ever see him but at dinner, & then his cheeks are flushed from over-fatigue of mind & body, & also from *forced* gaiety. I had today a most dreadful headache & a bad cough, both of which I attribute entirely to nervousness. Ld. Grimston took *me* in to dinner. How dull he is! The dressing up for our Turkish Tableau in the evening & the weight of my Turban did not improve my head. Lupo would act as a Black Boy & black her face—I never did see such an unaffected creature in my life. How I wish I were like her! Freddy was Sultan & looked the part admirably. Sir John Shelley left Combe immediately after dinner today. The whole thing went off admirably, & I felt in much better spirits than I have done for some time. But never did I look so ill, or never have I suffered so much from misery & agony of mind. I feel an undescribable weight on my spirits, & a sort of blank when I look beyond the present moment—& yet I know not why I shd. have these sensations, for I am almost sure that he does care for me; & altho' it may be much better for us not to marry now, yet, should we both remain in the same mind, Mama does not say she will ever object to it. But I think I shall feel much happier when I have had a satisfactory explanation with him, which as yet I have not had—& he does not know but what I *hate* him! After the Tableau they made me sing a little, & then we danced. Ld. Arthur made himself particularly amiable, but I dread Mama's telling him all, which I know she will, & he always is annoyed (Dieu sait pourquoi) at *any* flirtation; & I foretell that he will advise her to leave Combe. Altho' I felt in better spirits tonight, I still think that August looks wretched.

William Stanley and Rowland Errington.
Details from an engraving of Sir Francis Grant's *Melton Breakfast*

Augustus Craven
Detail from a painting by J. E. Ferneley

Friday, January 4, 1833

As the Hunters were not to start before 10 that morning I settled to be ready with Lupo to Breakfast with them. Ld. Arthur was also amongst the early risers. After that Lupo & I went to practise together, & Ld. Arthur & Grimbo [Grimston] came to listen to us. The former went away before Luncheon—evidently not wishing to see any more of *things*. Ld. Craven told me that the *Lead-Bird* [Grimston] was much *struck* with me—Quelle bêtise! After Luncheon, when I went to put my things on, they had some *fun* with him. They made out that I had 10,000 £ a yr.—that is, they made it out by saying that there was 2,000 £'s worth of *singing*, 3,000-do-of *Beauty*, 3,000-do-of *amiable qualities*, & the rest down in money. This excessive *Goose* at last said "Well, I don't see how I could do better." When I came down Ld. Craven told me all this, & said that *Grinder* was such a *born idiot* that he knew he could easily persuade him to propose. I begged he would do no such thing. When we were walking Freddy & *Grinder* joined us. I strenuously avoided coming in contact with the latter, as I could hardly keep my countenance—Freddy was so very absurd. In the even. I sang as usual, & then we danced. Lupo told August abt. the fun with Grimbo, but I did not think he *took* the *joke*, for he turned the subject immediately.

Saturday, January 5, 1833

My cough was very bad indeed. The Gentlemen went out Hunting. The weather was very cold, & morning visitors kept us in till dusk; but although it was very late Lupo & I took a run in the Shrubberies & talked a great deal about sailing. I am sure I shd. rather like that sort of life, every now & then. Sir John & Lady Pollen arrived before dinner. I am prepared to like them both very much. Freddy Gordon also arrived for dinner. Poor Freddy [Craven] hurt his arm out Hunting. It is now nearly a week since Uffy has dined with us. I heard Ldy. Pollen make some remark abt. me to August at dinner, & the very consciousness of it made me turn scarlet. This

evening I think all the Gentlemen excepting August & Ld.
Craven were a little *groggy*, & the row was tremendous.
Lady Craven was immensely annoyed at it, & I do not think
they will be so again.

Sunday, January 6, 1833

This day was lovely, & we all went to morning Church
except Mama & Lady Pollen. After which we talked in the
Drawing room until Luncheon. We afterwards walked to see
the Stables, where dear *Grand Duke* looked more lovely than
ever. We then went to see the Cutter that arrived last night.
It is a perfect miniature of the Menai, & will look pretty on
the water. It will hold 60 people. August & I had a great
deal of conversation for the first time since *that* wretched
Sunday night, & I have the satisfaction of thinking that we
understood each other all the better for it. I tried to express a
wish about his giving up North America, but he talks as if his
plans were now irrevocably settled. I persuaded him not to
Hunt so much, which he says he did to please Mama & get
out of *my* way! I wrote in my room until dinner. In the even.
we all talked very agreeably, & I felt happier than I have
done for some time. Poor Freddy was also today obliged to
give up dining with us.

Monday, January 7, 1833

The day was very wet, therefore we did not go out. The
Gentlemen went out Shooting—all such figures—but I
thought August became his brigand style of dress. We were
to have a Twelfth Cake tonight, so Lupo & I amused ourselves in selecting the Characters. We had settled that
August & I shd. draw King & Queen, & when he came in we
told him so. But before dinner Dapper said to me that she
thought it best not to settle it so, but to leave it to chance, as
Mama might not like it. I upon 2d. thoughts agreed with her.
Lord Craven dined with us today, which I was charmed at, as
I like him so very much—& then when he is not there August
is obliged to sit at the head of the table, ce qui ne *m'arrange*

pas. When the cake was brought round after dinner, *Uffy*
drew King & I Queen. Poor August *was sold cheap*—& his
face was *impayable*. We had great fun with the Mottos.
Augustus gave me one to which he wanted an answer, but I
gave him none & kept the Motto—which was 'Tu *sembles* te
plaire avec moi—*m'aimeras*-tu de *bonne foi?*' I now evidently
see that he thinks I *flirt* with him pour passer le temps & to
make a fool of him. Oh! If he only [knew] how I dread the
very suspicion of his going to North America! After dinner
we shook the names of several Gentlemen & Ladies in two
hats. *Stroker* fell to my lot the 1st time, then Lord Craven,
et pour dernier report, Auguste—such I trust will be my fate.
After this I sung a little, & then we danced. The Gentlemen
were all very *quiet* tonight—that is, very *noisy* but very *sober*.
Chowder [Fred Gordon], as he is called, is the best fun in the
world, & *Boots* [Talbot] is the most plain, matter of fact youth
possible. Altho' cousin to Poll [Sir John Pollen], he hates him
most cordially, & indeed, I think there is not much love lost
upon him here. This evening, as usual, I danced the Quadrille
with Mon Auguste. He then asked me to dance a Country
dance with him. I said "Yes" sans y songer, but on 2d.
thoughts I told him that I would not dance *twice* with him, &
therefore threw him over. He looked immensely disgusted &
rather angry I thought. I was cruel enough to laugh at his
look of dismay.

Augustus's feelings for Cou were too strong to admit of him
being teased by her. A little chaff induced in him a fit of Byronic
sulks and a threat to remain forever in North America.

Tuesday, January 8, 1833
When Lupo & I were practising this morning Freddy &
August came into the room, & we both set about bullying the
latter so unmercifully about the Country dance last night that
he left the room very sulky, & went & drove his team to
Coventry. In the evening we acted 'Meditation', which went
off à merveille. Oh! how wretchedly disagreeable he made

191

himself to his sister & I—trying in every possible way to hurt & annoy us. Talking of going to North America as of a thing quite settled, & telling Lupo that as probably he should not return for a year or two—if he did *ever*—that he left her Paul as a Keepsake. We neither of us answered much, but Lupo's eyes were filled with tears, & I was so low & nervous that several times I felt on the point of leaving the room for fear of exposing myself. He then said that he had given orders to his Valet to pack up his things as he was going to Melton on Thursday morning, stating that it was impossible for him to Hunt from such a distance. Lupo then appealed to me to persuade him not to go. He said that a word from me wd. be a *law*—but that he could not *flatter* himself that *I* cared. My feelings got the better of me, & I told him that his going away wd. make me wretched. Upon which he said *"Then*, Miss Smythe, I will stay." I afterwards repented having said anything upon the subject, as I am quite convinced that everything he said this evening was to discover what effect it wd. produce on me. If he cd. but know that I care for him & *him alone*. . . . I went to bed angry & hurt with his conduct.

Wednesday, January 9, 1833

The Hounds were to meet here this morning, therefore we were all down at Breakfast before ten. I took care to be very cold to August, & merely asked him whether he was in the same *amiable* humour he had been in the preceding night. The truth was he was anything but well, & had been troubled with the *Blue Devils*. He looks wretchedly ill, & I own it makes me miserable. They had but a short run, & when they came in they made Lupo & I go & look at dear Grand Duke, that August had brought into the Cloisters. He afterwards came & talked to us for a little in the Music Room. We rowed him immensely about last night, but, poor fellow! he looks so ill that I quite forgave him. Fred Gordon & Mr. Talbot, who, unluckily, had put their heads in at the door, went into the D. room saying that they had left August very well occupied with Miss Smythe in the North Parlour. This, of course, displeased Mama. Major Wyndham came this morning. I am sure he is a disagreeable person, & after all I had heard of him I am much disappointed. In the evening they made me sing. Grimbo is always very attentive by the Piano Forte. We then danced. After one Quadrille with August, a Valse was proposed. He asked me to valse with him. Without thinking I said "Yes". Mama came up to me, & said she insisted on my not dancing again with him. This it appears Uffy overheard, & repeated it to his Brother the next day. However, luckily for me, Dapper objected to the Valse & another Quadrille was proposed. August again asked me, but I refused & danced it with Grimbo. I never saw anyone *look so sold*. He left the room for a short time, & on his return Grimbo nearly *poked* his eye out with the door. I think both the Lead Bird & Chowder were *three* Sheets in *the wind* tonight. The former took leave of us tonight, & said he hoped to have the pleasure of often dancing with me in London. I rather fancy that Lady Verulam will not much approve of his *patronising* a *Miss Smythe*.

Cou had never been to a dance in the country before—sophisticated Brighton did not count—so that the Coventry Ball next day was a new experience. Her brief observation about middle-class and provincial society remind us that in the eyes of Elizabeth Bennett in *Pride and Prejudice*, she and Augustus would probably have been on the enemy side. Still, she danced with 'one or two quizzes'—that is, 'freaks'—and the two lovers undoubtedly made themselves more agreeable than Darcy and Miss Bingley at Meryton.

During the Ball she was able to have a brief explanation with Augustus.

Thursday, January 10, 1833
   This is the day of the Coventry Ball, at which Lord Craven is Steward. August was very unwell indeed, with a shocking feverish cold. He came & talked with his Sister & I in the

North Parlour. Our conversation was rather décousue, & I felt reserved. I cannot account for the sensation, but some days I feel as if nothing could annoy or flurry me, & as if things were perfectly indifferent to me. Our conversation in the Nth. Pr. today was not discovered, so that I escaped une gronderie—altho' I must say that Mama is very amiable when once I get to talk to her, & every night I excite myself dreadfully by sitting up with her. We all dined at four & were dressed & set out at a little *before nine*! When we arrived August was ready to hand me out of the carriage, & escorted me into the Ball Room. What a set of *quizzes* were assembled there! I had never been at a *bal de province* before, & I own I was very much amused, & should have been more so if my thoughts were not so completely engrossed with one subject. I danced the first Quadrille with *him*, & we talked a good deal. I, for the 1st. time, hazarded myself to give him Mama's answer, because he had just said that he shd. go to America as there was no use in his remaining in England while I was unmarried. When I told him what Mama said abt. our not knowing sufficient of each other, I never saw anyone's countenance brighten up so. He said "Then I may still hope that I shall be happy at some future day." His spirits altered completely, & we talked in the same agreeable way that we used to do formerly—without that sort of gêne that we have experienced lately. I then danced with Freddy. Whenever I sat down he was always at my side. I also danced with a Capt. Adams & one or two quizzes—but I honestly own that I so much preferred sitting down talking to August that I wd. much rather not have danced. I *honored* him with another Quadrille. Mama was in the best humor possible. But when Country dances & Reels were proposed I declined dancing, & sat down again by Mama to talk to August. Ld. Craven (who always is goodnatured) went & sat the other side of Mama & kept her attention entirely engaged. I thought August wd. have died at this piece of *Manoeuvring*, & I was in a sad fright for fear Mama shd. hear him laugh, & call his Brother '*Good Recorder*'. Once or twice Mama

194

looked round, upon which he hid himself as much as he possibly could, & said he was doing a bit of *Woodcock*. In short, he was in one of his mad freaks, & nothing could keep him quiet. He has now promised me not to go to America & also that he will sell Syphon—for really he has such bad luck that I am always in the greatest fright when he goes out Hunting. He amused me much by calling me his '*best* Miss Smythe' tonight. In short I enjoyed myself amazingly, only I saw a storm *impending* in Mama's countenance. We got home about half past one, & sat down to a regular dinner. I will not attempt to describe the sort of row that they made. Fred Gordon's & Freddy's elegant joke of 'A poke in the eye with a burnt stick' made its début tonight. I could not see the wit of it, & as I did not hear all the words *distinctly* I looked rather grave—upon which they teazed me to death. We staid up till past three, & when I got to my room I had a long lecture from Mama for making myself so particular. But really I feel it impossible for it to be otherwise, as even if I did *not prefer* talking to him I never have an opportunity given me of talking to anyone *else*—& I have very difficult Cards to play.

Friday, January 11, 1833

The day was lovely, & after Breakfast we Ladies took a long walk across the Park to see the new Boat on the water. Poor dear August was dreadfully ill, & did not get up till very late. He was to have driven us to see the *Adams'*, but was not able. Mr. Talbot supplied his place. When we came back we found him laying on the Sopha, looking miserable. They wished him much not to come into dinner, but he insisted, & I never saw anyone appear in such agony as he did the whole time. Captn. Adams of the Scotch Greys dined here. In the evening *he* was so ill that he left the Nth. Parlour directly. This made the rest of the evening a complete blank to me. We danced, but I was so low that the row Freddy & Chowder made made me quite cross, & I told them they were only fit for a Public House—which affronted them dreadfully.

195

Saturday, January 12, 1833

We went out walking early; dear August was a little better. He staid in the Drawing Room the whole day, & after Luncheon Mama & I were left alone with him. We talked together very agreeably. In the evening he was able to dance.

The high-spirited mocking of the lovers by Fred Gordon and Freddy Craven gave rise to another embarrassing demonstration on the part of Mama.

Sunday, January 13, 1833

After Breakfast I wrote to Elizabeth & told her the state of things. Dear August is decidedly better, & he now takes so much more care of himself, which he tells me is all owing to our conversation at the Coventry Ball. We all went to Evening Church, & as the day was very dull we did not go out walking. Mama staid writing in her room before dinner. I went down stairs, but August did not talk at all. At dinner we had a little conversation together, & in the evening he sat by me talking. Freddy & Chowder who, by the way, are the greatest bores in the world, laughed & began across the room, talking *at us*. All of a sudden Mama jumped up & desired me to go & play. We were both at opposite ends of the room in an instant—the whole break up was done so quickly that we have since compared it to a shell thrown into the Citadel at Antwerp. Every one, of course, saw this, & I for some moments hardly knew where I was standing; & really we were talking de la pluie et du beau temps—perhaps the only time our conversation had been *indifferent*, for Lady Pollen, who was close by us, said she could hear every word we said. I sung after this, but he remained at a respectful distance from the Piano Forte & never spoke to me again during the Evening—which was a very disagreeable one owing to Chowder. I think him quite impertinent, & I wonder August allows it. Both him & Freddy had a long lecture this morning from him, but they do not seem to have profitted by it. We were to have gone to Leamington, driven by August tomorrow, but owing to their jokes we have given it up. Mama & I had a long conversation together at night, but I somehow cannot succeed in pleasing her in my conduct, & I own that I am harassed to death—& yet I know that the very thought of going away drives me wild. It was entirely owing to their jokes that Mama interrupted us tonight.

Monday, January 14, 1833

Augustus staid at home all day, as he really is not well enough for Hunting. I saw he hardly dared speak to me, & Lupo told me he was miserable, so I told her Mama's motive last night, & she owned that they really were too odious. She repeated this to August, who again begins to talk of North America—inshort I dare not *think* of things, & try to bewilder myself in talking & laughing. General Johnston arrived before dinner—a very stupid looking old Bachelor. But we had *heaps* of *fun* with Lady Pollen about him, because Sir John *let out* to the Gentlemen *after dinner* that he had been Lady P's *First Love*—so that is the name he goes by. After dinner Uncle Berkeley arrived. He is such a nice person & so very agreeable. We danced, & afterwards talked very agreeably—infinitely more sociable than we ever have done. They are going out Hunting tomorrow, & I have promised to come down to Breakfast.

Tuesday, January 15, 1833

I got up very early, but owing to Lupo's not fetching me I did not get down until *they* were gone. Poor August received, before he started, the news of the sudden death of his Stud Groom, which distressed him immensely. He therefore rode to Leicester instead of Hunting. We walked in the morn & Mama had a long conversation with Lady Pollen; & to my horror she has just informed me that it has decided her to leave this place on Friday. At this intelligence I had not a word to say. I felt it was a death blow—but what could

197

I do? One cannot remain here for ever, & if really it is, as Lady Pollen represents, that Lady Craven does not wish us to stay longer—as she thinks it so exciting for August—why, it is better to go. Whichever way I reason with myself on the subject I find no other alternative. Therefore I am going to endeavour not to think about it, & to keep up my spirits as well as I can for the next three days. I have not courage to tell Lupo today. August was dreadfully seedy & tired on his return—& no wonder, for he had ridden 90 miles. I know he exerts himself so much beyond his strength, & the thought makes me miserable. We danced in the evening & played a round game. I endeavoured to be lively with August, for he has seen so many disagreeable things today. He got rather better at last. Uncle Berkeley made himself, as usual, charming.

Wednesday, January 16, 1833

I had a most awful headache, & would not walk with them in the morning. I told Lupo of our going away—& she, poor dear, began crying. I was positively wretched. After Breakfast the Gentlemen went out shooting. Lord Craven, who is never ready, came & sat with Mama & I for an hour at least. At last, who should walk into the room but August, who we thought miles off, shooting. He said that when he got half way he found he had gone out *without his Gun*! Such an absurd excuse to give for returning—I very nearly laughed in his face. At Luncheon Mama told *Uffy* that we were going away on Friday. I never saw anyone look so surprised. August did not say a word, but his Brother entreated Mama to change her mind. We went in the afternoon to pay a visit at Lord Hood's—only Dapper, Lupo & I. At our return the Gentlemen were not come in from shooting, & my head was so violently bad that I laid down on my bed untill dinner. I talked very little at dinner, for I really felt too low to exert myself. However, in the even. we acted the Turkish Tableau. After that they made me sing. I had seen August in earnest conversation with Uncle Berkeley before I sat down to the

Piano Forte—evidently about me—& whilst I was singing, & he was looking most wretched, leaning over me, I heard Uncle B. say to Dapper "Ah! poor Augustus". We then danced—I, of course, with him. Our conversation now *flags* a little, as we are both in wretched spirits, but I think he will not go to North America. After dancing, we three talked whilst the Whist was going on. He has promised me to come up to Town on the 25th. of February in hopes of a Ball being given at Devonshire House on that night.

As the time approached for her to leave Combe & Augustus, Cou gave vent to her feelings by teasing him more than ever. Love can suspend one's sense of reality, and some of her jokes taken in earnest, wounded him to the heart. The more tragic he became the more she teased: cruelty was the only form of love-making allowed to her.

Thursday, January 17, 1833

The day was very dull. Mama talked of going on Saturday instead of tomorrow, which at any rate will give me one day more. Whilst Lupo & I were practising in the North Parlour August rushed in, said he wanted to speak to Lupo, came up to her—& immediately darted out of the room again. I had never turned my head, & only thought him very cracked. Lupo & I agreed he had an attack of *Hydrophobia*, so he went by that name the whole day. However, he declares that I looked so cold that it awed him away. We walked after luncheon. The Gentlemen all went down to the Boat. I told Lady Pollen of our departure being postponed until Saturday. When Lady Craven joined us, she told her, upon which Dapper embraced me most affectionately & said that she had never mentioned the subject to Mama, as of course it was very awkward for her to do so, but that nothing could make her more wretched than the thought of our going, & yet she felt it was better for both that we should separate for a short time. Augustus hardly spoke a word before dinner, & at dinner I took the opportunity of snubbing him. It really was very cruel of me, for I said everything I possibly could most heartless—said that I never would marry but for ambition etc—*invited him* to come & see me *when* I *was* Lady *Hillsborough*. Inshort the truth was that my spirits were so dreadful that, fearing I might make a fool of myself, I talked as much nonsense as I possibly could. However I saw he did not consider it in that light, & looked *daggers* at me. Mama was *unusually gracious* to him, & he said he thought he was 'upish' in that quarter. In the middle of dinner she asked him if he would drive us to Leamington tomorrow. I never saw anyone look so pleased at a request. After dinner I told Lupo of my conduct, & when the Gentlemen came out He went & talked to General Johnston, & never attempted to come near me. I could not help laughing, as, altho' I perfectly deserved it, it was so like a child quarrelling with its own *bread* & *butter*. When I began to sing, however, he made his appearance as usual close by my side—or rather, leaning over the desk. He asked in *such* a humble tone for 'We met'. I believe I never was in finer voice than tonight, & I sang for a long time. After that was over I *was* much *surprised* at his asking me to dance with him. Mama even could not help laughing at the '*Lover's Quarrel*'. We made it up during the Quadrille, for really I do believe that his feelings were hurt. I told him I did not *believe* he *did* care or *could* care about me. His answer was that he never should love anyone but me, & that if I chose I might publish it to the whole world, & glory in my *triumph*. Oh! how harassing these conversations are to me. I am always in fear & dread, as Mama watches me, & tonight was very much irritated at our having talked so much. We afterwards played a Round Game & became very good friends. Lupo & I prepared to go to bed before the others as it was very late & they had not finished their Whist. As we were going out of the room August seized hold of my hand & pressed it most affectionately to his heart. I never saw him look so handsome. I talked a little in Lupo's room, & then went to bed. Mama & I had, as usual, a long conversation together; & I really believe that for my health it is a very good thing I am going away, altho' I know I shall fret myself immensely in London.

Friday, January 18, 1833

As the morning was very tolerable we three set out for Leamington. If I had been in good spirits I should have enjoyed this little frisk of all things. He drove us beautifully; & whilst we were paying the Haymans a visit he put up at the Inn. We found Fanny & her father very comfortable in a nut shell. When Augustus came to fetch us we made him come up, as Fanny said she was at Hooton at the time he was flirting with Maria [Stanley], when his Regt. was quartered at Chester. When we got home we sat talking in the drawing room until dinner. I could hardly believe that this was the last time I shd. find myself there—at least, not the last time of my *life*, I hope. At dinner when I came down, I found that Lady Pollen had taken the seat next August that Mama generally has, which I was *rather* glad of—but I certainly did not take advantage of it, for I was, if possible, *worse* than yesterday. I said everything I could to annoy him (an *amiable* motive certainly). Speaking of Stroker, he said "If you see him in Town, Miss Smythe, *pray* send *him here.*" Upon which I said de l'air le plus déterminé "Oh, no, for I must have *some one* to *flirt* with in London." I never shall forget the look of misery he gave me when I made this speech. But this did not soften me, for I went on 19 to the dozen. Towards the end of dinner he did not speak a word, & I saw what effect my conduct had had. I had teased him about *Long Lupo* [Lady Louisa Lascelles]—inshort about everything I could think of. When the Gentlemen came into the Nth. Parlour he went & sat down on the furthest sofa, & called Lupo to talk to him. I *was then* in an agony; & reproached myself most dreadfully. Pour passer le temps I talked to Freddy. At last Lupo came back to me & said that he was greatly distracted— that he certainly could not bear to remain in England. Inshort, at last, just as I was going to sing for the last time, he came up to the Piano Forte, & I begged he would forgive me—as everything I had said was merely to *teaze* him & drive away my own wretched thoughts. He then said that he would forget & forgive it all since it really was not meant in earnest, but that it would be utterly impossible to describe the misery he went through from the time I left the dining room. I promised to believe all he said, & never again to treat him thus cruelly. I then sang, but my voice trembled shockingly. Poor August's eyes were filled with tears. Freddy & Chowder made more row than usual, but everything seemed to remind me that this was the last evening. When I had done singing Dapper laughed & said "My dear August, you look the picture of misery." We then danced. He said "This will probably be the last time we shall have an opportunity of telling each other whether we love each other. I have told you the real state of my feelings, but never have you given me reason to hope that my love is returned." Oh! these words! Shall I ever forget them! I told him that if ever I had preferred anyone it certainly was him, & that I felt now as if I shd. not alter; but that I was so young & giddy that I thought it infinitely better to wait & know more of one another. He then asked me if I would allow him to talk to me after the dancing was over. They made up two Whist tables, so that no-one was left out but us three. We therefore established ourselves together on the sofa. We none of us were gay, but nervous—which made one laugh sans le vouloir. At last our conversation took a serious turn, which was much better. He said "I have vainly endeavoured to get Miss Smythe to call me by my Christian name, & I am the only one of the family to whom she is so formal." Lupo said that with her I always called him August—& I felt as if I could not bring the word out. At last he called me 'Cou'— & seized my hand—which he kept firmly locked within his own during the whole of our conversation. At last he asked Lupo how she would like *me* for a sister-in-law. At this we both laughed, & Lupo said that in that case I shd. be *Uffy's* wife. Upon which he said "No, *my dear Georgina*, if you are Lupo's sister-in-law you will be *my* wife"—to which I said

"Yes". Oh, how the mere thought of this makes me happy! At last I called him Augustus—I really thought he would have *squeezed* my hand to death. But we have now agreed when we are talking *together* to call each other by our names. After this we had a Round Game, altho' it was then two o'clock. However, we were none of us in a Card humour, & soon gave it up. I asked him whether I should see him in the morning. His answer was "How can you ask *such* a question, *dear Georgina?*" We soon prepared to go to bed, & we took leave of dear Lady Craven, who was most affectionate to me. When I got into my room I felt as if from that moment until they came to Town my life would be a blank. I could not help giving way to my tears, for never have I been treated so kindly in my life, or found such kind friends. I should be a most ungrateful girl were I ever to forget these happy days. May these dear friends always continue to enjoy the happiness they do now—& my most fervent wish is that they may *all* meet with their reward, both in this world & in the next. The thought that before this time tomorrow I shall be far away from them was indeed a wretched one for me. I leave one behind to whom I am truly & sincerely attached, & I only hope & trust that if it should never be my lot to be united to him, (that) he will find one who is as much devoted to him as I am. But the thought of being forgotten by him, or of being *forced* to marry another, drives me frantic—altho' one can never answer for what *may* happen. I do not feel at all inclined to sleep, but I must go to bed & endeavor to compose my thoughts.

Saturday, January 19, 1833

As it was dreadfully late when I went to bed I slept until they came to call me at 9 o'clock; & when I saw the dull, grey morning, & saw all the bustle & fuss attendant on departure my courage quite failed me. However, I dressed as quick as I could, & Lupo came to me. Poor dear girl! She could hardly speak, & I endeavoured to talk of anything but of the present, as my heart felt so heavy that I know I shd.

have made a *fool* of myself. Mama was not quite dressed, so we went down. We found poor August in the Drawingroom, who looked something too wretched. He said that he never could forget my kind manner last night, that it was quite a consolation to him. But Mama came down almost immediately, & I was not at all inclined to have any conversation—& during Breakfast we made a very silent Quartett. I am quite sure that now Mama is very sorry to go. She was rather in a hurry to get off, & therefore we could not wait to take leave of the dear amiable Host; but I always think that the shorter parting scenes are the better. Freddy came into the room just as we were preparing to go. When I went to embrace my dearest Lupo I thought I could not have commanded myself, for she burst out crying. We neither of us could utter. Poor August, as eldest, was obliged to take Mama to the carriage, & Freddy took me. This was perhaps much better for us both, as I shd. not have known what to say. The tears were running down my face when I got to the carriage, & when I had taken leave of Freddy I took dear August's hand to get into the carriage, but could not speak a word. I turned my head Round once, just before we were off, & there he was standing, seemingly in a reverie & unable to move. Another instant, & the whole scene vanished from my sight. Oh! what a journey this was of wretchedness & misery. Would that I could entirely forget it! I felt that the present & even the future were a perfect blank to me, & that the recollection of the past made me miserable, as it had completely centred all my affections on one individual, who I am not allowed to marry—at least, not at *present*. We arrived in Town about 8 o'clock. Oh! how difficult it would be to describe the misery of my feelings.

Above) Lady Louisa Craven ('Lupo'). Detail from an engraving
Below L.) Lord Craven. Detail of a painting by James Hayter
Below R.) Frederick Craven. Detail of a drawing by James Swinton

Combe Abbey from the west and Clarendon Park from the east
Recent photographs by Richard Buckle

BACK TO GREAT CUMBERLAND PLACE

Frost and wretchedness in London – Rowland asks no questions – Augustus arrives – He sails for France – The Duke of Orleans in love with Cou – Mama gives in – Engaged at last – Another wedding at St. George's.

After Cou's return to London the journal begins to peter out. It had served its purpose as a confidante during the difficult weeks at Clarendon and Combe. Luckily, though, Cou takes up her pen three or four times more to tell the happy ending.

April, May, 1833

As I have not written my journal very regularly from the day of my return to Town up to this time, Good Friday, April 5th, I shall just note what principal events occurred during this time. I own that I was too wretched to enter into the spirit of anything. Errington dined with us the day after our return to Town, & started from this door for Melton. His manner is totally altered. He asked no *questions,* but was evidently dying to *know* everything. We never said a word & he went away unsatisfied. Minney was in Town for two or three days, & then returned to Brighton. Every one is full of my reported marriage, & nobody will believe what one says upon the subject. Both Mama & I were confined to the house for the first fortnight with the most dreadful colds & coughs. A severe frost came on as soon as we came to Town, & lasted for some time. My sole pleasure was writing to Lupo & hearing from her. She was very amiable in telling me all that could interest me—altho' certainly we shd. both have communicated *more* had we not known that our letters were *seen*.

Cou had been too preoccupied with her own affairs to record that Louisa's first child, little Freddy, was born in March.

Here we are arrived at the 26th. May, & there is a great blank in my Journal—& yet for the last month my life has been anything but a blank. On the contrary, I have been happy in some respects, very happy—but in others, worried, agitated & excited. Till Augustus came to Town, of course, I enjoyed nothing. The long-looked-for Ball on the 25th of February did not take place, owing to the Duke of Devonshire being very ill. On the 24th, which was a Sunday, & a very rainy day, we heard a Cabriolet drive to the door, but not feeling the least interest as to who it was I did not stir. Presently the door opened & they announced "Mr. Craven"— & August rushed in! It would be difficult to describe how I felt. Certainly surprise made me nearly speechless. I know that in my manner I was formal, for I felt *paralysed*. He was dreadfully agitated, & seemed hardly to know whether to sit or stand.

The chronology of the journal is here a little hard to follow. In reckoning backwards to find the date Augustus came to London Cou forgot it was not a Leap Year: he must have arrived on Sunday, February 23. In March he was off on the *Menai*, sailing through the Needles to Dartmouth and Falmouth, down the west coast of France by Ushant and Isle Dieu, to Bordeaux.

Meanwhile Cou had a new admirer in the duc d'Orleans, son and heir of King Louis Philippe, who was in London on a visit. On May 17 Mrs. Fitzherbert wrote to Minney: 'Mrs. Wat says the Duke of Orleans is very much in love with Cou. She dances constantly with him and [he] says she is the prettiest girl in England. I fear if true [this] will turn the poor girl's head. Mrs. Wat is delighted and has just taken a Box at the Opera though she has not received as yet her money. I think the lawyers use her very ill but I also think her expenses are not in the least diminished. I tremble for what may happen. . . .' Cou does not mention her Royal admirer in what remains of the journal.

June 1833

I never had spirits to sit down & write my Journal once this season. It would merely have recalled wretched feelings & days that I wish now to forget forever—as, from having been the most miserable of beings, I am now the happiest. My fate is decided, & I am to be married the end of January. It was settled at Lady Elizabeth Feilding's Ball on the 28th of June, where I went in the lowest spirits, everything having gone wrong for the last few days, particularly the preceding one, which we had passed on board the Menai—when I had gone through a most harassing scene with him. The fact was, he never in his life had summoned enough courage to speak to Mama upon the subject, & only heard second hand different things she had said to Lord Craven—which only tended to irritate him more against her. I had vainly endeavored during the whole Season to persuade him to speak to her, but in vain. I knew that of course no other person's interference would be of any avail, & as he did not chuse to adopt this course I told him that if he could make up his mind to break the thing off, it had much better be done immediately—& this was the cause of everything going so wrong before Lady E. Feilding's Ball, where Mama began herself by saying that she had been told that he went about abusing her. And so from that a long conversation ensued between them, which I was determined not to interrupt in any way, as I felt convinced that they would get on very well together, & he was quite sure to plead his cause well. I therefore danced in the mean time with Ld. Hillsborough & Ld. Douglas, & when I returned to Mama he took me by the hand & said "Mrs. Smythe has given us leave to declare our marriage to the world!" Oh! what were my feelings at this moment! I could scarcely believe that Mama had really consented—but it was so—& I was the happiest being on earth. He had pleaded his cause so well that she had almost been obliged to say *yes*. I do not think it was *voluntary*, but she felt that we had persevered so long & that we really seemed attached, that there was no hope of having the thing broke off. He wanted to gain her consent to be married this Autumn, but that she wd. not agree to, & therefore it is settled for the last week in January. But I feel so completely happy that waiting 6 months seems nothing. The more I know of Augustus the more confidence I feel as to the prospect of my being thoroughly happy. Mama, indeed, has strangely altered her opinion of him, & is gradually getting to like him very much. He has under every circumstance shewn her the greatest respect, & I know that many has been the time when he has had the strongest battle with his feelings upon that subject. However, that is past & gone by, & I trust that they will now become the greatest friends. He told me that he should always behave towards Mama as he had done to his own Mother, & that she should never have to repent of the consent she had given. My life since that night has of course been widely different from what I felt previously. Even before this we lived a great deal with the family, but we both used to act in fear & trembling, consequently none of the parties that we made together were near so pleasant as they might otherwise have been.

Saturday, June 29, 1833

The day after Lady E.F.'s was Saturday the 29th. That night we went to the Opera. Lady Craven & Lupo received me most affectionately & when Augustus came he was the happiest of people. They asked us to dine en famille with them the next day & we accepted.

Sunday, June 30, 1833

I hardly could compose my feelings today. I can with such difficulty bring myself to believe that the thing is *really* declared, altho' in our *own minds* it has been settled for several months, & if Mama had refused her consent at the end of this season some *desperate* measure would certainly have been resorted to by us—for never were two people so ill used in every way. I cannot say I cared the least for what I *myself* suffered, but I must confess that it was as much as I *could* bear to see him treated as he was generally. I only wonder that he did not resent it, & I think his conduct on this subject is one of the greatest proofs he could possibly give of his attachment to me. He called this morning & was very well received by Mama—indeed I think that now she will see how useless it is to *snub* him in any way. Our dinner in Charles St. was charming as usual, & all the family were most kind & affectionate to me. I had a good deal of conversation with Augustus, who was in high force.

Monday, July 1, 1833

Mama went this morning to Aunt Fitzherbert, to inform her of it. I drove a little in the Park with Aunt Cha, & talked to Augustus. We dined with Lou, where he also dined. The party consisted of the Throckmortons, the Duchesse de Cannizaro ['the Countess'], George Villiers [Lord Villiers] & Ld. Marcus Hill. It was excessively lively & vive. The *Countess* asked us *all* to dine with her at Wimbledon next Sunday—& turning to August & I, she said "And you will find a little *wood* to walk about in, *little things*." They made me sing in the evening, & we settled to ride tomorrow.

Tuesday, July 2, 1833

Augustus called here to fetch me for riding, & brought us Lady Craven's Opera Box, as they were gone to the Duke of Somerset's Breakfast. The Bathursts called about 5, & we took a most delightful ride into the country, which under *existing circumstances*, is much pleasanter than the Park. The Bathursts & Aunt Cha came with us to the Opera, to which I *now never attend much*, as I am otherwise engaged.

Wednesday, July 3, 1833

I went & sat with Aunt Fitzt., who is quite put out that Mama should defer the marriage for so long, & wishes very much she could hurry it. The Bathursts dined here, & we then went to Almack's. We always have now to chaperone Georgy Bentinck, or else I am sure I do not know *why* I still continue to go to Balls—excepting that Mama is not yet *quite* enough reconciled to the thing to consent to his spending his evenings quietly here, which wd. in every sense be more agreeable. Few, if any, of my former partners ask me now to dance, & as he has a great objection to Valsing I generally now refuse —for I think it but fair that I should give in to him a little when he has gone through so much for my sake. We remained very late at Almack's as we could not get the carriage, & Mama was rather cross on returning home at his having remained with us the whole evening. I cannot submit to these extraordinary caprices on her part, as it is so unmerited. I am always very resolute & calm when I speak to her on the subject, & I have found that manner succeed.

Thursday, July 4, 1833

I rode with the Bathursts. He met us in the Park—as, on account of Mama's ill-humour last night, I would not allow him to call & fetch me. We rode in the Park today, & in the evening went to a large party at Lady Londonderry's. The crowd & heat were intense; & shortly after we arrived we fell in with all the Cravens. Lady Craven was on August's arm, & he wished us much to stay with them, but Mama was in one of her *fidgetty* humours, looking for God knows *what* or *who*, & said she must go round the rooms. August darted a look at her as if he could have *eat her up*, & turned away. I did not expect to see him again, but however, we met very often, & I found—

Cou's journal, like Louisa's, ends in mid-sentence. So we leave Mama in a fidgety mood, ranging about the rooms of Holdernesse House—in search of whom? Perhaps the Duke of Orleans?

On July 13 we find Mrs. Fitzherbert writing to George Dawson-Damer: 'The Duke of Orleans . . . has taken a great deal of notice of Cou, and constantly dances with her and all sorts of remarks have been made and all sorts of falsehoods have been propagated, which has been very unpleasant, both with respect to the mother and daughter and I am heartily glad he is going away. Mrs. Wat tells me he has pressed them very much to spend next winter in Paris and that he will make it very pleasant to them. In the meantime it has been announced in the newspapers that she is going to marry Craven. I wrote Minney word that Mrs. Wat had got a Box at the Opera but this is false. She was there last night with Ly. Craven. There is a mystery about this affair that I cannot penetrate for I don't like asking questions. . . .'

The duc d'Orleans was painted by James Holmes during his visit to England, possibly at the instigation of Cou. He died in a carriage accident a few years later.

Cou and Augustus were married at St. George's, Hanover Square on December 23, 1833. Among their wedding guests were Louisa and Frederick Hervey-Bathurst, Lady Craven, Louisa Craven, Lord Craven, Rowland Errington, Lord Munster, George and Minney Dawson-Damer, Lord Arthur Hill, Lord Grimston, Francis Molyneux, Fred Gordon and Poodle Byng. There was a 'déjeuné' afterwards in Cumberland Place.

EPILOGUE

Cou was nineteen and Augustus twenty-three at the time of their wedding. The young couple were only to enjoy two and a half years of happiness together, for Augustus Craven died in July 1836.

Within three weeks of their marriage they were at Combe, and Augustus was hunting almost daily. He rode with the Atherstone, the Quandon, the Warwickshire and Squire Osbaldistone's hounds. Lord Craven, Freddy and Uncle Berkeley, Sir John Pollen, Lord Villiers, Lord Grimston, Fred Gordon, Rowland Errington and Frederick Hervey-Bathurst are mentioned in his note-book as having hunted with him during the winter. The only reference to Cou is on Tuesday, February 11, 1834, when there was a meet at Combe 'Mrs. Craven riding Woodpecker. The hounds went away from the sidings through Brandon Wood, and lost at Birberry. I did not follow them but took Mrs. Craven home. . . .' Mrs. Wat was staying in the house-party until March 3. On March 17 the Augustus Cravens left Combe for London. At this time he kept between a dozen and fifteen horses, mostly listed as hunters, with four grooms and a coachman.

The Cravens made their home at Brambridge, and it was here that their two sons, William George and Walter Keppell were born in 1835 and 1836.

Augustus died on July 26, 1836. As a boy I remember looking at one of the pictures of him by Ferneley, the one in which his horse seems on the point of coming a cropper into a ditch. This belonged to my great-uncle Caryl Craven, and now hangs in the Duke of Northumberland's study at Syon. My uncle told me that Augustus Craven broke his neck or killed himself out hunting, and I assumed this picture must have been painted as a record of his doing this, and thought how morbid his family must have been to commission it. Either Uncle Caryl was not telling the truth, or I misunderstood him, for there is a letter from Mrs. Fitzherbert to Maryanne Jerning-ham, dated August 4, 1836, in which she writes: 'I am sure you will be shocked to hear Augustus Craven is dead. He had been ill some time though he was not thought in danger till two days before he expired. It is impossible to describe the deep grief and distress this has occasioned everyone that knew them. As to poor Charlotte [Cou] her state of misery is beyond anything. So young and so happy as she was, to see all her comfort and happiness destroyed. He had just completed a twenty-fifth year, she her twenty-second and what makes it more melancholy he died on her birthday. . . .' My guess is that Augustus wore himself out by his exertions in the hunting field, and died, perhaps, of an illness brought on by a bad fall.

Cou continued to live at Brambridge for some years after her husband's death. There she was within a morning's drive of Louisa at Clarendon. No doubt Mama and Aunt Cha paid her long visits.

Cousin Fanny Hayman had married, two months before Cou's wedding, the seventeenth Lord Somerville, later an Admiral: by him she had seven children, of whom two have descendants living today.

Cou's first love, John Trotter, had also married in 1833 one of Lord Ravensworth's daughters, Charlotte Amelia Liddell: their grandson now lives at Mells Park, near Frome.

Elizabeth Brudenell-Bruce, Cou's great friend, married in the same year the affable Dane, Count Christian Danniskiold-Samsøe, who had danced attendance on both the Smythe girls in earlier seasons.

In 1833 Lord Albert Conyngham married as his first wife, Henrietta Maria Forester, sister of 'le beau Cecile', of Mrs. Robert Smith, who had died of cholera in 1832, and of Lady Bradford and Lady Chesterfield: on the death of his Uncle Denison he inherited two and a half million, changed his name to Denison and was made Lord Londesborough. He was the ancestor of Edith, Osbert and Sacheverell Sitwell.

Lord Craven married Lady Emily Grimston, daughter of Lord Verulam and sister of 'Grimbo', in 1835: from this marriage descend the subsequent Earls of Craven. Lupo Craven, having refused Tom Brand (later Lord Dacre) because he never opened a book, married, in 1836, the rich Sir George Johnstone, nephew of the Smythe's old friend, the musical 'Countess', later Duchess of Cannizaro. She had two sons by this marriage, from the second of whom the present Johnstone baronet descends. On Sir George's dying five years later, she married Alexander Oswald of Auchencruive, by whom she had no children. Freddy Craven never married.

In the spring of 1836 that attractive 'mauvais sujet', Uncle Berkeley Craven, committed suicide, 'after losing more than he could pay'. Another (great-great-great) uncle of mine, Charles Greville, wrote in his diary: 'It is the first instance of a man of rank and station in society making such an exit. He had originally a large landed estate, strictly entailed, got into difficulties, was obliged to go abroad, compromised with his creditors and returned, fell into fresh difficulties, involved himself inextricably with betting, and went on with a determination to shoot himself if his speculations failed, and so did. He was very popular, had been extremely handsome in his youth, and was a fellow of infinite humour and good humour.'

Aunt Haggerston also died in 1836. None of her Stanley grandsons had yet married, but Maria Williams-Bulkeley had already given birth to two sons; in the next few years she was to have two more. William Stanley never married—he was too busy dissipating the family fortune. Rowland Errington married Julia Macdonald in 1839, and in 1863 succeeded his brother as eleventh Baronet, though with the name Errington, not Stanley. The youngest brother John married in 1841 Maria, only daughter of Baron de Talleyrand: they had no children. John succeeded Rowland as the twelfth and last Baronet in 1876. The only one of these brothers to have children was Rowland: he had three daughters. The eldest never married, and the youngest married Lord Pollington, son of the Earl of Mexborough, but had no children: however, the second, Ethel, married in 1876 Captain Evelyn Baring, by whom she had two sons, and it is through her and the Bulkeleys that the line of Aunt Haggerston and of the ancient house of Stanley is carried on. Captain Baring became the first Earl of Cromer: he was 'the maker of modern Egypt' at the end of the nineteenth century. The present Lord Cromer is his grandson, and the great-grandson of Cou's devoted cousin Rowley: the Baring family flourishes.

In 1837 'Mountain' Hillsborough married Caroline Frances, daughter of Lord Combermere: he succeeded his father as fourth Marquess of Downshire in 1845, and subsequent Marquesses descend from him.

Mrs. Fitzherbert died peacefully at Brighton on March 27, 1837 at seven in the evening. The Dawson-Damers were with her. She was buried in the Roman Catholic chapel of St. John the Baptist in Kemp Town on April 6. Her two adopted daughters, Minney Seymour and Maryanne Jerningham waited in the church, while Edward Jerningham, George Dawson-Damer, Frederick Hervey-Bathurst, Munster, Colonel Gurwood, George and Frederick Seymour and some of the sixteen servants followed the hearse.

Louisa was staying at Brambridge with Cou at the time of the funeral, and Frederick preserved the letters both sisters wrote to him.

Louisa wrote:

Sunday.

How glad I am you went to Brighton. I was *convinced* they would be pleased at yr. going, and even had they not been it was I am sure the right thing to do. I almost wish I had been with you, though it would have been a mournful scene for me, but I should have liked once more to have beheld her features, though from Minney's letter to Cou I fear you were *almost* too late.

Were you present at the reading of the Will? I suppose so, as Minney mentions the arrival of the executors on Friday I think. I am not surprised at Brighton being the place she fixed upon for her Funeral, as it was her favorite home. Minney mentions the Will & says the jewellery is at the

215

Bank & will not be opened till after the Funeral. Anxious, dearest Fredk., as we are for you to return to us, I hope you will wait at Brighton & return to us on Thursday, as we wd. rather hear through you than from any one else of any little memento our dearest Aunt has left us. You, my darling Frederick, know how much I loved her & prized her affection, & your kind heart must deplore her loss. She was my kindest friend, & the person in whom I felt the most confidence. I feel as if I had really lost a second home, so much, as you know, did I enjoy being in her house. Poor Minney, I shall always be fond of her, from having been the favorite of Aunt Fitz.

I am surprised there is nothing left to Gurwood. The idea of both houses being sold rather gives one a turn. As it is to be the case I shall like to purchase several things out of Tilney Street, as I shall like to have things that have belonged to her, though I shall prize nothing equal to her last gift to me at Brighton. . . . Little Freddy is to come to us tomorrow . . . How did you find Ly. Fremantle? She must have felt poor Aunt Fitzherbert's death very much. They had been such old friends. Write me every particular, dearest Frederick, & believe me Yr. devotedly affect.

Louisa.

You will say everything kind from me both to the Damers & Jerninghams, & you will tell them they will I hope on our return to Clarendon spend some time with us . . .

Cou was anxious to secure Haselhurst, Mrs. Fitzherbert's cook who had been with her thirteen years. She wrote:

My dear Frederick. I wished to join one line to Lou's letter saying how much I shd. like to have Haselhurst if she is not already engaged to Minney or Marianne.

I should only wish her to be Cook in my establishment, but I think she wd. be such a comfort to me, & such a good manager. Beside when I leave home & take Sharpe with me, she will be a trustworthy person to leave in the house. I don't know what poor Aunt Fitz gave her, but perhaps you wd. kindly find out for me, as I wd. give her the same unless it is exorbitant. But you will be the best judge of that. Perhaps you could speak to her yourself if it wd. not be a great trouble. I am *very* sorry that poor Gurwood shd. not have been remembered. Probably he will be left one of the Souvenirs. I am very grateful of her kind remembrance of me. We are anxious to know what the result of the remainder of the Will is, & if the Box is opened immediately after the Funeral I suppose you will await to see it. I am in a great dilemma about the Jerninghams. Do they expect to be invited here? Thank Minney for her letter, & persuade her to come here as soon as she can. I trust we shall be able to get many Souvenirs of dear Aunt Fitzt. when all the contents of Tilney St. are sold. We shall be very glad indeed to see you back again.

Ever yrs. affecty.
Georgina Craven

Sunday.

In a codicil to her will, dated March 28, 1836, Mrs. Fitzherbert had written: 'To my dear sister-in-law Mrs. Wat Smythe one thousand pounds legacy. To my two nieces Lady Bathurst and Mrs. Craven one thousand pounds each. I have ever felt for them both as great an interest and very sincere affection and had in a former will left them considerable legacies. Since that period they have been greatly provided for, and do not stand in need of any assistance from me.'

Colonel Gurwood, referred to in the letters of Louisa and Cou, was one of Mrs. Fitzherbert's executors. He edited the Duke of Wellington's Despatches, but suffered from a kind of persecution mania, and cut his throat in 1845.

Minney's son Lionel succeeded his uncle as fourth Earl of Portarlington: her daughters married Lord Fortescue, Colonel Haygarth, Captain Sutton and Sir John Leslie. The present Lords Portarlington and Fortescue, and Sir Shane Leslie, biographer of Mrs. Fitzherbert, therefore descend from her. She died in 1848.

Mrs. Fitzherbert's other adopted daughter, Maryanne Jerningham, had two sons and two daughters who survived infancy. As her husband's elder brother died without heirs, her two sons succeeded in turn as tenth and eleventh Lords Stafford. In 1858 her daughter Emily married Basil Thomas Fitzherbert of Swynnerton, thus uniting the family of Jerningham to that of Mrs. Fitzherbert's second husband. As Minney's two sons died unmarried, the Stafford title passed to her eldest Fitzherbert grandson, whose descendant, Lord Stafford, now represents both these ancient Catholic families. Maryanne died at Versailles in 1859 and was buried at Cossey in Norfolk.

Louisa, who proved such a devoted wife to Frederick Hervey-Bathurst, and bore him a son and a daughter, died in 1840. She was only thirty. Sir Frederick married again five years later, and had eight more children. Louisa's line continues; and it was her grandson, the son of 'Little Freddy', the late Sir Frederick Hervey-Bathurst, who first showed me her journal and the miniatures by Holmes.

Mrs. Wat Smythe kept on Great Cumberland Place after the marriage of her two daughters, and died there in 1849. She left most of her property to Cou's elder son, William Craven.

Of the half-dozen principal characters in our story Sir Frederick was the last survivor. His grandson, who died while this book was in course of preparation, remembered him well as a gruff old gentleman. The late Sir Frederick supplied me with the following information and I am happy to be able to include in this book a paragraph written by the grandson of Frederick and Louisa. 'Sir Frederick Hervey-Bathurst was a great cricketer, and made his debut at Lord's in 1831. His "tiger" who went to Lord's with him, told me that when he went in people were asked to stand further back because he hit so hard. He was a fast bowler with a very low delivery—what would now be called almost underhand. He played nineteen times in Gentlemen and Players between 1831 and 1854 inclusive; and in his forty-seventh year, 1853, Sir Frederick and Mr. Kempson bowled all through the Gentlemen and Players without a change.'

Sir Frederick was outlasted, however, by his old rival Ossulston, who married Lady Olivia Montagu, daughter of the sixth Duke of Manchester, in 1850, succeeded as sixth Earl of Tankerville in 1859, and died in 1899. The present Lord Tankerville and his family descend from him.

On October 19, 1844, Cou married again. Her second husband was a Frenchman, five years younger than herself, Edmond-Michel-Philibert de Caumont, marquis de la Force. The marriage was celebrated in the *mairie* of Chanelay, near Paris, by the mayor, François-Philibert-Bertrand-Nonpar, duc de Caumont-la Force, the bridegroom's grandfather, whom he was later to succeed in the dukedom. Cou's two brothers-in-law, who had presumably looked after her interests since the death of Augustus, cannot have disapproved of this second marriage, for both Frederick Hervey-Bathurst and Lord Craven crossed the Channel to attend the ceremony. Cou had now married into one of the oldest families in France, and was eventually to be a duchess: nevertheless, from this moment obscurity enfolds her. She certainly lived mainly, if not entirely, in France, but no trace of her name or her husband's can be found in any fashionable paper of the period. Mystery surrounds her husband. His father was a soldier, his mother a Russian, Princess Catherine Galitzine: of himself I can discover nothing. Was he handsome and dashing like Augustus Craven? No portrait has survived. Knowing Cou as we now do, it strikes us as improbable that she should marry in order to become a duchess: on the other hand, that La Force married her for her money is not impossible. I cannot help feeling there was something wrong about him. They lived at the Château de Créteil, an attractive village near Paris, now a busy industrial suburb, of which Edmond was for a time mayor. This seems his only claim to distinction. He and Cou had no children. He died and was buried at Créteil in 1857. When his widow followed him to the cemetery ten years later, she was buried in a separate grave.

Cou's husband was succeeded in the dukedom by his uncle, whose grandson is the present duc de la Force, a distinguished historian and Member of the Académie Française.

Twice widowed, Cou continued to live at Créteil. Her elder son, William, had gone from Oxford, where he was supposed to be the richest commoner in the University, into the Life Guards. Her younger son, Walter, went into the Navy.

Walter married in 1864 the Contessa Elisabetta Oldofredi-Tadini, and went to live in Italy. His wife's mother had been a Terzi, her grandmother a Galitzine, so he was marrying a connection of the La Force family. Of his four children, none of whom married, the last survivor, Mary Craven, died at the age of ninety while this book was still in preparation, after sending me photographs of portraits of Wat Smythe and of Cou as a widow.

My great-grandfather, William George Craven, was tall, handsome and spoilt. In considering his life one remembers Uncle Berkeley and Cou's observation about the Berkeleys and the Cravens not being good blood. He had beautiful manners and an excess of charm: but this did not prevent Lord Clarendon referring to him in a letter to the Duchess of Manchester as 'that double barrelled brute'. Although his father, Augustus, as a younger son had only been allotted London property instead of an estate, this property had increased enormously in value. Some of it was off Regent Street, some of it in Paddington, where there is a Craven Road, and some near Charing Cross where there is a Craven Street: much of it still belongs to my cousin Violet Wimbush. When William Craven came of age he had at least twenty thousand a year; but by the time he died in 1906 he is said to have lost three fortunes. Of his many extravagances the Turf was probably the greatest. (His racing colours were scarlet and white.) Was he stupid, ill-advised or merely unlucky? His stud apparently only lost him money.

In 1857, the year of his step-father's death, William Craven married Lady Mary Yorke, youngest daughter of the fourth Earl of Hardwicke. Her mother had been Susan Liddell, whom the Smythes met at Ravensworth in 1830, and whose parents had given breakfasts in the walled garden of Percy's Cross. More 'bad blood', perhaps, to mix with that of Craven and Berkeley!—though some of the Yorkes were staid and respectable sailors or lawyers (the first Lord Chancellor Hardwicke's mother had been a relation of Edward Gibbon), more of them were weak, feckless and devoted to pleasure. Mary was as beautiful as her husband was handsome. They were said to be the best-looking couple in England: but with all their gifts of birth, wealth and beauty their marriage seems to have been doomed from the start. Mary Craven had a sweet, loving nature, and was adored by her family, but there may have been something weak or simple about her. In the portraits by Watts and other painters her wide staring eyes and petulant mouth reveal a childish side to her character.

From the beginning William Craven made no effort to be faithful to his wife. Beautiful, admired and neglected, she eventually took a lover and had a son by him. Craven, so charming to everyone else, was ruthless to her and turned her out of the house. She went to live in Paris, where, I believe, she was for some time kept by a Frenchman. Later she embraced the Roman Catholic faith and died insane in a religious institution at the age of fifty-three. Her children by William Craven continued to see her intermittently up to the time of her death, and were devoted to her.

There were four children. Augustus, the eldest, got into the hands of moneylenders, sold the reversion to his inheritance —which his father subsequently bought back—and was disinherited. He married two or three times. The only child of his second wife, my cousin Violet Craven, who was brought up with me, married in 1935 Roland Wimbush, by whom she has two children. She has inherited William Craven's London property; and when she came into it she sold the site of Charing Cross Station to pay death duties. The second child of William and Mary Craven was my grandmother, Constance Georgina, who married Captain Francis Sandford of the Grenadier Guards, and had four daughters. The third child, Caryl, never married. The fourth, Isobel, married as his second wife the Earl of March, later Duke of Richmond, and died young, leaving two daughters.

Georgina Smythe had one grandchild living when I began to edit her journal: Mary Craven, the daughter of her younger son Walter. All Georgina's other descendants derive from her elder son, William. She has seven great-granddaughters living: Mrs. Roland Wimbush, Miss Eva Sandford, Mrs. Robert Thomas, Mrs. Christopher Buckle, the Hon. Mrs. Patrick Kinnaird, Lady Muriel Derek-Jones and Helen, Duchess of Northumberland. She has twelve great-great-grandchildren: Jennifer Wimbush, John Wimbush, Lady Dalrymple-White, Richard Buckle, John Beckwith, Mrs. George Dusgate, Mrs. John Talbot, the Duke of Northumberland, the Duchess of Hamilton, the Countess of Ellesmere, Lord Richard Percy and Lord Geoffrey Percy. Finally she has fifteen great-great-great-grandchildren: Jan Dalrymple-White, William Beckwith, Richard Dusgate, Richard Elwes, Gillian Elwes, Edward Elwes, Lady Caroline Percy, Lady Victoria Percy, Lady Julia Percy, Earl Percy, the Marquess of Douglas and Clydesdale, Lord James Douglas-Hamilton, Lord Hugh Douglas-Hamilton, Lord Patrick Douglas-Hamilton and Lord David Douglas-Hamilton.

✢　　✢　　✢

Nobody in my family knew, or if it was once known, nobody remembered, that Cou's son, the extravagant William, had published a novel. Yet, thanks once again to Mr. Kersley, here it is lying in front of me, *The Margravine, A Story of the Turf*, by W. G. Craven (Chapman & Hall, 1870). It is odd that this racing man should have had literary ambitions. Did he write the book unaided? The story is quite well told and the conversations are often entertaining. Did the young millionaire, temporarily broke, retire to the country and turn out a novel in exchange for a few hundred pounds? Was it a *roman à clef* designed to justify his conduct over some scandal that had turned society against him? Although much of the sensational story is clearly invented, it is natural that the inexperienced author should draw upon his own friends and surroundings for certain characters and descriptions. The hero, Charlie Delval, 'as fine a specimen of an Englishman as you might wish to see', had in common with

William Craven that his father had died when he was a child, and that his mother lived on the Marne near Paris. It may therefore be permissible to assume that in the few paragraphs he devoted to Mrs. Delval, who dies in chapter five, her son is giving us a miniature of Cou towards the end of her life.

'Mrs. Delval was the personification of a charming woman. Never spoilt by the world, she made herself popular amongst those who approached her, by her winning smiles and graceful manners. She was not a striking beauty, but her regular features and well-proportioned figure caused her to be admired by many. . . . Mrs. Delval . . . left alone, and no longer caring to live in circles which reminded her of more happy times, migrated to France. Here she took a lease of one of those villas on the banks of the Marne which cluster around Nogent, a small village lying some nine miles east of the centre of Paris, and on the outskirts of the Bois de Vincennes. La Maison Gaultier was built in the time of Louis XVI, and was originally intended for a *pavillon de chasse.* Placed in the middle of about six acres of well-laid-out grounds, it was capable of holding a much larger establishment than Mrs. Delval thought it necessary to keep. Herself a good scholar, she devoted her time to the early education of her children. . . . Mrs. Delval had surrounded herself with a small circle of friends from the environs of Nogent, Vincennes, and the other adjoining towns, from whom she was most disinclined to part; added to which her reminiscences of England were not of the most agreeable nature. Her children were too fond of her to let a shadow cross her path or cloud her generally placid countenance. . . .'

Cou's simple tomb in the main avenue of the cemetery at Créteil bears the following inscription:

CI GIT
LA DUCHESSE DE CAUMONT LA FORCE
NEE GEORGINA HENRIETTE SMYTHE
VEUVE DE L'HONORABLE AUGUSTUS CRAVEN
DECEDEE A SON CHATEAU DE CRETEIL
LE 11 DECEMBRE 1867

Cou had survived by thirty-one years the husband with whom she fell in love on board the *Menai* at Greenwich during that fine summer of 1832. Yet their posterity seems secure; and in the pages of this journal, now open for the whole world to read, Cou and Augustus may perhaps be said to live happily ever after.

GENEALOGICAL TABLES
AND BIOGRAPHICAL NOTES

FAMILY OF THE FIRST WALTER SMYTHE

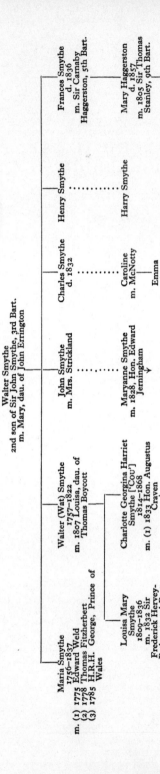

Walter Smythe
2nd son of Sir John Smythe, 3rd Bart.
m. Mary, dau. of John Errington

Maria Smythe
1756–1837
m. (1) 1775 Edward Weld
(2) 1778 Thomas Fitzherbert
(3) 1785 H.R.H. George, Prince of Wales

Walter (Wat) Smythe
1757–1822
m. 1807 Louisa, dau. of Thomas Boycott

John Smythe
m. Mrs. Strickland

Charles Smythe
d. 1832

Henry Smythe

Frances Smythe
d. 1836
m. Sir Carnaby Haggerston, 5th Bart.

Louisa Mary Smythe
1809–1836
m. 1832 Sir Frederick Hervey-Bathurst, 3rd Bart.
↓

Charlotte Georgina Harriet Smythe ['Cou']
1814–1868
m. (1) 1833 Hon. Augustus Craven
↓

Maryanne Smythe
m. 1828, Hon. Edward Jerningham
↓

Caroline
m. McNotty

Emma

Harry Smythe

Mary Haggerston
d. 1857
m. 1805 Sir Thomas Stanley, 9th Bart.

William Stanley
1807–1863,
10th Bart.

Rowland Errington
1809–1876,
11th Bart.
↓

John Stanley
1810–1806,
12th Bart.

Maria Stanley
18 –1899
m. 1832 Sir Richard Williams-Bulkeley, 10th Bart.
↓

NOTE

Descents shown in dotted lines denote presumed illegitimacy. The only marriages given are those which had taken place before Cou's. An arrow indicates that a family continues.

DESCENDANTS OF GEORGE AUGUSTUS CRAVEN AND
CHARLOTTE GEORGINA HARRIET SMYTHE

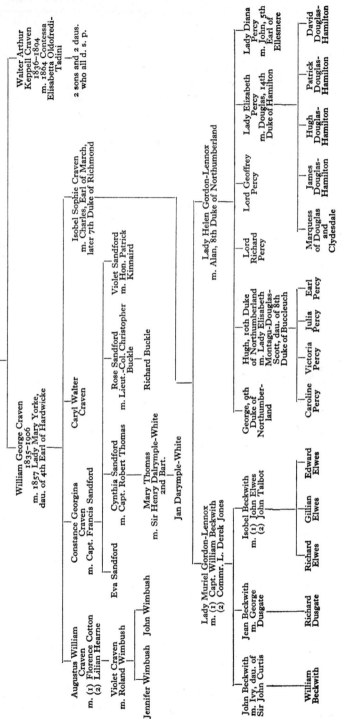

BIOGRAPHICAL NOTES

ADALBERT, Heinrich Wilhelm, Prince, of Prussia (1811–1873), son of Prince Friedrich Wilhelm and grandson of King Friedrich Wilhelm II; renounced the Greek crown in 1831; Inspector General of Artillery; Admiral; Inspector General of the Navy ; *d.unm.*

ALVANLEY, William Arden, 2nd Baron (1789–1849); *s.* his father 1804; *d. unm.* One of the most amusing and best natured of the club-men and dandies.

ANSON, Hon. George (1797–1857), 2nd son of Thomas, 1st Lord Anson; *m.* 1830 Hon. Isabella Forester, dau. of 1st Baron Forester. Later Major-Gen.; Commander-in-Chief in India, where he died.

ANSPACH, Brandenburg and Bayreuth, Margravine of, *b.* Lady Elizabeth Berkeley (1750–1828), dau. of the 4th Earl of Berkeley; *m.* (1) in 1767 William, 6th Baron Craven, by whom she had 2 sons, the 7th Baron and 1st Earl of Craven (of the 2nd creation), and Henry Augustus Berkeley Craven. (Her youngest son, Keppel Craven, the antiquarian, is presumably not admitted to be by her husband, as Burke's Peerage omits to mention him.) Her daughters married the 2nd Earl of Sefton and the Hon. Frederick St. John. She *m.* (2) H.S.H. Christian Frederick, Margrave of Anspach, Brandenburg and Bayreuth. She was a great traveller, and died at her villa in Naples, having been made Princess Berkeley in the Holy Roman Empire by the Pope. Authoress of memoirs and numerous plays; an enthusiastic amateur actress.

ASHLEY, (-Cooper) Hon. Anthony Lionel (1813–1836), 6th son of the 6th Earl of Shaftesbury. Brother of the philanthropic Earl and of William and John Ashley.

ASHLEY, (-Cooper) Hon. Anthony William (1803–1877), 2nd son of the 6th Earl of Shaftesbury, and younger brother to the philanthropist; *m.* 1831 Maria Anne, eldest dau. of Col. Hugh Duncan Baillie of Tarradale; *d.s.p.*

BAGOT, Emily Georgina (*d.* 1848), 2nd, but at this time eldest surviving dau. of Sir Charles Bagot, G.C.B., P.C., M.P., by Mary, eldest dau. of 3rd Earl of Mornington; *m.* 1837 George, 10th Earl of Winchilsea; *d.s.p.* Both Louisa and Georgina Smythe speak of Miss Bagot, who was evidently unusually intelligent and attractive.

BATHURST, Selina Mary, only dau. of Sir Frederick Anne Hervey-Bathurst, 2nd Bart., sister to Sir Frederick, the 3rd Bart.; *m.* (but not till 1870) Capt. Thomas Bulkeley of Clewer Lodge.

BEAUCLERK, Charlotte (*d.* 1852), elder dau. of John Beauclerk, great-grandson of the 1st Duke of St. Albans, and of Mary Fitzhugh; *d. unm.*

BEAUCHAMP, Richard Seymour, Viscount, later Earl of Yarmouth, and finally 4th Marquess of Hertford (1800–1870); K.G., Capt. in the army; *d. unm.*

BEDFORD, Duchess of (1781-1853), *b.* Georgina, 5th daughter of Alexander, 4th Duke of Gordon; *m.* 1803, as his 2nd wife, John, 6th Duke of Bedford, K.G.

BERKELEY, Lady Elizabeth. *See* ANSPACH.

BORINGDON, Edmund Parker, Viscount (1810–1864), later 2nd Earl of Morley; *s.* his father 1840; *m.* 1842 Harriet, dau. of Montagu Parker, widow of William Coryton.

BOYCOTT, Charlotte (*d.* 1842), 6th dau. of Thomas Boycott and Jane Puleston; *d. unm.* The diarists' 'Aunt Cha', who stayed often at Gt. Cumberland Place.

BOYCOTT, Thomas, of Rudge (1734–1798), son of the Rev. Richard Boycott and Gertrude Jenkins; *m.* Jane, dau. of John Puleston of Pickhill (who *d.* 1803), by whom he had 3 sons and 7 daughters. Maternal grandfather of the diarists.

BOYCOTT, Thomas (1771–1856), of Boycott, Hinton and Rudge, son of Thomas Boycott and Jane, youngest dau. of John Puleston of Pickhill, Denbigh; *m.* 1801, Jane, eldest dau. of Thomas Tarleton of Bolesworth Castle. He had 1 son, who predeceased him, and 4 daus. Uncle of the diarists.

BOYCOTT, Thomas (1806–1827), only son of the above; *d.s.p. and unm.* First cousin of the diarists.

BOWEN, Mrs. (*d.* 1830), Sophia, 4th dau. of Thomas Boycott and Jane Puleston; *m.* 1810 William Bowen, M.D. In *Burke's Landed Gentry* the date of her death is wrongly given as 1848.

BRUDENELL-BRUCE, Lady Elizabeth (1807–1847), youngest dau. of the 1st Marquess of Ailesbury; *m.* 1833 Count Christian Danniskiold-Samsøe. Georgina Smythe's closest friend.

BULKELEY, Sir Richard Williams-, 10th Bart. (1801–1875); *m.* (1) 1828, Charlotte Mary, dau. of William Lewis Hughes, 1st Lord Dinorben, who died childless in 1829; (2) 1832, Maria Frances, only dau. of Sir Thomas Stanley. Bart. They had 4 sons.

BYNG, Frederick Gerald (1784–1871), 5th son of the 5th Viscount Torrington; *m.* Catherine Neville. Clerk of the Foreign Office and gentleman usher of the Privy Chamber. One of the most popular men-about-town of the period, and a great friend of Mrs. Fitzherbert's. Known as 'the Poodle'.

CANNIZARO, Duchess of. *See* SAN ANTONIO.

CAROLINE, Queen (1767–1821), *née* Princess Caroline Amelia Elizabeth, 2nd dau. of Charles William Ferdinand, Duke of Brunswick-Wölfenbuttel; *m.* 1821 George, Prince of Wales, by whom she had an only dau.

CASTLEREAGH, Frederick William Robert Stewart, Viscount, later 4th Marquess of Londonderry (1805–1872), only son of Charles William, 3rd Marquess of Londonderry by his first wife; *m.* 1846 Elizabeth Frances Charlotte, dau. of Robert, 3rd Earl of Roden, and widow of Richard, 6th Viscount Powerscourt; *s.* his father in 1854; K.P., P.C. Dying childless, he was succeeded by his half-brother. He was the nephew of the great statesman.

CAVENDISH, George Henry (1810–1880), 2nd son of William Cavendish by Louisa, dau. of the 1st Lord Lismore, and grandson of George Augustus Henry, 1st Earl of Burlington; *m.* 1833 Lady Louisa Lascelles, youngest dau. of 2nd Earl of Harewood. His brother succeeded the bachelor Duke as 7th Duke of Devonshire.

CHARLOTTE, Queen (1744–1818), *née* Princess Charlotte Sophia, dau. of Charles Louis Frederick, Duke of Mecklenburg-Strelitz; *m.* 1761 King George III, by whom she had 9 sons (2 of whom died in infancy) and 6 daus.

CHARLOTTE AUGUSTA, Princess (1796–1817), only dau. of George, Prince of Wales (later King George IV), and Princess Caroline (of Brunswick); *m.* 1816 Prince Leopold George Frederick of Saxe-Coburg, 3rd son of Francis Antony Frederick, reigning Duke of Saxe-Coburg-Saalfeld. She died giving birth to a still-born son.

CHESTERFIELD, George Stanhope, 6th Earl of (1805–1866); *s.* his father in 1815; *m.* 1830 Anne Elizabeth, eldest dau. of Cecil, 1st Lord Forester.

CLARENCE AND ST. ANDREWS, Prince William Henry, Duke of, Earl of Munster, later King William IV (1765–1837), 3rd son of King George III. After living for years with Mrs. Jordan, the actress, and having children by her, he married 1818 Princess Adelaide Louisa Theresa Caroline Amelia, dau. of George Frederick Charles, reigning Duke of Saxe-Meiningen, by whom he had 2 daus. who died in infancy.

CONYNGHAM, Lord Albert (1805–1860), later 1st Lord Londesborough; 3rd son of the 3rd Baron and 1st Marquess Conyngham; *m.* (1) 1833 Henrietta Maria Weld, dau. of the 1st Lord Forester, by whom (who died 1841) he had 2 sons and 4 daus., and (2) Ursula Lucy Grace, dau. of the Hon. Charles Bridgeman, by whom he had 4 sons and 2 daus. He changed his name to Denison on inheriting from his Uncle William Joseph Denison of Denbies, M.P., and was created a Baron in 1850. Author of *Wanderings in search of Health*; and a great collector of antiquities. Great-grandfather of Dame Edith, Sir Osbert and Mr. Sacheverell Sitwell.

CONYNGHAM, Marchioness of (1769–1861), *née* Elizabeth, dau. of Joseph Denison; *m.* 1794 Henry, 3rd Baron and 1st Marquess Conyngham, by whom she had 3 sons and 2 daus. The last favourite of George IV.

COSBY, Thomas Phillips (*b.* 1803), son of Thomas Cosby of Stradbally Hall, Queen's County; Capt. Royal Horse Guards; *d. unm.*

COX, Mr. Either Henry Richard Cox (*b.* 1804), eldest son of Richard Henry Cox of Hillingdon and Charlotte Fitzhugh, who *d. unm.* or Frederick William Cox, his brother, who *m.* 1834 the Hon. Fanny Pitt-Rivers, dau. of Horace William, 3rd Lord Rivers.

CRAVEN, Elizabeth, Lady (wife of 6th Baron). *See* ANSPACH.

CRAVEN, Hon. George Augustus (1810–1836), 2nd son of the 1st Earl of Craven; *m*. 1833 Charlotte Georgina Harriet Smythe, the diarist, by whom he had 2 sons.

CRAVEN, Hon. Henry Augustus Berkeley (1776–1836), 2nd son of the 6th Baron Craven and Lady Elizabeth Berkeley, later Margravine of Anspach; *m*. 1829 Marie-Clarisse Trebhault, whom he seems not to have taken about with him, and about whom nothing is known.

CRAVEN, Hon. Frederick Keppel (1812–1864), youngest son of the 1st Earl of Craven; *d. unm.*

CRAVEN, Countess of (1782–1860), Louisa, dau. of John Brunton of Norwich, a celebrated actress; *m*. 1807 William, 7th Baron Craven and 1st Earl of Craven by the 2nd creation. She was mother of the 2nd Earl, of Augustus Craven, Frederick Craven and Lady Louisa Craven.

CRAVEN, Lady Louisa Elizabeth Frederica (*d*. 1858), only dau. of the 1st Earl of Craven; *m*. (1) 1840 Sir George Johnstone, 7th Bart., by whom she had 2 sons, and (2) 1844 Alexander Oswald of Auchencruive.

CRAVEN, William, 2nd Earl of Craven (1809–1866); *s*. his father 1825; *m*. 1835 Lady Emily Mary Grimston, dau. of the 1st Earl of Verulam, by whom he had 4 sons and 5 daus. Lord Lieutenant of Warwickshire, Recorder of Coventry, High Steward of Newbury.

DANNISKIOLD-SAMSØE, Count Christian Conrad Sophus (1800–1886); *m*. (1) 1833 Lady Elizabeth Brudenell-Bruce, dau. of the 1st Marquess of Ailesbury; and (2) 1850 Hofdame Anna Amalie Louise Øllegard von Zytphen.

DAWSON-DAMER, Hon. George Lionel (1788–1856), 3rd son of the 1st Earl of Portarlington by Lady Caroline Stuart, dau. of the 3rd Earl of Bute; *m*. 1825 Mary Georgiana Seymour, dau. of Lord Hugh Seymour. Assumed in 1829 the additional surname of Damer on inheriting from his aunt, Lady Caroline Damer. Lieut.-Col., M.P.

DAWSON-DAMER, the Hon. Mrs. (1798–1848) Mary Georgiana, 2nd dau. of Admiral Lord Hugh Seymour and Lady Anne Waldegrave; *m*. 1825 George Lionel Dawson, 3rd son of the 1st Earl of Portarlington, who assumed the surname Damer on the death of his Aunt Lady Caroline Damer.

DELISLE, Mlle; governess and companion of the diarist, Georgina Smythe, from *c*. 1830 to 1832.

DEVONSHIRE, William Spencer Cavendish, 6th Duke of (1790–1858), only son of William, 5th Duke, by his 1st wife Lady Georgiana Spencer; K.G., K.S.A., K.A.N., D.C.L., P.C.; *d. unm.* The patron of Paxton, who built the 'Crystal Palace' for the Great Exhibition.

DINO, Duchesse de (1792–1862), Dorothea, 3rd dau. of the Duke of Courland; *m.* 1809 Edmond, Comte de Périgord, the nephew of Talleyrand. Her mother had been Talleyrand's mistress, and she may have been his daughter. Likewise *she* was probably Talleyrand's mistress, and her third child, Pauline, may have been Talleyrand's. She lived apart from her husband and kept house for Talleyrand. In London she was accorded the honours of an Ambassadress, which was exceptional for any but an Ambassador's wife. Their Embassy was in Hanover Square. She was a brilliant and attractive woman.

D'ORSAY, Alfred de Grimaud, Comte (1801-1852); son of General d'Orsay and Eléonore de Franquemont, daughter of the Duke of Würtemberg by Anne Franchi (known as 'la belle Sullivan', later Mme. Craufurd); *m.* 1827 Lady Harriet Gardner, only legitimate dau. of Charles, 1st Earl of Blessington; *d.s.p.* The famous dandy, friend of Lord and Lady Blessington; an amateur artist.

DOUGLAS AND CLYDESDALE, William Alexander Anthony Archibald Douglas-Hamilton, Earl of, later 11th Duke of Hamilton, 8th of Brandon (1811–1863); *m.* 1843 Princess Mary of Baden, youngest daughter of Charles Louis Frederick, reigning Duke of Baden, cousin of the Emperor Napoleon III; *s.* his father 1852. Father of the 12th Duke of Hamilton and of a daughter who married the Prince of Monaco.

EDWARDES, Hon. William, later 3rd Baron Kensington (1801–1872), second son of 2nd Baron Kensington; *m.* 1833 Laura Jane, dau. of Cuthbert Ellison of Hepburn; *s.* his father 1852.

ELPHINSTONE, Hon. Georgiana Augusta Henrietta (*d.* 1892), only child of the second marriage of George, 1st Viscount Keith and Hester, dau. of Henry Thrale and Dr. Johnson's friend; *m.* 1831 Augustus John Villiers, 2nd son of the 5th Earl of Jersey. He died in 1847 and she *m.* in 1870 Lord William Godolphin Osborne, son of the 5th Duke of Leeds. There were no children by either marriage.

ELPHINSTONE, John 13th Baron (1807–1860); *s.* his father in 1813; Capt. Royal Horse Guards; Governor of Madras and Bombay; *cr.* Peer of Great Britain 1859; P.C., G.C.H., G.C.B.; *d. unm.*

ERRINGTON, Rowland Stanley-Massey-Stanley (1809–1876), assumed the name of Errington in 1819, later 11th Bart.; 2nd son of Sir Thomas Stanley-Massey-Stanley and Maria Haggerston; *m.* 1839 Julia, eldest dau. of Sir John Macdonald, K.C.B., by whom he had 3 daus., Claudine Stanley, who *d. unm.* 1864, Ethel, who *m.* 1876 Capt. Evelyn Baring, later 1st Earl of Cromer, and Venetia, who *m.* 1867 Viscount Pollington, son of the Earl of Mexborough. The diarists' first cousin once removed.

ESTERHAZY, Princess. The wife of Prince Paul Anton Esterhazy (1786–1866), the Austrian diplomat who was Ambassador in London from 1815–18 and from 1830–38. One of the Leaders of London society and a Lady Patroness of Almack's.

FARQUHAR, Lady Sybella Martha, only dau. and heir of the Rev. Morton Rockcliffe; *m.* 1809 Sir Thomas Harvie Farquhar, 2nd Bart. Their 2 eldest daus. married the Hon. Charles Grey, son of the great Lord Grey, and George Clive, M.P., in 1836 and 1835.

FITZCLARENCE, George Augustus Frederick, later 1st Earl of Munster (1794–1842), eldest natural child of William, Duke of Clarence (later King William IV) and Mrs. Jordan; *m.* 1819 Mary Wyndham, natural dau. of George, Earl of Egremont, by whom he had 4 sons and 3 daus. Major-Genl., A.D.C. to Queen Victoria, Lieut. of the Tower, Governor of Windsor Castle. Committed suicide.

FITZGIBBON, Lady Louisa Isabella Georgina, 2nd dau. of the 3rd and last Earl of Clare; *m.* 1847 the Hon. Gerald Normanby Dillon.

FITZHARRIS, Lady (1807–1876), *née* Lady Corisande Emma Bennet, only dau. of 5th Earl of Tankerville; *m.* 1830, James Howard Harris, Lord Fitzharris, later 3rd Earl of Malmesbury.

FITZHERBERT, Mrs. (1756–1837), *née* Mary Anne (or Maria) Smythe, elder dau. and eldest child of Walter Smythe of Brambridge by Mary Errington; *m.* (1) in 1775 Edward Weld of Lulworth Castle, (2) 1778 Thomas Fitzherbert of Norbury, (3) 1785 secretly George, Prince of Wales. She is supposed to have died childless, although it is possible that Maryanne Smythe was her child by the Prince.

FITZROY, Lord James (1804–1834), 3rd son of George Henry, 4th Duke of Grafton, by his wife Charlotte Maria, dau. of the 2nd Earl Waldegrave; *d. unm.*

FLAVIGNY, Maurice, vicomte (later comte) de (1804–1873). A diplomat. His sister Maria, comtesse d'Agoult was the mistress of Liszt, by whom she had 3 children, including Cosima Wagner.

FORESTER, Hon. George Cecil Weld Forester, later 3rd Baron Forester (1807–1886), 2nd son of the 1st Baron; M.P. and later a General in the Army; Comptroller of the Household 1852 and in 1858–59; *m.* 1862 the Hon. Mary Anne, dau. of Edward Jervis, 2nd Viscount St. Vincent, and widow of Colonel D. O. Dyce; *s.* his brother in 1874. His sisters married Robert Smith, Lord Albert Conyngham, Lord Chesterfield and Lord Bradford.

FORESTER, Hon. Isabella Elizabeth Annabella (*d.* 1858), 3rd dau. of the 1st Baron Forester; *m.* 1830 Hon. George Anson.

FREMANTLE, Capt. John (*b.* 1790), son of Stephen Francis William Fremantle, and nephew of Sir William Fremantle; Coldstream Guards, A.D.C. to Wellington at Waterloo, later C.B. and Major-Gen.; *m.* 1829 Agnes, 3rd dau. of David Lyon.

FREMANTLE, Cecilia Mary (*d.* 1871), 2nd dau. of Sir Thomas Francis Fremantle, G.C.B., Admiral of the Blue, an elder brother of the Sir William Fremantle who married the grandmother of Frederick Hervey-Bathurst; *m.* 1844 Lord William Hervey, son of the 1st Marquess of Bristol. Her eldest brother, Thomas Fremantle, who was created a Bart. in 1821, became 1st Lord Cottesloe.

FREMANTLE, Lady (*d.* 1841), *née* Selina Mary Elwell, dau. and heir of Sir John Elwell, Bart.; *m.* (1) 1779 Felton Lionel Hervey, a grandson of the

1st Earl of Bristol, by whom she had 2 sons, and (2) 1797 the Right
Hon. Sir William Henry Fremantle, Treasurer to the Household, Deputy
Ranger of Windsor Great Park. She was grandmother of Sir Frederick
Hervey-Bathurst, who married Louisa Smythe.

FREMANTLE, Sir Thomas Francis, 1st Bart., later 1st Lord Cottlesloe
(1798–1890), eldest son of Sir Thomas Francis Fremantle, G.C.B., Vice
Admiral of the Blue, and Elizabeth, co-heir of Sir Richard Wynne of
Falkingham; *m.* 1824 Louisa Elizabeth, dau. of Field-Marshal Sir George
Nugent, 1st Bart.; *cr.* Bart. 1821; M.P. 1827–46; Secretary to the
Treasury 1834–35 and 1841–45; Secretary at War 1844–45; Secretary
for Ireland 1845–46; *cr.* 1874 1st Baron Cottesloe.

FREMANTLE, Sir William Henry (1766–1850), youngest son of John
Fremantle of Aston Abbots; *m.* 1797 as her second husband Selina Mary,
daughter of Sir Thomas Elwell, Bart., and widow of Felton Hervey;
G.C.H., P.C., Treasurer to the Household, Deputy Ranger of Windsor
Great Park.

GEORGE IV, King, George Augustus Frederick, Prince of Wales (1762–
1830), eldest son of King George III; *m.* 1795 his first cousin, Princess
Caroline Amelia Elizabeth, 2nd daughter of Charles William Ferdinand,
Duke of Brunswick-Wölfenbuttel, by whom he had a dau., Charlotte
Augusta (1796–1817); Regent 1811; *s.* his father as King January 29,
1820; Crowned July 19, 1821.

GORDON, Lord Francis Arthur (1808–1857), 6th son of George, 9th
Marquess of Huntly; *m.* 1835 Isabel, only child of Lieut.-Gen. Sir William
Keir Grant, K.C.B.; later Lieut.-Col. 1st Life Guards.

GORTCHAKOFF, Prince Alexander Mikhailovitch (1798–1883). Russian
diplomat. Later Minister in Germany and Austria, Minister of Foreign
Affairs, Chancellor of the Empire.

GREVILLE, Brooke (1798–1884), 3rd son of Henry Francis Greville;
m. 1856 Emilie, dau. of Charles Bouchey. 1st Cousin of the diarists Charles
and Henry Greville.

GREVILLE, Charles Cavendish Fulke (1794–1865), eldest son of Charles
Greville and Lady Charlotte Greville, dau. of the 3rd Duke of Portland;
Clerk of the Privy Council, Secretary for Jamaica; *d. unm.*; After Pepys
and Evelyn perhaps the most interesting of the English diarists.

GREVILLE, Henry (1801–1872), youngest son of Charles Greville and
Lady Charlotte Bentinck, dau. of the 3rd Duke of Portland; brother of
Charles Greville the diarist; *d. unm.* An amateur of music, particularly
singing, of painting and the theatre.

GRIMSTON, James Walter, Lord Grimston, later 2nd Earl of Verulam
(1809–1895); *m.* 1844 Elizabeth Joanna, dau. of Major Sir Richard
Weyland of Woodeaton; *s.* his father 1845.

GROEBEN, Graf Karl von der (1788–1876); *m.* 1831 Thusnelda von
Dornberg; by whom he had 5 sons, all of whom entered the Prussian
Army; later a general of Cavalry.

HAGGERSTON, Lady (*d.* 1836), Frances, younger dau. of Walter Smythe and Mary Errington; *m.* Sir Carnaby Haggerston, 5th Bart., by whom she had one dau. Mary, later Lady Stanley. Aunt of Louisa and Georgina Smythe.

HAYMAN, Frances Louisa (Fanny) (*d.* 1885), only dau. of John Hayman and Frances Boycott; *m.* 1833 the Hon. Kenelm Somerville, R.N., later Admiral Lord Somerville, by whom she had 7 children. She has Blackett descendants living.

HERTFORD, Francis Charles Seymour, 3rd Marquess of (1777–1842); K.G.; *m.* 1798 Maria Fagniani, illegit. dau. of the Duke of Queensberry. Caricatured as Lord Steyne in *Vanity Fair* and as Lord Monmouth in *Coningsby*, he collected many of the treasures now in the Wallace Collection.

HERTFORD, 4th Marquess of. *See* BEAUCHAMP, Viscount.

HERVEY, Elizabeth, youngest dau. of Felton Lionel Hervey and Selina Elwell (later Lady Fremantle); *d. unm.* Aunt to Sir Frederick Hervey-Bathurst.

HERVEY-BATHURST, Sir Frederick Hutchinson, 3rd Bart. (1807–1881), eldest son of Sir Frederick Anne Hervey-Bathurst and Jane, dau. of John Hutchinson (who died 1827); grandson of Felton Lionel Hervey and the Lady Fremantle who appears in the diaries; great-grandson of the Hon. Felton Hervey, who was 8th son of the 1st Earl of Bristol by his second wife; *m.* (1) May 14, 1832 Louisa Smythe, by whom (who *d.* 1840) he had a son and a daughter; (2) 1845 Clare Emily, youngest dau. of Sir Richard Brooke of Norton, by whom (who *d.* 1867) he had more children.

HERVEY, Lionel Charles (*d.* 1842), 3rd son of Felton Lionel Hervey and the later Lady Fremantle, uncle to Sir Frederick; *m.* Frances Mary, dau. of Vice-Admiral Thomas Wells.

HILL, Lord Arthur Moyses William, later 2nd Baron Sandys (1792–1860), 2nd son of the 2nd Marquess of Downshire; *s.* his mother as Baron Sandys in 1836; Lieut.-Gen., Colonel 7th Dragoon Guards and Scots Greys; *d. unm.*

HILL, Lord Arthur Marcus Cecil, later 3rd Baron Sandys (1798-1863), 3rd son of the 2nd Marquess of Downshire; *m.* 1837, Louisa, dau. of Joseph Blake; *s.* his brother (Lord Arthur) as Baron Sandys 1860.

HILLSBOROUGH, Arthur Wills Blundell Sandys Trumbull Windsor Hill, Earl of Hillsborough, later 4th Marquess of Downshire (1812–1868), son of the 3rd Marquess by Lady Maria Windsor-Clive, dau. of the 5th Earl of Plymouth; *m.* 1839 Caroline Frances, dau. of Stapleton Cotton, 1st Viscount Combermere; K.P.

HOLMES, James (1777–1860). Miniaturist and water-colour painter, a favourite artist of George IV.

JERNINGHAM, Hon. Edward (1804–1849), 2nd son of Sir George William Jerningham, 7th Baronet, who obtained, in 1824, a reversal of the attainder of his ancestor, Sir William Howard, 1st Baron and Viscount

Stafford, and became 8th Baron Stafford; Lieut., Dragoon Guards; *m.* 1828 Maryanne Smythe.

JERNINGHAM, the Misses. The eldest daughter of Lord Stafford having *m.* Lord Lovat in 1823, and another having died in 1815, there remained: Hon. Frances Sophia (1803–1838), who *d. unm.*; Georgina, her twin, who *d. unm.* 1841; Laura Maria (1811–1886), who *m.* 1829 Hon. Robert Edward Petre, but died a nun; and Isabella Maria (1815–1847), who *d. unm.*

JERNINGHAM, The Hon. Mrs. *See* SMYTHE, Maryanne.

KEITH, Viscountess (1762-1857), Hester, dau. and heiress of Henry Thrale and of Dr. Johnson's Mrs. Thrale; *m.* as his second wife George Keith Elphinstone, 1st Viscount Keith. Her dau., Georgiana, was to be Louisa Smythe's most intimate friend. Lord Keith's only dau. by his first wife became Baroness Keith on her father's death: she *m.* the Count de Flahaut, Talleyrand's son, the diplomatist, and one of her daughters married the 4th Marquess of Lansdowne.

KERRY, William Thomas Fitzmaurice, Earl of (1811–1836), son of 3rd Marquess of Lansdowne; *m.* 1834 Lady Augusta Lavinia Priscilla Ponsonby, 2nd dau. of 4th Earl of Bessborough; M.P. When he died without inheriting he left an only dau., Mary, who married Sir Philip Percy Egerton Herbert, and his posterity continues in the family of the Lords Powis.

KNIGHTON, Sir William (1776–1836); Keeper of the Privy Purse to George IV, and one of his executors.

LAHARPE, Mlle. Governess to Georgina Smythe until 1827.

LANE-FOX, Mrs; Georgina Henrietta, dau. of Edward Pery Buckley; *m.* 1814 George Lane-Fox, M.P., of Bramham.

LASCELLES, Lady Louisa (*d.* 1886), 4th dau. of 2nd Earl of Harewood; *m.* 1835 Lord George Henry Cavendish, M.P.

LEVESON-GOWER, Edward (1807–1853), 2nd son of John Leveson-Gower; grandson of Admiral John Leveson-Gower, the 2nd son of the 1st Earl Gower. An officer in the Army; *m.* 1839 Frances Cecilia, dau. of Dr. William Powell.

LIDDELL, Hon. Thomas (1800–1856); 2nd son of Thomas Henry, 1st Baron Ravensworth; *m.* 1843 Caroline Elizabeth Keppel, eldest dau. of George, 5th Viscount Barrington.

LIEVEN, Dorothea Christoforovna, Princess (1785–1857); dau. of General Benckendorff; *m.* 1800 Count (later Prince) Lieven, Russian Ambassador in London from 1812 to 1834. A queen of London society; mistress of Metternich and Guizot.

LIEVEN, Prince Paul Petrovitch; 2nd son of Prince Lieven, the Russian Ambassador.

Londonderry, Marchioness of (1800–1865); *née* Frances, dau. of Sir Henry Vane-Tempest; *m.* 1819 as his 2nd wife Charles William Stewart, who *s.* in 1822 his half-brother, the statesman, as 3rd Marquess of Londonderry; step-mother of Lord Castlereagh.

Luttrell, Henry Lawes (1765–1851); natural son of the 2nd Earl of Carhampton; Wit and the author of occasional verses, *d. unm.*

Macdonald, Capt. James William Bosville (1810–1882); 2nd son of the 3rd Baron Macdonald and Louisa Maria La Coast, natural dau. of the Duke of Gloucester and Lady Almeria Carpenter; Later C.B., Lieut.-Gen., Colonel of the 21st Hussars; *m.* 1859 Elizabeth Nina, dau. of the 3rd Lord Wallscourt.

Margravine, The. *See* Anspach.

Molyneux, Hon. Francis (1805–1886); 4th son of William Philip, 2nd Earl of Sefton, the Whig politician; *m.* 1842 Lady Georgiana Jemima Ashburnham.

Mornay, Charles-Henri de, later comte (1803–1878). In the French Diplomatic Service.

Munster, Earl of. *See* Fitzclarence.

Orleans, Ferdinand-Philippe, duc de (1810–1842). Eldest son of King Louis-Philippe; *m.* Princess Helen of Mecklenburg; *d.* in a carriage accident.

d'Orsay, Comte Alfred. *See* D'Orsay.

Ossulston, Charles Augustus Bennet, Lord, later 6th Earl of Tankerville (1810–1899), son of 5th Earl and Corisande de Gramont; *m.* 1850 Lady Olivia Montagu, eldest dau. of George, 6th Duke of Manchester; *s.* his father in 1859.

Peyton, Lady (*d.* 1857), *née* Harriet, dau. of Thomas Fitzhugh; *m.* (1) James Bradshaw, (2) in 1803 Sir Henry Peyton, 2nd Bart.

Pollen, Lady (*d.* 1877); *née* Charlotte Elizabeth, only dau. of the Rev. John Craven; *m.* 1819 Sir John Walter Pollen, 2nd Bart.

Porchester, Henry John George Herbert, Lord, later 3rd Earl of Carnarvon (1800–1849); *m.* 1830 Henrietta Maria Anna, eldest dau. of Lord Henry Thomas Molyneux Howard, niece of the 12th Duke of Norfolk; *s.* his father 1833.

Radnor, William Pleydell Bouverie, 3rd Earl of (1779–1869); *m.* (1) 1801 Catherine, only dau. of Henry, Earl of Lincoln; and (2) 1814 Anne Judith, 3rd dau. of Sir Henry Mildmay, 3rd Bart.

Radnor, Countess of (1790–1851); *née* Anne Judith, 3rd dau. of Sir Henry St. John Mildmay, 3rd Bart.; *m.* 1814 as his 2nd wife William, 3rd Earl of Radnor.

RAVENSWORTH, Lady (1773–1845); *née* Maria Susannah, dau. of John Simpson of Bradley, and grand-dau. maternally of the 8th Earl of Strathmore; *m.* 1796 Sir Thomas Henry Liddell, 6th Bart., created in 1821 Baron Ravensworth.

ROGERS, Samuel (1763–1855); Banker, poet and art collector.

DE ROOS, Henry William Fitzgerald, 22nd Baron (1793–1839); son of Lord Henry Fitzgerald (son of the 23rd Duke of Leinster), and of Charlotte Boyle, 21st Baroness de Roos; *s.* his mother 1831; *d. unm.*

DE ROOS, Olivia (1807–1885); 3rd dau. of Lord Henry Fitzgerald; *m.* 1833 Henry Richard Charles Wellesley, later 1st. Earl Cowley, K.G.

RUSSELL, Francis (1793–1832); eldest son of William Russell, posthumous 3rd son of Francis, Marquess of Tavistock; *d. unm.*

RYDER, Lady Louisa (*d.* 1899); youngest dau. of the 1st Earl of Harrowby; *m.* 1833 the Hon. George Fortescue.

ST. ALBANS, Duchess of (1777–1837); *née* Harriot, dau. of Lieut. Matthew Mellon; *m.* (1) 1815 Thomas Coutts; and (2) 1827 9th Duke of St. Albans.

SALISBURY, Marchioness of (1802–1839); *née* Frances Mary, dau. and heir of Bamber Gascoyne; *m.* 1821 James Brownlow William, 2nd Marquess of Salisbury, K.G.

SEFTON, Countess of (1769–1851). Maria Margaret, dau. of 1st Earl of Craven; *m.* 1792 William, 2nd Earl of Sefton.

SEYMOUR, Francis George Hugh, later 5th Marquess of Hertford (1812–1884); elder son of Admiral Sir George Francis Seymour; *m.* 1839 Lady Emily Murray, dau. of the 3rd Earl of Mansfield; later G.C.B., P.C., D.L., M.P., General, equerry to the Prince Consort, groom-in-waiting to Queen Victoria, Deputy Ranger of Windsor Great Park, Lord Chamberlain; *s.* his cousin 1870.

SEYMOUR, Frederick Charles William (1797–1856); 5th son of Admiral Lord Hugh Seymour and Lady Anne Horatia Waldegrave; *m.* (1) Lady Mary Gordon, dau. of George, Marquess of Huntly, and (2) 1832 Lady Augusta Hervey, eldest dau. of the 1st Marquess of Bristol.

SEYMOUR, Mary Georgiana (Minney). *See* DAWSON-DAMER, the Hon. Mrs.

SHELLEY, Sir John 6th Bart. (1772–1852); *s.* his father 1783; *m.* 1807 Frances, heiress of Thomas Winckley.

SHELLEY, John Villiers, later 7th Bart. (1808–1867); eldest son of Sir John Shelley, 6th Bart.; *m.* 1832 Louisa Elizabeth Anne, dau. of the Rev. Samuel Johnes-Knight; *s.* his father 1852.

SMYTHE, Charles (*d.* 1832), 3rd son of Walter Smythe of Brambridge and Mary Errington.

SMYTHE, Harry. Supposedly an illegitimate son of Henry Smythe, youngest brother of Wat Smythe.

SMYTHE, John, 2nd son of Walter Smythe of Brambridge and Mary Errington; *m.* the widow Strickland.

SMYTHE, Maryanne (*c.* 1806–1859), natural dau. either of George, Prince of Wales and Mrs. Fitzherbert, or of John Smythe and an unknown mother; *m.* 1828 the Hon. Edward Jerningham.

SMYTHE, Walter (Wat) (1757–1822); eldest son of Walter Smythe of Brambridge, and Mary Errington; *m.* 1807 Louisa, youngest dau. of Thomas Boycott of Rudge, by whom he had 2 daus., Louisa Mary and Charlotte Georgina Harriet, the two diarists.

SMYTHE, Mrs. Wat (1778–1849), *née* Louisa Victoria Sobieska Foxhunting-Moll, youngest dau. of Thomas Boycott of Rudge, Shropshire, and Jane Puleston; *m.* 1807 Walter Smythe of Brambridge; mother of the two diarists.

SOMERSET, Edward Adolphus St. Maur, 11th Duke of (1775–1855); *m.* (1) 1800 Lady Charlotte Douglas-Hamilton, dau. of 9th Duke of Hamilton who *d.* 1827, and (2) 1836 Margaret, dau. of Sir Michael Shaw-Stewart, Bart.

STANLEY-MASSEY-STANLEY, John, later 12th Bart. (1810–1893); 3rd son of Sir Thomas Stanley-Massey-Stanley and Maria Haggerston; *m.* 1841 Maria, only dau. of Baron de Talleyrand; changed his name to Errington and *s.* his brother Rowland as 12th and last Bart., 1875.

STANLEY-MASSEY-STANLEY, Lady (*d.* 1857); *née* Mary, dau. of Sir Carnaby Haggerston and Frances Smythe; *m.* 1805 Sir Thomas Stanley, 9th Bart; mother of Maria, who *m.* Sir Richard Bulkeley, and first cousin to the two diarists.

STANLEY-MASSEY-STANLEY, Maria (*d.* 1899); only dau. of Sir Thomas Stanley and Mary Haggerston; *m.* 1832 Sir Richard Williams-Bulkeley, 10th Bart; ancestress of the present Williams-Bulkeleys.

STANLEY-MASSEY-STANLEY, Sir Thomas, 9th Bart. (*d.* 1841); 2nd son of Sir Thomas Stanley, 7th Bart. and Catherine, dau. of William Salvin of Croxdale; *m.* 1805 Mary, only dau. of Sir Carnaby Haggerston, 5th Bart.; *s.* his elder brother in 1803.

STANLEY-MASSEY-STANLEY, William Thomas, later 10th Bart. (1807–1863); eldest son of Sir Thomas Stanley-Massey-Stanley and Mary Haggerston; *s.* his father in 1841; *d.s.p.*

STRACHAN, Lady (*c.* 1790–1868), *née* Louisa Dillon; *m.* (1) 1812 Admiral Sir Richard Strachan, and (2) Picalillo; created Marchesa di Salza by the King of Naples. A successful courtesan.

TAGLIONI, Marie (1804–1884), creator of *La Sylphide* and the greatest ballerina of the Romantic era.

TALBOT, George Gustavus Chetwynd- (1810–1896), 5th son of 2nd Earl Talbot; in Holy Orders; *m.* 1842 Emily Sarah, 2nd dau. of Henry Elwes of Colesbourne, Gloucestershire.

TANKERVILLE, Countess of (1782–1865), *née* Corisande, dau. of duc de Gramont; *m.* 1806 Charles Augustus Bennet, Lord Ossulston, later 5th Earl of Tankerville. Her parents were emigrés from the French Revolution, and she had been brought up at Devonshire House. Her brother married d'Orsay's sister.

TOLSTOY, Count. Russian diplomat and nephew of Princess Lieven.

TROTTER, John (*d.* 1870), of Dyrham Park, Hertford; Capt. 2nd Life Guards; *m.* 1833 Charlotte Amelia Liddell, dau. of Henry Thomas, 1st Baron Ravensworth.

VILLIERS, Charles Pelham (1802–1898); 3rd son of George, 3rd son of 1st Earl of Clarendon; Judge-advocated general, M.P., President of the Poor Law Board; *d. unm.*

VILLIERS, George Augustus Frederick Child-, Lord Villiers, later 6th Earl of Jersey (1808–1859); *m.* 1841 Julia, eldest dau. of the Rt. Hon. Sir Robert Peel, 2nd Bart.; *s.* his father 1859 and *d.* three weeks later.

VILLIERS, Thomas Hyde (1801–1832), 2nd son of George, 3rd son of 1st Earl of Clarendon; Clerk in the Colonial Office; M.P.; Secretary to the Board of Control. The 4th Earl—the statesman—was his brother.

WELLINGTON, Arthur, Wellesley, 1st Duke of (1769–1852); 3rd son of the 1st Earl of Mornington; *m.* 1806 Catherine Pakenham, 3rd dau. of the 2nd Baron Longford. Victor of Assaye, Vimiera. Talavera, Busaco, Fuentes d'Onoro, Ciudad Rodrigo, Badajoz, Salamanca, Vittoria, Orthez, Toulouse, Quatre-Bras and Waterloo; K.G., Field-Marshal, Prime Minister, etc.

WILLIAM IV, King. *See* CLARENCE AND ST. ANDREWS, Duke of.

WORTLEY, Lady Georgina (1804–1884), *née* Georgina Ryder, 3rd dau. of Dudley, 1st Earl of Harrowby; *m.* 1825 the Hon. John Stuart-Wortley, later 2nd Lord Wharncliffe.